From Aid to
Re-Colonization

ALSO BY TIBOR MENDE

World Power in the Balance
Southeast Asia Between Two Worlds
Conversations with Nehru
China and Her Shadow
The Chinese Revolution

From Aid to Re-Colonization

Lessons of a Failure

TIBOR MENDE

PANTHEON BOOKS
A Division of Random House, New York

FIRST AMERICAN EDITION

 Published in the United States by Pantheon Books, a division of Random House, Inc., New York, and simultaneously in Canada by Random House of Canada Limited, Toronto. Originally published in France as *De l'Aide à la Recolonisation: Les Leçons d'un Échec* by Éditions du Seuil.

Library of Congress Cataloging in Publication Data

Mende, Tibor.
From Aid to Re-Colonization.

Translation of De l'aide à la recolonisation.
Includes bibliographical references.
1. Economic assistance. 2. International economic relations. I. Title.
HC60.M37513 338.91 72-10911
ISBN 0-394-48197-6

Manufactured in the United States of America by
Haddon Craftsmen, Scranton, Pennsylvania

9 8 7 6 5 4 3 2

FOREWORD

This book has been written for the informed reader and not for specialists. It is an ambitious attempt to reappraise an immense subject, that of the relationship of the industrial powers of the North Temperate Zone of the world with the former colonial countries making up its southern half. The extent of the material renders generalizations unavoidable, and they are of course always contestable. Yet on a subject that has become so cliché-ridden, it may perhaps be helpful to be controversial.

The first half of this volume tries to survey and to analyze the North-South relationship since 1947. The second attempts to draw conclusions and formulate suggestions for the future which it is hoped some readers may consider constructive. The role of the introductory and concluding remarks is to place the whole subject within its global setting.

The expressions "developed" and "developing" countries have been avoided, partly because they are no more than polite fictions and mainly because their constant utilization, as in international documents, is rather monotonous. Instead, on the one hand, economically advanced, industrial, high-income, or rich countries, and on the other hand, underdeveloped, low-income, formerly colonial, economically backward, or poor countries, are referred to as practically synonymous.

Explanatory or statistical notes and those containing details of source material referred to are numbered and can be found at the end of the book.

T.M.

Geneva, January 1972

Contents

Foreword v

Introduction ix

Part One

I. The Inimitable Original 3

II. A Distorting Encounter 13

III. From Ideal to Practice 29

IV. The Cost of Being Generous and of Being Aided 42

V. Who Aids Whom and Why? 67

VI. The Mercenaries of the Status Quo 86

VII. *Trahison des Clercs*—North-South Version 130

VIII. A New Phase 159

Part Two

IX. In Search of the Favorable Wind 167

X. The Pillar of Fundamental Needs 175

XI. The Temptation of Voluntary Quarantine 194

XII. Institutions, Intentions, and Practice 213

XIII. Palliatives and Alternatives 228

Concluding Remarks 264

Appendix 1: *How the Communists Do It* 278

Appendix 2: *Aid Flows—Statistical Table* 291

Notes 293

Index 309

About the Author 319

INTRODUCTION

An unprecedented and significant chapter in international relations is coming to its end. Its life-span has been unexpectedly short. It signifies retreat from a bold and ill-conceived enterprise. Moreover, what was noble in its original motivation has become progressively submerged by other considerations which, inevitably, have led to mutual recrimination and to the present disenchantment.

The essence of that chapter has been the attempt to recast the industrially advanced countries' relations with the former colonial areas, emerging through the gate of independence as the underdeveloped southern half of our globe. The experiment itself rested on a double assumption. On the one hand, it was built on the belief that, through successive stages, the economically backward regions could repeat the Western world's own experience of economic development. The other assumption was that the wealthiest industrial states could set off and speed the economic development of the materially backward countries by offering part of the funds compulsorily collected from their taxpayers to governments of the new sovereign states in the form of gifts or loans. In both of these assumptions the rich countries were prompted by complex considerations ranging from the selfish to the altruistic. And as a rule, they professed to believe that the people constituting the governments at the receiving end would use the funds put at their disposal for the improvement of the lives of their citizens and for the modernization of their states.

Those who, for varying reasons, were opposed to the experiment have no difficulty, with the aid of hindsight, in describing it as a quixotic enterprise that attempted the impossible and tried to do so with inadequate means. Others, more favorably disposed, have maintained that the modesty of resources devoted to the experiment and growing contradictions in both its execution and its motivations have been short-circuiting whatever chances of success it may have had. Between the two poles, like most historical enterprises, the original experiment too will outlive its real utility. It will linger on half dead, kept alive by habit, inertia, and vested interests. Yet it is irrevocably a closed chapter.

It is closed not merely because of its theoretical shortcomings or the modesty of the means employed but also, and perhaps mainly, because the entire world political context in which the original experiment was conceived has radically changed.

The past quarter-century has seen the dispersal of power all around the North Temperate Zone. Centered first in the North Atlantic area, it yielded to a bipolar world. But this bipolar world, with its cold war setting —which for so long has provided the rigid framework for the ideas and the practices of relations between the rich and poor countries—has itself ceded its place to a multipolar constellation. Moreover, this transformation has been unfolding simultaneously with an ever-increasing integration among the industrial powers of the North Temperate Zone themselves. An ever more integrated industrial world now finds itself face to face with a splintered and economically backward numerical majority, united only in its common resentment against the economically advanced minority's privileges.

The ideas and methods hitherto mobilized in the service of the emancipation of the underdeveloped countries are by now severely battered. They did, however, add up to at least a tentative response to the challenge of an unprecedented set of problems in international relations. They produced a novel network of international engagements. But as the rethinking of the original methods and ideas becomes unpostponable, the response ought not be disengagement or withdrawal but rather an attempt to make the new endeavors consistent with the realities of the multipolar world emerging from the cold war.

To do so, a whole series of questions await constructive answers. The really relevant, basic ones—whether or not gifts and foreign aid in general can stimulate development, whether the rulers who received the gifts have been desirous and capable of using them for the desired end, or whether the assumptions of the economists, the theoreticians, the administrators, and the aid establishment as a whole have been built on observable facts—are only beginning to be asked. In the meantime, the one thing that has remained unchanged is the problem itself. In fact, each day it grows even more terrifying and monumental than it was when decolonization revealed it.

Influenced by the lessons learned, when and in what form the North-South problem will be confronted again in earnest is probably the second major problem of our times. The first, of course, is the accommodation in the making whereby the nuclear powers of the North Temperate Zone may avoid destroying each other and by doing so may even open the way towards common endeavors. Within such a context, the second problem may be their relations with the majority of mankind in the

Southern Hemisphere, an ever-increasing proportion of which is unable to satisfy even its elementary material requirements. Moreover, the second may very well condition the first.

Against such a background, it may seem almost blasphemous to ask why the future of the North-South relationship should be of such great concern to the materially advanced countries of the North.

Aid-giving as a part of international relations has not been widely challenged. Not even public opinion or legislatures in the rich countries have in their majority turned against the practice the burden of which they are supposed to carry. And this is the more significant as a whole series of interrelated developments seem to contradict this fairly general acquiescence.

One of them is directly connected with the very concept of the modern welfare state.

If we go back to its origins, we discover as its major motivating force a desire for the equalization of opportunity. Gradually it was also discovered that there was no incompatibility between egalitarian reforms and economic growth. Indeed, welfare reforms turned out to be highly productive both directly and in their indirect stabilizing influence. The redistributional reforms within the national framework, however, tended to encourage latent nationalistic sentiments. As Gunnar Myrdal pointed out some time ago, the welfare state implied intervention to correct the effects of blind market forces. Inevitably, this enhanced the importance of the national state. It alone could do the legislating, the taxing, and the regulating which was a prerequisite of the redistributive enterprise. The cumulative effect was the intensification of organizational and human relations within the national community and the focusing of people's attention on what was happening within it. Inside that framework people came to understand each other's motives, aspirations, and reactions. In brief, within the national framework they discovered both the inevitability and the advantages of their interdependence.

But simultaneously the outside world acquired more and more the characteristics of an unpredictable and dangerous entity, one beyond the familiar network of interdependence thus created. In this sense, the psychological sequels of the welfare state's evolution appreciably accentuated latent opposition between the safe and familiar on the one hand and the insecure and uncertain on the other. Indirectly, then, they tended to stimulate a kind of mental isolationism at the expense of an international outlook. This evolution, of course, has been in marked contrast with technological possibilities or with the growing integration of the industrialized world. As a defensive reflex perhaps, the new isolationist sentiment has been reluctantly expanded and transplanted to the limits of the emerging larger socio-economic frames imposed by technological progress. The place of the isolationist welfare state is being taken by the equally inward-looking regional entity. And the process continues up to the limits of what may seem plausibly familiar, the Common Market or an Atlantic Community today and, who knows, a white man's world tomorrow. Once the frontiers of this familiarity are reached, in the form of either cultural or racial barriers, the isolationist sentiment again coagulates around the core of the relatively familiar. Once again it becomes less and less flexible as a geographically broadened reflex of self-defense. The conflict of the familiar and the unknown is thus magnified up to the limits of technologically imposed larger dimensions.

This mental process, however, has evolved parallel with the technological transformation of our societies.

Out of a mass of economic, social, and technological changes a totally new system is emerging. It imposes new modes of social behavior. It shapes its own set of new values. It begins to amount to a new culture. But in the meantime, the Southern Hemisphere, by and large, has remained locked in its struggle to enter its first industrial revolution. This way, the psychocultural distance between the welfare units of the North Temperate Zone and of the materially backward countries of the Southern Hemisphere has been acquiring a new meaning. It is expressed less in calories or in per capita incomes than by an ever deeper grievance fed by the sense of humiliation caused by dependence and blocked horizons—a far more formidable barrier to communications than the mere material gap. The distance separating the familiar and the uncertain steadily broadens.

A related development has been unfolding in the purely technological field. The advanced industrial world's dependence on the raw materials of the Southern Hemisphere is no longer to be taken for granted. Ignoring, for the moment, that important parts of the industrial world might opt for slower economic growth involving diminished dependence on basic materials, the three continental units of the Northern Hemisphere—the United States, the Soviet Union, and China—either within their borders or in their easily accessible frontier areas, possess most of the essential raw materials their continued prosperity requires. The industrial areas as a whole—and Europe and Japan in particular—may soon engage in the exchange of a large volume of their industrial products against some of the natural resources of the Soviet Union and China. Moreover, all of them are fast developing manufacturing techniques and technology which enable them to achieve important economies in the quantities of raw materials they require, to replace them with synthetic and artificial products, or to prolong their usefulness through processes of recycling. Combined, these developments may considerably reduce the technologically advanced countries' dependence on raw materials imported from the former colonial areas.

To be sure, it is still cheaper within the prevailing international trading system to rely on imported ingredients. But should cost considerations be disregarded, their replacement is becoming technically feasible. Indeed, within the foreseeable future even the oil of the Southern Hemisphere may know a similar fate in face of the discovery of new deposits in the Northern Hemisphere and of the atomic and other new sources of energy likely to be produced at competitive prices.

Moreover, we are only at the beginning of the process. Plastics is only the first of the new industries producing "materials" for specific purposes and tailor-made qualities. It represents merely the beginning of the breakaway from traditional basic materials which, for thousands of years, have provided the parameters of man's creativity. He is about to cease to create from basic materials and begin to produce materials to serve the ends of his creativity. Provided the ecological problem is confronted in time and with the technological ingenuity it calls for, the ultimate prospect may very well be liberation from geographically located material resources, a development of incalculable consequences for the centuries-old relationship between economic entities, and the world-wide division of labor it produced.

Indeed, if some cosmic accident should sever the southern from the northern half of our globe, modern technology would soon enable the North Temperate Zone to adjust to the new situation without serious, long-term effects on its material prosperity. It would take time and would not be without serious temporary dislocations. In monetary terms it would certainly be costly. But it could be done.

But that is not all. Recent developments in military techniques, too, would have to be considered. Military power being more and more the product of advanced technology and of the ability to produce totally new materials, the industrially advanced world cannot fail to find in these developments further encouragement for its inward-looking inclinations. On the basis of some recent experiences, it may be argued that even this overwhelming technological superiority is helpless in the face of human qualities expressed in determination and the will to resist. This may be true, though only on condition that the full destructive potentiality is not utilized. Moreover, within the North-South context it is the defensive potentiality that really matters. In that sense, there can be little doubt that the advanced industrial societies' military-technological power is certainly in a position to protect them against physical destruction, against any outside force menacing their organizational functioning, or at least to render any serious challenge utterly suicidal. And the resultant strengthening of prevailing sentiments of invulnerability inevitably renders assertions of North-South interdependence the less convincing.

The mirror-image of such developments has been the steady erosion of the materially backward countries' prestige and bargaining power. The underdeveloped world is far less influential than it once was. It no longer throws up leaders capable of commanding a world-wide audience. Courted by the big powers at the height of the cold war, today the underdeveloped countries' views are little sought and even less heeded. On the international plane the political and economic concessions they have obtained have been marginal. Even in the rare situations where they have agreed policies, rather than to threaten they now have to persuade. If after Bandung the industrial countries reacted with an uneasy mixture of guilt and fear, fifteen years later the meeting of fifty-four nonaligned countries in Lusaka was barely noticed in the world press. The danger that the industrial North will continue the exploitation of the underdeveloped countries is a probability. But that the rich world may be tempted simply to ignore most of them is, henceforth, a distinct possibility.

The impact of such political, economic, and technological changes has been reinforced by the painful discovery that opulence did not usher in the oft-announced "end of ideology." The young are in search of a purpose. Managers, scientists, and intellectuals question their role in society. Chronic inflation brings strikes and echoes of the class war. And balance-of-payments difficulties focus attention on internal economic problems. All combined seem to conspire to intensify the collective, inward-looking sentiments of the materially advanced North. Yet paradoxically, and certainly encouragingly, a countertendency begins to assert itself all over the Western world, and in the United States in particular. It has its roots both in the obvious, inherent dangers of the mental isolation of the rich, and in the domestic ramifications of development policies calling for the rethinking of this particular aspect of international relations and of the engagements it has produced. Indeed, this new debate may go a long way to explain the persistence of the conviction that the future of North-South relations is still of capital importance.

But to ascertain how solid or how durable the conviction really is, it may be helpful to turn to the aims and the motivations of the postcolonial aid experiment.

There has been confusion all along about its aims. Some believed that the task was to help the underdeveloped countries catch up with the material levels of the industrialized ones. But the application of elementary arithmetic soon revealed the vanity of an exercise whose effectiveness would have to be measured in decades if not in centuries. The second aim, then, became to narrow the dangerous gap dividing the rich from the poor world. In some exceptional cases, and provided the rich countries' progress slowed down, this ought not to be impossible. Yet the acceleration of the rich countries' economic progress, brought about by technological innovation combined with appropriate economic policies, has rendered even this more modest goal almost unattainable. There remained a third and double aim. On the one hand, it was believed that by helping economic progress, aid-donors might lessen the probability of violent social and political upheavals capable of detonating conflicts in which they might find themselves involved. On the other hand, aid revealed itself as a convenient instrument to stabilize existing power bases and at least to prolong the status quo. This double objective, so it would seem, is still among the main aims of those shaping the policies of the aid-providing countries.

But there has been comparable uncertainty about the motivations of aid policies. With numerous variants, the arguments invoked have belonged to one of three main categories: the commercial, the strategic, and the moral.

The commercial or market argument rests on the deep-seated and still justifiable proposition that the underdeveloped countries represent both an indispensable source of essential commodities and raw materials and an irreplaceable market for at least some of the exports of the industrial states. To maintain and to expand the international system of trade, so the argument runs, it is indispensable to ensure the continued interdependence of the rich and the low-income countries. It is true, of course, that the volume of trade between the industrialized and the underdeveloped countries has grown considerably during the postwar years. But it is equally true that such trade represents a steadily declining share of the over-all commerce between nations. By now it accounts for less than a fifth of the total. Trade in the modern world is increasingly trade between the rich, and in manufactured goods.

All this said, it is obvious that commodities and raw materials can still be obtained at much more advantageous terms from the Southern Hemisphere than from alternative sources in the North. It is equally evident that, at least for some industries, the underdeveloped countries' markets offer great possibilities. Further, any rise in purchasing power resulting from economic progress would inevitably help transform the potential market of half of mankind into a real one capable of absorbing increasing quantities of both consumer goods and capital equipment. Nevertheless, for want of rapid economic progress, trade with the underdeveloped countries does not grow in proportion to the numerical promise of their potential consumers. Moreover, if inhibiting political considerations were one day set aside, trade within the North, between the Western industrial states and Japan on the one hand and the Soviet Union and China on the other, would yield far more spectacular results than anything that could be expected from exchanges with the underdeveloped countries at their present and foreseeable rate of economic progress.

The so-called strategic argument carries greater weight. It is made up of several related components.

In its simplest form it maintains that, in a world of big power competition, hostility from a state in the Southern Hemisphere may lead to its according military privileges to one or a group of Northern powers to the detriment of the others. Inversely, friendship and close collaboration with a country in the South might procure port facilities, air, land, or electronic bases, or, in case of war, might induce it to offer strategic support or even to ally itself with the war effort of the friendly Northern powers.

This argument also has its ideological projections. Regimes identifying themselves with the ideological options of a Northern power are more likely to listen to its advice, to go along with its political attitudes, or to favor and support its moves involving psychological or physical pressure. Last but not least, ideologically sympathizing Southern states are more likely than others to give the private investors of the Northern powers preferential treatment and thus to reinforce the factors which maintain them within the sphere of influence of those given great powers.

Finally, there is that aspect of the strategic argument which is concerned with continuity, violence, and the threat to international order. Economic progress, it is argued, will produce mature and stable regimes, and therefore to help bring it about is an indispensable insurance policy against spreading chaos and the breakdown of orderly international relations. This is now beginning to be threatened by events in various underdeveloped regions of the world. There are local wars and menacing international complications. There is a rise in the tempo and seriousness of violence, involving such acts as sabotage of essential installations, kidnappings, and the hijacking of planes, to all of which the complex organizational structure of the advanced industrial countries is particularly vulnerable. What is more, the possibility exists that some underdeveloped countries, not necessarily ruled by rational men, might even acquire relatively cheap but highly effective biological, bacteriological, or even nuclear arms. All this could bring about situations either uncontrollable by the great powers or capable of upsetting their security.

None of these arguments, however, is fully convincing. There have been only too many occasions to confirm that aid rarely begets gratitude and may rather have the opposite effect. Neither the Soviet Union's experience with Indonesia, the United States' with Pakistan, nor France's with Algeria seems to prove that economic aid is instrumental in securing lasting strategic advantages. As for ideological affinity, it can be durable only if based on spontaneous and effective coincidence of options. Otherwise, the imposition of ideological preferences unavoidably secretes an internal opposition likely to weaken collaboration even below the level that might have been attained without interference. In any case, Western concern for non-Communist development as much as Communist concern for the noncapitalist type of development was prompted by the assumption that economic aid would produce quick results and, by implication, proportionately rapid political commitment. By now it has become clear that in most cases development will be so slow that its ultimate ideological outcome has barely more than academic interest. And in the case of privileges secured for private investors, here too experience has shown that while it may be transitionally profitable, its durability will certainly be endangered whenever it goes beyond the recipient country's demonstrable self-interest.

That an underdeveloped country might employ modern, highly lethal arms against an industrial power cannot entirely be ruled out. But in view of the annihilating retaliation this would inevitably provoke, it is difficult to imagine that such a decision could be taken by logically reasoning individuals. If so, it is equally unlikely that mere economic aid or other material advantages would deflect them from their irrationality. Yet so long as at least one of the major military powers of the North considers it in its interest to push a minor country to suicide in order to serve its own design to harm the other great powers, the possibility cannot be discounted. That an underdeveloped country could obtain dangerously offensive, ultramodern weapons from a disgruntled power, though unlikely, is not impossible. Indeed, combined with accumulating racial resentment in the contemporary world and with the political opportunities this offers to a nonwhite major power, the possibility of such a course cannot lightly be discarded. The riposte to such a hypothetical constellation of circumstances, however, is not in the bribing or the forcible recruiting into subservience of unwilling partners, but rather in the removal of the grievance which might provide the temptation. The Soviet Union appears already more inclined to collaborate with its former rivals in the maintenance of world order than to exploit disorder to its own advantage. Offered similar participation and cooperation in the international community, China may very well follow the same path.

Sabotage, kidnappings, or the hijacking of airplanes, which so forcefully symbolize spreading chaos for newspaper readers, are almost without exception the acts of individuals or of desperate and disgruntled minorities prompted much less by international political or strategic considerations than by revolt against injustices within their own communities. Their acts, moreover, disproportionately disrupting as they may be for the highly integrated industrial societies, hardly ever seriously menace their security or their basic, world-wide interests.

But the core of the "strategic" argument, namely that collaboration between North and South is likely to produce and to maintain mature, responsible, and stable regimes, is the most vulnerable to confrontation with observable evidence. To begin with, practically all the major armed conflicts of the past decades have been set off by states with a far higher standard of living than any of the underdeveloped countries are likely to achieve within the foreseeable future. A full belly does not exorcise the temptation to violence. Moreover, only totally static societies are really stable. Imposed stability, on the other hand, provokes unrest and disruption. As a matter of fact, development creates its own appetites and is incompatible with the absence of often violent change. Indeed, development and even mere economic progress in most underdeveloped countries involve structural changes which, in view of the nature of the present ruling elites, cannot usually be brought about by pacific means alone. Development is synonymous with mutation and change and so with the acceptance of instability. As a rule, its course is not calculable. The only realistic antidote is power to limit its extent and curtail its spread whenever it may overflow into external adventure. The United States and the Soviet Union have already learned that lesson and under its impact have partially tempered their rivalry. If the great powers of the North really desire development to occur in the Southern Hemisphere, they will have to be prepared to live with prolonged instability over large areas of the world. To do so, it would be more in their interest to heal the grievances dividing them which prolong their rivalry, and not to attempt to impose stability on a hemisphere sick of intolerable deformations which are unhealable merely by peaceful means.

And this brings us to the third, to the moral argument.

The scandal of degrading and avoidable poverty surrounding the industrialized world's opulence is obvious. It is visible on television screens. It can hardly be ignored without courting bad conscience. Nor can it easily be dissociated from the kind of internal order three centuries of Western supremacy have helped to bring about. "For nations as for individuals, greed is the most evident form of moral under-development"—in the words of Pope Paul VI's encyclical *Populorum Progressio*—and in a world split North-South, the unthinking rich may have to face "the wrath of the poor" on an international rather than a national scale.

It is thus understandable that moral indignation in face of the prevailing situation can powerfully reinforce or even replace the vulnerable chain of spurious economic, political, and military arguments habitually invoked in the interest of greater cooperation between the rich and the poor world. Luckily there are many millions of both modest and prominent individuals in the rich countries whose imagination reaches out to the destitution and the agony of others living in distant lands. Yet even those in the industrialized countries who are sensitive to this moral obligation are torn between two contradictory sentiments. On the one hand, there is a vague sense of guilt due both to colonial history and to half-conscious awareness of benefitting from an international order which tends to prolong or even to reinforce exploitation. On the other hand, there is lurking fear of an emerging demographic minority status, potentially the more menacing as it may be backed by racial resentment. As a result, and notwithstanding the moral imperative, existing feelings of solidarity still hover ambiguously somewhere halfway between outdated paternalism and a still-fragile sense of international solidarity.

Nonetheless, it is the moral argument that has proved to be the most effective in moving opinion in support of aid. Yet in justification of their policies, aid-giving governments have tended to mobilize the particular half-truths which at a given moment, commercially, politically, strategically, or before their legislatures, best served their short-term interests. It is significant to note in this connection that in the past few years aid appropriations have declined most sharply in the United States where they have been most regularly justified on national security grounds. In contrast, they have notably increased in the Scandinavian countries (in Sweden in particular), where it is rather the moral argument which has most frequently been invoked.

In the meantime, however, primarily under the impact of scientific and technological developments, the North-South division and the moral challenge it poses have been acquiring new dimensions and a novel quality.

The conditioning impact of advanced technology and of electronics in particular on everyday life, on social organization, or on mass communications is shaping new attitudes and a corresponding new set of values. Our ability to act and to reason are extended and multiplied to a degree that is bound to transform our social environment from education to leisure, to biology, to the electronically manipulated techniques of mind-molding and government. For the time being the United States is the country which has undergone in this sense the most far-reaching changes. And if it may be questioned whether even Western Europe and the United States are still living the same sociocultural phase, it is clear that the gap separating the industrialized and the underdeveloped areas of the world is increasing. As the income gap continues to widen, its corollary, the psychocultural moving apart, is likely to acquire spectacular proportions. Yet simultaneously the spreading network of electronic communications will inevitably produce, in Kenneth Boulding's words, "a world super-culture, and the relations between this super-culture and the more traditional national and regional cultures of the past remains the great question mark of the next fifty years."

What will be the likely consequences?

As before, tiny privileged minorities will adapt to the new cosmopolitan superculture. But they will constitute mere sociocultural outposts incapable of interacting with the local environment. The majorities, deprived of access but inevitably informed of the new realities, will be the more intensely conscious of their privation. Mere dictatorships relying on unifying doctrines will be in no position to confront the resulting frustration and even less to offer lasting solutions. The parameters of material possibilities will still be prohibitive. Since they cannot attain the level of development of the advanced world, there may come an upsurge of conscious rejection of both its ideologies and its values. A mixture of xenophobia and racial hatred could provide the emotional force to fuel its vehemence. It might mean the end of any possibility of dialogue. It might also bring the end of any agreed set of human values. And in their convulsive frustration parts of the underdeveloped world may turn to movements of rejection and salvation, leading to a situation resembling, on an immensely magnified scale, the xenophobic, messianic disorders which punctuated the agony of the Manchu dynasty in China.

With such possibilities ahead of us, we may be going towards a socio-economic fractioning of the world, with a technologically robotized pragmatic core and an industrially advanced outer circle trying to harmonize its traditions with technological imperatives, both surrounded by impoverished masses in perpetual, fragmenting turmoil, driven by racial and regional passions, and in chronic revolt against the very psychosocial base on which the prosperity and way of living of the opulent minority has been built. Moreover, the strains and dangers of the resulting schisms would further be accentuated by the gradual disappearance of history's traditional shock-absorbers of distance and time.

Within such a hypothetical world environment, with imaginative thinking on the wane in mechanized and standardized societies, it is conceivable that the emission of new ideological waves would become the almost exclusive privilege of the rebellious, searching, and turbulent majority. At a given moment there might even arise the question which of the two psychological and sociocultural frameworks would be more conducive to the toleration of genuine human values, to the preservation of the variety and spontaneity of the human personality, or to the provision of conditions for a life humane enough to be worth living.

In a situation of this kind the major danger the prosperous minority of mankind would face would be the almost inevitable defensive reflex. With the *rentier*'s self-righteous and sterile mentality, anxiously awaiting the end of the storm behind his locked doors, it would demand the prolongation of the status quo and the protection of comfort and security. To succeed, it would be tempted to isolate itself from the movements and the ideas aiming at more than mere technological change. The price of such a defensive reflex might well be fossilized attitudes, mental sclerosis, and intellectual suffocation. It would be a very different danger from those now analyzed by military, political, and economic specialists.

To scrutinize the future is always a perilous enterprise. Yet those tempted to brush aside such speculations as exaggerated and remote might well ponder their heralding symptoms already around us.

Shorn of their coating of both hypocrisy and sentimentalism, the basic facts of the North-South relationship are fairly clear. To begin with, before the end of this century about seven billion people, nearly double the present world population, will be seeking by ever-expanding economic activities to maintain or to emulate living standards now the privilege of only a minority. In the second place, there is both the earth's finite capacity to support ever-mounting levels of production and consumption, and society's limited capacity to endure the physical, psychological, and ecological consequences of such an incalculable technological onslaught.

Indeed, the situation resembles that in a vast building where a minority living in the few spacious and comfortable apartments cohabits with a steadily multiplying crowd packed into far more numerous but much less comfortable rooms. Quite apart from the inevitable resentments, strains, and incidents, all have to obey certain rules. They have to rely on the same common services such as heat, light, and running water. They have a joint interest in keeping odors and noise at reasonable levels, the stairway free, the elevators in working order, the water reservoir clean and full, the rubbish chutes functioning, and television sets fitted so as to enable others to use theirs. The lodgers have no other place to go to, and no conceivable transformation or extension of the building could offer comfort to all. Thus arrangements have to be worked out in order to maintain a bearable situation. But with numbers growing each day, not even the most equitable distribution of space could offer a durable over-all remedy. In some acute moments charity will have its role to play. But it will solve no basic problem. The solution, if any, will not be merely in the field of the quantitative. Indeed, any satisfactory arrangement will ultimately have to rely on the new dimension of tolerance. And it is in this sense that the "moral imperative" returns.

But unlike the lodgers in that crowded building, we have to face the inadequacy of our comprehension of the very problems to be confronted. Synthetic and fashionable development doctrines have at best offered partial answers only. Can we fully identify the reasons which have led this first experiment in aid to its failure? Do we know enough about the particular mixture of motives, circumstances, and aims which induce apparently inert societies to embark on their own transformation? Can we define the real impact of external factors on their endeavors? Or can we ever command the objectivity to assess to what extent our own experiences are or are not relevant to their reality and to their aspirations?

It is not sure that unequivocal answers to such and similar questions will ever be forthcoming. What is certain is that without at least tentative answers there is little hope of building a new rationale for a more realistic confrontation of the problems arising from the coexistence of an immensely strong and materially comfortable minority with a destitute, vulnerable, and increasingly restless multitude.

And without such a new and coherent approach, the prospects for the remaining quarter of this turbulent century, which at last holds out the promise of peace among the potentially most destructive powers, will not be very reassuring.

Part ONE

I | *The Inimitable Original*

In most cases, underdevelopment today is lived by non-Westerners. But most of those who analyze its symptoms or build theories about its origins and elimination are Westerners or westernized intellectuals from economically backward countries. This is one of the remarkable features of the current widespread discussion of development.

Leisure, humanitarian inclinations, the predilection for synthesis, as much as the playful satisfaction of applying advanced mathematical tools to apparently realistic tasks, have all played their role. Relative ignorance of the underdeveloped countries' history, on the other hand, has made it easier to believe that their past or present situation resembles earlier stages of the history of the now technologically advanced states. Underlying all this has been the flattering and egocentric notion that underdevelopment is degradation, a deviation from a norm which must be analyzed and its future evolution envisaged in comparison with what has happened in Western societies.

By and large, then, two main schools have emerged in development economics. Their underlying ideas are, respectively, the "dual economy" and, resulting from the effort to view the problem in its historical perspective, the theory of the "stages" of development. There have been of course numerous variants, some attempting to harmonize the two. Yet both schools have this in common: they take the Western experience as their basis of comparison.

In the first school, the underdeveloped society under the microscope is divided into a "traditional" and a "modern" sector, with the implication that the latter sector assimilates Western forms and responds to Western types of stimuli while the former, the larger one, does not. The theorizing in this case is about the respective roles of the two sectors, about their interaction in producing balanced or unbalanced growth, and, in a larger perspective, about the spread of one at the expense of the other. In the "stages" approach, there are neat definitions of the various grades to be negotiated before the society in question reaches the economic nirvana of high per capita consumption of automobiles, washing machines, and other rewards of the consumer society.

Both conceptions assume that economic progress made by the West in the wake of its industrial revolution will be reproduced in comparable stages—though it is hoped much shorter ones than in the original process. In both approaches it is implicit that the underdeveloped countries of today are waiting for their own "take-off" at the end of history's runway, just as the now advanced countries waited at a given moment of their past before taking off into their own industrial revolution. The Communist approach is basically identical, though with its indispensable ideological ingredients.* That the planes are essentially comparable is taken for granted by both Western and Communist theories. That the engines or even the design of the aircraft now awaiting take-off may have undergone basic modifications during the two

*See Appendix 1, pp. 278–90.

centuries of delay is rarely considered. That during the same period traffic rules and the character of the frustrated pilots may have changed, or that, as a result of increased traffic, obstacles may have appeared on the runway itself, is frequently overlooked.

Within such a mental framework, then, modernization involves successive stages that each developing society must undergo in a more or less determined sequence. As a consequence, the concepts usually employed when theorizing about development tend to become metaphors, and analysis, in its turn, an unconscious exercise in attempting to force facts into forms shaped by comparisons.

As for the prototype itself, its origins are in the economic and political breakthrough which occurred first in England and later in France at the end of the eighteenth century and the beginning of the nineteenth. Though it has been abundantly described, we are still far from certain either about its origins or about the real determinants of its dynamics. Nonetheless, forgetting for a moment the millions of grown-ups and children who paid for its success with their hopes, their health, and even their lives, the story unfolds with fairytale logic and consistency. It leads up to the happy end, mercifully shorn of its incidental ugliness by history's ability to forget. In retrospect, the chain of developments, the interplay of indispensable components, the suitable answers to successive challenges—in a word, the smoothness of the whole process—tend indeed to lend reality to the perfection and the purposeful precision of a veritable laboratory model.

The scene having been prepared for the great play, as it were, politics, economic concepts, values, and social structures entered a period of metamorphosis as if inspired by people's sudden awakening to the fact that they might after all shape their economic and social environment to their own advantage. "Traditional" society began to undergo significant modifications. Owing to geography, to natural resources and to cheap communications, to trading opportunities offered by overseas conquest and to the commercial arts they fostered, as well as to suitable developments in the institutional, social, and political fields, England got ready for its take-off—the first, whose variants provided much of the economic and social history of modern times.

The most impressive feature of the process was no doubt its cumulative and self-reinforcing nature. The favorable interaction of simultaneous progress in agriculture and industry was the curtain-raiser. But following upon this early phase, developments unfolded as if an invisible magician had been carrying around a spark from each stimulated sector to awaken the dormant potentialities of the remaining ones. Indeed, the "diffusion effect," or "structural intercommunication," as economists call it, appears to have been the key to what amounted to almost generalized advance on all fronts.

It would seem that it was growing demand that spurred technical progress and its practical application, and that only after this did the population begin to expand with greater speed. Looking for the causes of this higher demand, however, much evidence indicates that a major cause was the fast growth in the quantity of food available. In England in the second half of the seventeenth century, the output of wheat on each hectare had grown three times faster than during previous centuries. By the beginning of the eighteenth century, thanks to more advanced methods of production, there was already a sizable surplus of grain for export. And from 1760 onward structural changes symbolized by the "enclosures" further accelerated the growth of agricultural output. Developments in France were similiar, though somewhat slower, the transformation beginning around 1750. If during the first half of the eighteenth century the annual increase of agricultural production was well below 0.5 percent, it grew to nearly 1.5 percent during the third quarter of the same century.[1] In fact, the early history of the industrial revolutions of both Great Britain and France clearly suggests a likely sequence: more food, a larger number of industrial workers, greater abundance of manufactured goods, and only subsequently more people. Indeed, though far from rich in good land, Britain began to import a sizable proportion of its food requirements only in 1840, more than sixty years after the beginning of its industrial revolution. The history of the other advanced Western countries, like that of Japan, seems to confirm the sequence. But that was only the beginning of the cumulative process.

Improvement in agricultural productivity first helped to satisfy higher nutritional demands. Then, in a climate of wide variations, textiles constituted the next most urgent unsatisfied need. Cotton, introduced on a large scale for the first time, was particularly suitable for mechanical treatment. As a matter of fact, without machines built to transform cotton, there would probably not have been comparable progress towards the mechanization of the production of textiles made of traditional fibers. Moreover, the mechanization of textile production ruined the peasants who were part-time handloom operators and so forced them to enter the new mills. Simultaneously, it compelled the remaining, relatively efficient agriculturists to step up their productivity in order to make up for the loss of income the handlooms used to provide. In this way, the coming of cotton and its mechanical transformation not only stimulated higher productivity on the land but, at the same time, produced its own reservoirs of industrial labor.

The beginnings of agricultural modernization, in

their turn, created a growing demand for iron to supply the simple implements and other equipment needed on the land. As with textiles, here too technical innovation was required to take care of increasing demand. The answer was provided by coal. The expansion of the metal industry, on the other hand, further improved agricultural equipment and thereby productivity. Furthermore, the improvement in the quality of iron and the lowering of its price soon made it possible to replace wood by metal in textile machinery, which remained the chief utilizer of metal until the coming of the railroads.

At that point the dialogue between industry and agriculture began to broaden. Agriculture had accomplished its historic task. From there on, technical development occupied the driver's seat.

The textile mills, with their insatiable demand for driving energy, and the metal industry—thanks to the lower price of iron and the growth in the output of coal—had been preparing the ground for a more sophisticated and portable steam engine. This again, together with cheaper iron and more abundant coal, opened the way for the railroads and the consequent drastic lowering of the cost of land transport. Soon the same process was repeated on the oceans, and henceforth overseas markets could be supplied at even more competitive prices.

This wondrous story of spontaneous development and its diffusion through sector after sector in mutually stimulating interdependence went hand in hand with a comparably logical and interlocking chain of modifications in supporting structures and institutions.

During the first stages of the process, the investments required to finance industrialization were rather modest. In England at the beginning of the nineteenth century, the equivalent of four months' wages was required to put a person to work in the nascent industries. In France, it required six to eight months' wages. The new capitalists could therefore be of modest origin, and indeed often came from agriculture. In fact, the investment capital required in agriculture was at the time higher than that needed to engage in industrial production. It was possible for the man who worked his handloom to transfer his skills and aptitudes to mechanical production. Traditional techniques could still be integrated into the new activities. Not only was a large pool of experience thus available to advance to a higher level of mechanical application, but, almost automatically, a potential entrepreneurial class was in reserve, ready to man the new posts created by the process of mechanization. The modesty of the investments needed and the high profits to be reaped in their turn helped self-financing and, at that early stage at least, made reliance on sophisticated financial mechanisms not too urgent.

The lack of cheap transportation throughout this period had, of course, a tonic effect on the various productive activities just unfolding. The high cost of transport, in practice a forerunner of later protectionist policies or of the self-imposed isolation resorted to by some countries in transformation, provided a natural barrier behind which there was no alternative to self-reliance. The so-called diffusion effect was unhindered. Each newly developed sector could fully exert its stimulating influence on those about to be born or just beginning to get on their feet.

Imports of equipment had played only a negligible role in the early industrial revolutions. For some time techniques remained relatively simple, and almost to the end of the nineteenth century the installation and operation of machines could be taken care of by former artisans and craftsmen, whose experience and knowledge were still adaptable to the emerging new techniques. Imitation was still relatively easy. Thus in England, and during the industrial revolutions following its own, most of the machines could be built relying on indigenous mechanics and craftsmen with little recourse to science or to invention.

A comparable sequence was repeated, with greater or lesser variations, in one after the other of the Western countries: about half a century later in France and Belgium and—under vastly different circumstances—in the United States; one or two decades after that in Germany, Sweden, and Switzerland.

The time span between the first and the last take-off within the Western, industrially advanced community was less than a century. It was only towards the end of that hundred years that the really revolutionary economic and organizational changes began to crowd in. The phenomenal acceleration and cheapening of transportation, the fast-growing specialization in all economic activities, the rapid sophistication of science-based technology which finally broke the link between traditional crafts and modern techniques of production, and last but not least, the growth and consolidation of overseas empires, bringing about the world-wide division of labor, all combined to change circumstances beyond recognition within a few decades. Already Japan had had to elaborate its own distinct method of take-off, totally different from the model relied upon in the West. Russia and later China found themselves in the same predicament.

The rest of the story we are familiar with. The classic sequence of stages in the Western model has been abundantly analyzed. What we do not know is the nature of the particular constellation of circumstances which, one after the other, set off the extraordinary process. Though its successive phases are richly documented, we know next to nothing about the causes of its beginnings. Some have advanced the view that the explanation is to be found in the economic influence of Protestantism. Others have looked for the cause in reactions to national humiliation.[2] One interesting theory maintains that the industrial revolution occurred in Northwestern Europe because it was the "frontier region of Mediterranean civilization," and thus "severed from the institutional power system of its parent," was "less stifled than any other [civilization] by age-long accumulations of institutional dust, more susceptible by far than any other to change and innovation."[3] One hypothesis is as good as another. We just do not know what particular combination of preconditions generated the industrial revolution. Indeed, to proffer any key set of detonators would be very much like pretending to have an irrefutable answer to the question how to fall in love.

It is known that this is more likely to happen at a certain age. It may be influenced by character or temperament, and it may be conditioned by imagination or by past experience. The variables are infinite, and few generalizations are admissible. Nonetheless, if an imaginative and healthy adolescent is placed in suitable intimacy with an exceptionally agreeable and attractive young lady, the chances of a positive outcome are fairly high. Notwithstanding the uniqueness of Western industrialization, development economists will be delighted to see their theories confirmed in other situations. What happened with reassuring regularity in the West in the nineteenth century, they will note, is happening again. Taiwan, Israel, and Mexico are there to support their case. That such and similar examples are the result of historically improbable combinations of internal and external circumstances will leave their faith unshaken. Indeed, should our young man fail to react as expected, Communist economists will instinctively ask for larger doses of ideological hormones. Western development economists, for their part, undeterred by the modest dimensions and the even more modest numbers of the apparently successful cases, will continue to insist that the constellation of their prescribed preconditions, however unlikely, should somehow be re-created in all subsequent attempts.

At this point, however, it may be prudent to inquire whether the young man in question is not constitutionally and fundamentally different from what his observers would like him to be. For if that is the case, it may even be necessary to admit that neither the hormones nor the Western prescriptions are likely to produce the expected results.

II | *A Distorting Encounter*

THE BEAUTY, if that is the word, of the West's first industrial revolutions resided in their cumulative nature. As with spectacular fireworks, one detonation set off the next. And the positive chain reaction of mutually reinforcing outbursts ushered in an over-all pattern of self-generating and self-perpetuating development. But once the shifting of the European economic frontier began, the external impact was quite different. The chain reaction was still there, but it was neither mutually reinforcing nor positive in its effects. Often it spread havoc. Nearly always, it tended to be distorting.

This inversion of effects, of course, had a variety of causes. One of them was the inability of agriculture to play the dynamic role it had in the West as a prelude to industrialization. Rapid changes in production methods and the fast-growing investments implied by nascent technology were other causes. By the end of the nineteenth century the cost of maritime transport—freight rates and insurance combined—had fallen to about a tenth of what it was at its beginning.[1] This removal of the protective shield costly transport had amounted to was perhaps even more pervasive in its effects. But overshadowing them all was the spread of direct European control over the overseas societies exposed to change, causing their forcible submission to the rules of the international trading system.

In agriculture, if differences in methods and productivity between preindustrial Western Europe and Asia or some parts of Latin America were a matter of degree, the same could not be said of Africa south of the Sahara. While the transposition of the West's agricultural transformation to most of Africa was inconceivable, by contrast it was at least a theoretical possibility in the case of Asia and Latin America. Nevertheless, the West's agricultural revolutions, opening the gates for the industrial ones, all occurred within the Temperate Zone, whereas most of the areas now underdeveloped lie in tropical and subtropical regions. The new techniques ought to have been adapted to local conditions. In addition, both the fertility of tropical soils and the climatic and health conditions affecting the cultivators should have been considered.[2]

Such considerations apart, the West's agricultural revolutions, at their beginning at any rate, were characterized by the reduction of unplowed land, by the introduction of new crops, and above all, by higher yields on already cultivated land. Units of cultivation of adequate dimensions, then, were primordial. But in Asia, for example, conditions were quite different.

In the England of 1700 there were 1.5 people for every hectare of cultivated land. In France there were 1.1. In contrast, for China at the beginning of the nineteenth century the corresponding figure was estimated at 3.6. In India, with 3.8 cultivators per hectare, the density seems to have been even higher.[3] It was still greater in the Korea of the eighteenth century: nearly four times more cultivators for each hectare than in France at about the same time. By and large, it seems safe to assume that when the impact of the Western agricultural revolution might have reached it, population density on the land in

East Asia was already three to four times higher than in Western Europe, a fact that goes a long way to explain why the Western pattern could not have been applied with any chance of success.* Moreover, improvements in sanitary conditions were already beginning to accelerate population growth. When England and France embarked on their industrial revolutions, their populations were growing by less than 1 percent annually. With relatively small populations increasing at a moderate rate, there was a good chance that the newcomers would be absorbed into the rapidly growing industrial sector. Not so in Africa, Asia, or Latin America. India's population expanded by a yearly 1.5 percent after 1870 and gathered speed in the following decades. The rate was 2 percent for the Moslem population of Algeria, and 2.2 percent for Egypt after 1880. Between 1870 and 1913, it reached 2.9 percent in Latin America.[4]

It was against such a background that the rapid expansion of the plantation economy occurred in many areas. Commerce in what became typical plantation products began long before the West's agricultural revolution. High prices at the time justified even small-scale trade in these products and indeed this was at the origin of some colonial conquests. But the rapid lowering of freight rates and insurance costs quickly transformed the situation. Once luxury items, tropical products became accessible to the masses. If Great Britain imported only 42 tons of tea in 1700, this increased to 25,000 tons by 1850 and to more than ten times that quantity a century later.[5]

John Stuart Mill noted in 1852 that "colonies should be regarded as outlying agricultural or manufacturing establishments belonging to the larger community" where, as in the West Indies, "England finds it convenient to carry on the production of sugar, coffee and a few

*Japan was the only exception in the region. Between 1870 and 1910 its population increased by a yearly average of 0.9 percent only.

other tropical products."[6] Like some contemporary economists, he too considered the coming of plantation economy as the beginning of the Western type of industrialization. Yet, rather than spreading their modernizing impetus, plantations tended to remain alien enclaves, impoverishing rather than enriching the food-producing agriculture surrounding them.

Contemplating the impact of the West's industrial revolution on the tropical and subtropical regions of the world, this is one of the numerous examples we see of a change advantageous from the purely economic point of view but exacting a high social and political price heavy in its consequences and not measurable in merely economic terms.

Transport grew cheaper while purchasing power was rising fast in the West. The demand for plantation products expanded proportionately. France's imports of cocoa, for example, went up from 675 tons in 1831 to 57,000 tons in 1960. World production of coffee increased fivefold between 1840 and 1880, and more than doubled again during the following quarter-century. Consumption of rubber, like that of other raw materials feeding modern industry, mounted even faster: from 1,400 tons in the middle of the last century to twenty times that much forty years later;[7] or from 80,000 tons in 1910, when the automobile appeared, to almost 3 million tons by 1970.*

But the other side of the medal reveals a corresponding chain of equally significant developments, though of a very different nature.

To begin with, an important proportion of the most fertile lands was taken over for plantations. In some areas, as on Java for example, the peasantry was virtually forced to give priority to work on plantations over the

*The nearly 3 million tons of natural rubber consumed in 1970 accounted for only 40 percent of the world total. Over 60 percent was in the form of synthetic rubber.

satisfaction of its own food requirements. In other situations, where local labor was inadequate in numbers or not easily adaptable to organized work on plantations, foreigners were imported in large numbers. This led to the appearance of sizable minorities of alien ethnic origin, such as the Chinese in Malaya and in Southeast Asia in general, the Indians in Ceylon, and the Negro communities in the Caribbean and in both North and South America, or to forced migratory movements all over Africa. Moreover, whenever the combined impact of such measures produced shortages in basic foodstuffs, cereals from Temperate Zone countries began to be imported. Simultaneously, the rapid growth in the quantities of plantation products exported (together with those of the mines) lowered still faster the cost of return freight and so made even easier the importation of manufactured consumer goods. These in their turn fatally undermined whatever local industry survived and heralded the doom of local crafts and artisans.

As a rule, the plantations were controlled by foreigners who supplied both capital and managerial skills. Nearly always they imported the equipment they needed, controlled the export market, and repatriated most of their profits. Moreover, plantation techniques were not transferable to food production. Given the organizational separation of the plantations and the importing of practically all the modern equipment needed, this precluded even indirect modernizing effects on the food-producing agriculture of the host country. In addition, if the first roads and railroads facilitated the evacuation of plantation (and mining) products to the ports, the same roads and railroads helped to render still cheaper the distribution of imported consumer goods in the interior.

Even such a summary canvas may help to pinpoint the origins of the whole series of problems which, with the passage of time, were destined to grow to serious proportions.

Not only were the colonized areas unable to emulate the agricultural revolutions of their colonizers; they also found their traditional agrarian structures modified by imposed, extreme specialization on marketable but locally not consumable products. The tools provided by the new metal industries, which in the West had helped to increase productivity on the land, were not available. As for the modernization of methods involved in plantation cultivation, this could not spill over into the food-producing sectors and so had no cumulative effect on over-all economic progress. Indeed, not only did several of the colonized areas thus become dependent on imported food, but the massive entry of manufactured consumer goods helped to eliminate local artisans and thereby to destroy the decisive link in human skills in the process of industrialization. Furthermore, with profits being drained out of the country and plantations contributing little to the prosperity of the majority, the host countries' economies gradually became dependent on distant and narrowly controlled markets, and this without any corresponding influence over prices. Compelled to provide congenial settings for the new type of production, including even the appearance of large alien minorities, economic and political structures underwent far-reaching modifications which have deeply marked the evolution of the societies in question right up to this day.

The other gravitational pull altering the original shape of numerous traditional societies came from the mines. Here too, the reduction of transport costs was the motor of change. Earlier it had been taken for granted that transforming industries had to be in the proximity of mines. With the coming of the steamship, the railroad, and later on, the ore-carrying cargo vessel, even a separation of several thousand miles ceased to be economically prohibitive. The result was more and more intense exploitation of distant mineral deposits without corresponding progress in the establishment of local transforming industries. The underdeveloped countries continue to supply a growing proportion of the world's base metals but transform only a tiny part of them. The exceptions apply mainly to ores with low metal content, involving prohibitive transport charges. But when it comes to iron ore, for example, if the underdeveloped countries supply over a third of the non-Communist world's output, they still account for less than 4 percent of its production of steel. In fact, even in the industrial countries with immense reserves of metals in their soil, the tendency is still for the transforming industries to move to the ports and there to process the imported ores.

As was the case with plantations, mining operations were usually started by foreign companies and their profits and savings have been repatriated on a continuous and massive scale. Similarly, most of the equipment and other goods needed by the new enterprises were imported, as well as the specialists and the managerial personnel. The influence of the consumption habits of those working for the mining industries spread simultaneously with the cheapening of transport, and inevitably helped to stimulate demand for imported, manufactured consumer goods. Furthermore, the relatively advanced techniques employed in mineral exploitation did not spread to the surrounding economy any more than in the case of plantations and, in the same way, scarcely contributed to the modernization of the host economy as a whole. Here, too, there occurred no automatic interaction.

Thus, such developments in both agriculture and mineral exploitation not only failed to provide the required impetus to industrialization but, by eliminating artisans and traditional crafts, also helped to destroy the very pillar on which the West's transition to industrialization had been built. This was particularly marked in the fully colonized areas, though, to a lesser extent, other regions too were exposed to the same impact. In fact, industrial techniques underwent in the meantime rapid sophistication, and the simple integration of traditional skills gradually became impossible. Even imitation grew more and more difficult without the intervention of at least a certain degree of scientific reasoning. If in the West the iron founder, the locksmith, or the watchmaker could keep up with technical evolution, the traditional artisan of the underdeveloped countries was as a rule unable to construct his bridge leading to the building of a steam engine or the repair of a dynamo. It was too late to regain the ground lost. Once again the gap in the diffusion effect manifested itself with a vengeance, and dependence on imported machinery and equipment became more and more pronounced. Moreover, just when the radical lowering of freight rates disposed of the virtual protection of home markets, there occurred also an enormous increase in the burden of industrial investments.

If putting a man to work in industry in early nineteenth-century England was reckoned to cost the equivalent of three to four months' wages (and about twice that much in France), by the middle of the twentieth century in the United States it already required what he earned in thirty months. In 1951 a group of experts appointed by the United Nations estimated at $2,500 the amount of capital needed for each additional person to be absorbed into nonagricultural employment in a typical underdeveloped country.[8] This would correspond to about ten years' wages of the average Indian factory hand. In Western textile mills, for example, in 1945 it cost over $6,000 to create a new post. In up-to-date, automated spinning mills, the investment needed to employ an additional person is now estimated at up to $100,000, or more than an Indian worker would earn in four centuries.[9]

Even if one disregards for the moment the possible influence of aptitudes, climate, and other factors not easily calculable, such figures alone ought to go a long way to explain the relative paucity of entrepreneurial classes in most underdeveloped countries. To complete the picture, however, it must be remembered that during the early industrialization of the West the existence of large numbers of small industrial units provided a vast experimental ground for both technical and entrepreneurial talent. This school has not been open to the underdeveloped countries nor, as a consequence, the natural selection of talent it offered in both fields.

But the absence of economic cross-fertilization illustrated by such examples conveys hardly any impression of the numerous secondary effects of the distortions thus introduced. The growing difficulty in relying on self-financing was only one of them. The lack of suitable educational progress, due at least partly to the missing link in the economic process which might have stimulated it, was another. The demonstration effect of the rich countries' social legislation constituted an additional factor tending to inflate the cost of any large-scale economic enterprise.

As for organizational abilities and techniques—both essential ingredients and fruits of accelerated growth in the West—these had no chance to develop for want of comparable activities. Negotiating skills, naturally acquired by those at the center of the emerging global economic network, could not be assimilated. Such skills, of course, were also a part of the growing power of Western countries over the underdeveloped countries. The same applied also to the financial, banking, insurance, and transport mechanisms, all rapidly growing more complex. Though substantial utilizers in all these fields, the underdeveloped countries were offered few opportunities to prepare their specialists for them. The list could be lengthened without difficulty. It would merely help to confirm that the technical, scientific, and social progress which had transformed the industrial nations so radically and with such speed scarcely touched the surface of preindustrial societies.

It is not surprising that the areas which have experienced such a sequence of influences today face incomparably greater obstacles when they attempt to modernize than the countries of Western Europe had to confront at the time of their own early industrialization. Their demographic inflation in itself confers on their task a totally different dimension. Furthermore, the difference is not only quantitative, but has also its decisive qualitative aspects.

Indeed, an awareness of the direct consequences of the imposed collaboration of partners so manifestly unequal might lead one step nearer to the identification of the essence of underdevelopment.

Suspended, as it were, between the two poles of plantation and mine, the preindustrial societies grew both highly vulnerable to outside economic influences and excessively dependent on them. A number of other factors, though highly beneficial in themselves, compounded the mounting difficulties. Modern technology imported into labor-abundant societies brought unemployment and nearly always greater inequality. Parliamentary institutions, notwithstanding their merits in the milieu that had produced them, tended to consolidate the power of unrepresentative westernized elites and to divert scarce talent into sterile opposition. Paradoxically and most unfortunately, even Western hygiene and medicine aggravated the situation by introducing modern death rates long before birth rates could be tamed by modern methods. Newspapers, films, and radio, for their part, have been instrumental in the almost irresistible projection of alien consumption habits which have invariably stimulated material aspirations and patterns of demand which the existing economies could not possibly satisfy.

The simultaneous exposure of such distorted social structures to world market forces, subjecting the weaker to the formative influences of the stronger, exerted its full force. The trade that developed between such unequal partners could be neither free nor equitably distributed. Within such a context, capital movements and even imported knowledge and technology tended further to unbalance the preindustrial structures. Together with discriminating freight rates, with subsidized agricultural production in the rich countries, and with the punitive escalation of tariff structures calculated to hinder the underdeveloped countries' attempts to export their own raw materials in processed or manufactured forms, all were part of the system which has found its apotheosis in the prevailing world-wide division of labor. Its essence is that the former colonial countries are specialized in a narrow range of products whose long-term market possibilities are usually bad—mainly those of tropical agriculture, and of industries which are extractive and technologically stagnant—while the former colonial powers concentrate on industrial activities characterized by dynamic technological progress.

That the cumulative effect of this rigid and almost irreversible separation of roles fuels discontent and corrodes social cohesion in the underdeveloped countries is hardly surprising. And it is unlikely that the problems thus created will be faced with the required realism so long as they are defined in mainly economic terms. These are very inadequate guides, along the stages of descent from usually poor, sometimes prosperous, but more often merely balanced and viable societies, through the stagnation caused by institutional distortion and progressive impoverishment, to the deformity now commonly referred to as underdevelopment.

To indulge in metaphors, in the case of the Western industrial revolutions not only did the wheels of economic activity steadily expand in diameter but, simultaneously, they also developed cogs which smoothly interlocked with those of the neighboring wheels, bringing the entire formidable mechanism into mutually reinforcing, accelerating movement.

The evolution of the areas exposed to the Western impact, on the other hand, might be compared to a plant which suddenly finds itself surrounded by the dense network of a banyan tree's irresistible roots. The plant's growth is not arrested, but its course is narrowly determined; it has to twist its way between the inflexible branches and adapt its shape and direction to the openings left by the invading giant. Seeking its way, the plant is increasingly deflected. It is forced to lean on the intruding roots and, by doing so, is deprived of the possibility of acquiring the necessary experience to stand on its own feet. Gradually, distortion becomes its normal shape and the resulting deformation the price of its continued existence.

At this point the eyebrows of liberal economists will be raised into Gothic arches. If increases in national income are faster than population growth, they will object, will that not lead to higher standards of living and, as a consequence, to the gradual solution of existing economic, social, and political problems? And they will quote the standard list of star performers. It is distressingly short. And even so, a few can quickly be omitted as evidently exceptional. Whether it is Puerto Rico, Libya, Israel, Hong Kong, or Saudi Arabia, it is clear that the fast growth of their national product has been due to highly unusual circumstances unlikely to be repeated elsewhere and that they provide no model for countries less fortunately endowed with either natural resources or strategic, political, or human assets. As for the rest, there remain Mexico in Latin America, Malaysia and Thailand in Asia, South Korea and Taiwan in the proximity of Japan, and the Ivory Coast in Africa.[10]

It should not be overlooked that in each of these countries, as in many others not on the list, there have been real economic achievements and genuine progress either towards industrialization or in agricultural modernization. But it is equally clear that all of them have benefitted from a constellation of very exceptional factors on which the overwhelming majority of underdeveloped countries simply could not count.

Mexico inherited from its revolution an agriculture whose basic structures had been radically changed. It is the neighbor of the world's richest market and has a regular and very important tourist income. Relying on the defensive umbrella of its giant neighbor, it has wasted little on military expenditure and has been able to count on an exceptional volume of private foreign investments. Malaysia, exporting tin and rubber and importing much of its food, has benefitted for several years from the rising demand for its mining and plantation products and, in fact, has achieved Asia's second highest per capita income, after Japan. Thailand, even richer in natural resources, has reaped comparable advantages. Heavy foreign investments and income, connected with America's military presence in the region, were further contributory factors. The Ivory Coast's economic growth, built mainly on its plantation products, was favored both by its privileged relationship with the Common Market and by an exceptionally heavy inflow of foreign capital. As for Taiwan and South Korea, they have inherited infrastructures developed by Japanese colonization. They were flooded by American aid for political and strategic reasons, and both have greatly profited from the considerable financial fallout produced by the Korean and Vietnam wars. Previously, Taiwan received also the influx of capital, skills, and entrepreneurial talent fleeing China. Last but not least, South Korea as well as Taiwan has been much exposed to the radiating effects of Japan's extraordinary economic ascent and, more recently, to its growing tendency to transplant its labor-intensive industries to nearby low-wage areas.

Yet even so, in none of these cases has economic growth outpaced population expansion by more than 6.5 percent. Indeed, Taiwan aside, the per capita share of the growth of income even in these exceptional cases was not much above 4 percent. But how was this distributed? Has it helped to reduce inequality and unemployment, to eliminate illiteracy, or, in general, to further social justice? Has it alleviated economic vulnerability or extreme dependence on external forces and decisions? Has it advanced the solution of the economic, social, and political difficulties implicit in underdevelopment, or has it rather aggravated them?

This is really the heart of the matter: the difference between mere poverty and underdevelopment, or between economic growth and development.

While statistically measurable growth may attenuate poverty, at the same time it may also aggravate the symptoms of underdevelopment. In practice poverty and underdevelopment may—and only too often do—coincide. But in a historical perspective they are not synonymous. The first is quantifiable. The second is essentially qualitative; it is a state of mind and a cumulative process like development itself. Its definition has to rely more on the historian and the sociologist than on the economist alone. Poverty as such does not exclude development. Nor is continued underdevelopment incompatible with a growing national product. Yet underdevelopment is a historical phase with its specific internal and external constraints which obstruct progress towards self-reliance and spontaneous, balanced growth.

Experience seems to prove that the unchecked market forces at work on the international scene tend to perpetuate if not to accentuate inequality and underdevelopment. That the mere injection of foreign aid or technical assistance can tame this implacable trend has not yet been convincingly demonstrated. Indeed, the few non-Western countries which have achieved self-sustaining and autonomous development have done so at the price of a more or less prolonged isolation from the world economic system dominated by the West. Japan, after the Meiji Restoration, though poor in resources, industrialized and developed fast while insulating itself against unwanted outside influences. Latin America and Russia, though immensely richer in resources, failed to do so. In fact, Russia repeated Japan's achievement only after it too had cut itself off from the world system. And China, so it seems, is in process of copying their example. All these cases can of course be attributed to particular circumstances. No doubt these played their role. But to disregard Japan's, Russia's, and now China's path and, relying on a few dubious examples, to maintain that external aid can be decisive in ending underdevelopment, may justify methods as dangerously ambiguous as would be the treatment of a deformed spine by the provision of better crutches.

The problem of underdevelopment—and this is almost all we have learned about it during the past quarter-century—is far more complex than it was first believed to be. It has its roots in local history as much as in the world-wide economic environment. It does not lend itself either to hasty solutions or to spacious generalizations. Yet upon decolonization, the fear of disruption of traditional ties, demographic alarm in some regions, as well as political and strategic considerations in others, precipitated action. The future donors were only too disposed to overlook how complicated and deep-seated were the problems, the choices involved, and the consequences of their actions.

And so, the aid experiment got under way.

III From Ideal to Practice

THE HORROR AND WASTAGE of great wars inevitably secrete their antidote of idealism. The Second World War was no exception. Among the positive endeavors conceived as the slaughter and destruction came to an end, there was one that seemed to symbolize a decisive mutation in the social consciousness of sovereign nations. As the world dug itself out of the rubble, the victors decided to give institutional form to the overflowing of human solidarity across national borders. Nothing of the kind had ever existed before. People seemed to have become aware that their governments had a responsibility not only to promote the well-being of their own citizens but also to aid the just aspirations towards a better life of less fortunate masses in other lands.

Still better, the original formulation of the aim has clearly shown that its drafters were at least vaguely aware of the multidimensional complexity of development. Yet, notwithstanding the various institutions created for the task, a shift in emphasis soon became perceptible. Shorn of its original components one after the other, the whole undertaking was gradually reduced to a quantifiable economic operation. Its complexity disregarded, deprived of much that had been noble in its original purpose, the experiment became little more than the wielding of a mere economic instrument in the service of barely concealed political aims.

There was no conscious perversion involved, nor did any mastermind conceive or direct the metamorphosis. It was the outcome of the interplay of changing circumstances, of unforeseeable accidents or of pressures emanating from identifiable interests, and of the complicity of certain groups in the aided countries themselves. Combined, they provoked a series of uncoordinated modifications. One by one the generous was replaced by the selfish, the desirable by the expedient, and the imaginative by the shortsighted until the whole design acquired the shape and dimensions of what in retrospect may appear a great fraud.

Indeed, an attempt to retrace at least the main stages of this descent from ideal to practice is instructive, showing how excessive optimism was followed by disenchantment, then by discredit, and finally by the failure of the whole aid experiment.

"With a view to the creation of conditions of stability and well-being which are necessary for peaceful and friendly relations among nations based on respect for the principle of equal rights and self-determination of peoples," those who drew up the Charter of the United Nations in 1945 expected the organization to promote "*a*) higher standards of living, full employment, and conditions of economic and social progress and development; *b*) solutions of international economic, social, health, and related problems; and *c*) international cultural and educational co-operation." And all members signed their pledge "to take joint and separate action" for the achievement of these aims. According to this grand design, the Economic and Social Council was to be the coordinating center of a galaxy of United Nations special agencies, in the effort to help the nations of the world undertake a coordinated and world-wide offensive against poverty, unemployment, and the other economic and social causes of international tension and war.

It is worth noting that in this original statement of the ideal, in addition to higher standards of living equal emphasis was given to full employment and to the preconditions of progress and development, with acknowledgment of the complexity of a variety of related issues such as health, education, and human rights.

That was, one should remember, two years before the day when, to the accompaniment of military music, Lord Mountbatten and his troops left the subcontinent of India and thus inaugurated the period of decolonization. Simultaneously, the pillars of the aid edifice were erected. Because of the fluidity and the geographical dispersion of the process, however, its chronological definition is not easy.

To begin with, from the Bretton Woods Conference emerged the World Bank and the International Monetary Fund. But so far as the underdeveloped countries were concerned, it soon became clear that these institutions associated with the United Nations were to contribute to the charter's purposes on the basis of strict banking principles. The underdeveloped countries, of course, could not easily afford to borrow money at high interest rates, nor had they the experience or the expertise to put money quickly to work if they could get it at all. So, the United Nations proceeded to set up its Technical Assistance Board, which, in collaboration with its special agencies, was going to show the emerging countries what a number of desirable things they could have if only they could command the experts and the capital to make them work. Then the United Nations was given its Special Fund, to provide preinvestment grants and the infrastructure necessary for development, though the Fund has never been provided with anything like adequate means. And to complete the picture, later on the World Bank created its own International Development Agency (IDA)—in Lord Ritchie-Calder's words, its "softhearted side"—to provide cheap or interest-free loans from the profits it was making on its ordinary lending operations.

In the meantime, in 1950 a group of experts appointed by the secretary-general of the United Nations had attempted to spell out in detail the intentions of the charter. Their report, the first of its kind, prefigured two main aspects of the aid debate, which was destined to grow to monumental dimensions in the years to come. On the one hand, it gave a foretaste of the tenacious practice of global quantification. On the other, it spelled out with remarkable candor the structural preconditions of development.

"Economic progress will not occur unless the atmosphere is favourable to it," the experts warned. "The people of a country must desire progress, and their social, economic, legal and political institutions must be favourable to it." These words introduced a discussion of "the psychological and social prerequisites of progress."

> People may be unwilling to make the effort to produce wealth if the social prestige which they desire is more easily acquired in other ways. Thus, in feudal or aristocratic societies where power is inherited rather than earned, and where little respect is accorded to wealth which has been created in the first or second generation, the energies of ambitious men are not attracted so much to the production of wealth as to the acquisition of skills which may secure entry into the strongholds of power.

The discussion of the structural preconditions of development was carried even further:

> . . . in any society inequalities of wealth may deny equality of opportunity to the greater part of the population, and keep ignorant many persons who, given the opportunity,

> would contribute to raising the national income. This is at its worst where society is stratified by caste, colour, or creed, and where whole sections of the population are deprived of opportunity by law, by custom, or by chicanery. Rapid economic progress is seldom found in societies which do not have vertical mobility or where a section of society is seeking to maintain special privileges to itself. . . . There is a sense in which rapid economic progress is impossible without painful readjustments. . . . In our judgment, there are a number of under-developed countries where the concentration of economic and political power in the hands of a small class, whose main interest is in the preservation of its own wealth and privileges, rules out the prospect of much economic progress until a social revolution has effected a shift in the distribution of income and power.

And the warning was reiterated:

> There cannot be rapid economic progress unless the leaders of a country at all levels—politicians, teachers, engineers, business leaders, trade unionists, priests, journalists —desire economic progress for the country and are willing to pay its price, which is the creation of a society from which economic, political and social privileges have been eliminated.[1]

As for the quantitative part, the group of experts drew up a neat statistical table with precise estimates of the needs of the underdeveloped countries in the fields of agricultural and industrial development in Asia, Africa, and Latin America. They suggested that the industrial countries should transfer to the underdeveloped ones about $10 billion annually, amounting to some 3 percent of the combined national incomes at that moment of Western Europe, Australasia, the United States, and Canada. They also recommended that the underdeveloped countries should raise an equal amount from their own domestic savings: "An annual investment of about $19 billion, which is about 20 percent of the national income of these countries in 1949, might raise their national income by about 2½ percent per annum."

Two decades have elapsed since this report was published. The quantification game which it launched—that is, the calculation down to the second decimal of how much financial aid would be required by people as different from one another as the Laotians, the Congolese, and the Chileans in order that their national incomes should grow by a certain percentage—has become a flourishing academic pastime and has fatally infected the international organizations. As for the second theme—preconditions and necessary structural changes—this has received less and less emphasis as the years have gone by.

To explain this diminishing emphasis it is sufficient to recall the principal changes in international relations in the years following the publication of the report. By the end of 1949 Mao Tse-tung was in power in China. American policy towards Japan was undergoing rapid and spectacular change. The first rape of Czechoslovakia had occurred, and McCarthyism was spreading its paralyzing semantic terror over the United States. The Berlin blockade in Europe and the Korean War in Asia marked the crescendo of the cold war. During those years, within a decade following the publication of the United Nations Charter, ideal and reality had been forced into confrontation. As a result, each had to go its own way.

At this point, however, one has to recognize the immense formative influence of the Marshall Plan.

The United States emerged from the war with its economy not only undamaged but greatly expanded. As the other victors tended to their wounds, America was the major source of aid. In fact, in view of the towering predominance of the United States' national product among all nations, American aid for many years to come usually accounted for more than half of all the resources the advanced countries were to put at the service of their assistance efforts. The historical beginnings of the United States aid program were in the Marshall Plan, and ever since it has been persistently evoked both as the model of a successful aid and development effort and as its greatest achievement. For all these reasons, the Marshall Plan's motivation and operation influenced later American aid so decisively that it could hardly be overestimated.

In the late 1940s, the United States devoted nearly 3 percent of its national product to aiding Europe, most of it in the form of gifts. Yet if the originators of the Marshall Plan sought to root it in the instinctive generosity of the American people, they did so with a clear-cut objective: to help rebuild a Europe strong enough to resist the menace of Communism. And the two elements, the humanitarian and the defensive, have ever since provided the basic rationale of America's aid program in favor of the underdeveloped nations. The mixture has been at the back of the semantic confusion which has surrounded the subject and colored the pronouncements on aid of all postwar presidents.

Launching his "Point Four" program, President Truman stated: "Democracy alone can provide the vitalizing force to stir the peoples of the world into triumphant action, not only against their human oppressors but also against ancient enemies—hunger, misery, and despair." President Johnson was more outspoken: "Of course, our security and welfare shape our policies. But much of the energy of our effort has come from moral purposes. . . ." In 1961, in his Foreign Aid Message to Congress, President Kennedy expressed the view that "the economic collapse of those free but less developed nations which now stand poised between sustained growth and economic chaos would be disastrous to our national security, harmful to our comparative prosperity and offensive to our conscience." Later on, in his message to Congress in May 1969, President Nixon merely paraphrased the mixture used by his predecessors: "If we turn inward, if we adopt an attitude of letting the underdeveloped nations shift for themselves, we would soon see them shift away from the values so necessary to international stability. Moreover, we would lose the traditional concern for humanity which is so vital a part of the American spirit."

But the Marshall Plan was essentially a repair job. The effort was meant to be, and indeed turned out to be, self-liquidating. It involved the rehabilitation of modern and highly productive societies temporarily damaged by war. These possessed the techniques, the organizational ability, and the human resources needed to re-establish their prewar prosperity. Nonetheless, except for aid to the Philippines, this was the United States' first experience in institutionalized foreign aid, and it was inevitable that it should lastingly stamp American attitudes. Previously, the term "foreign aid" had been used to define a variety of activities, from missionary effort and disaster relief to postwar rehabilitation of refugees, or from military support to foreign investment and cultural exchange. But later on, that ambiguity carried over to new countries which, unlike postwar Europe, had started off with few if any of the essential requirements for building a modern state. Thus around 1950, when in the midst of the cold war United States foreign-aid budgets began to grow fast, the semantic ambiguity maintained by the interplay of generosity and interest tainted with hypocrisy decisions on both economic and political levels. Rehabilitation was confused with development and emancipation with friendly alignment.

Characteristic American optimism also played its role. What was accomplished within a few years in Western Europe, it was believed, could be repeated in the underdeveloped countries. The model was there: the countries of Western Europe had "developed," so the economically backward countries had merely to follow in their footsteps. As a matter of fact, during the forties and fifties foreign aid was considered a transitory phenomenon. United States foreign-aid legislation was of one-year duration, and in extending the Mutual Security Act in 1953, Congress expressly stipulated that economic aid was to end within two years and military aid one year after. Part of the explanation was that aid had come to be considered a mere short-term instrument of foreign policy, and it was not by accident that the Agency for International Development operated within the State Department. Another part of the explanation may have been in the frequency of elections in the United States and in the resulting greater sensitivity of congressmen to public reaction: they had to offer specific results for their constituents' money and votes. Yet if they looked to the polls for guidance, increasingly they found foreign aid far below such domestic interests as cheaper health services, better roads, or more recently, protection against industrial pollution.

Notwithstanding this inconsistency in the two major motivating elements, these had been catering, as it were, to two distinct needs. Generosity and anticommunism appealed to the average American's pride and sense of mission. Political, economic, and strategic interests, on the other hand, moved Congress, which with the passage of time became increasingly unwilling to vote any economic assistance unless it was coupled with a military-assistance bill.[2] This became a marriage of convenience, an inevitable compromise to save a political orphan from complete neglect.

The evolution of the aid story from ideal to compromise followed a similar course in the case of the former colonial powers.

In the autumn of 1950, for example, facing up to the economic problems of the newly independent Asian members of the British Commonwealth, there appeared the Colombo Plan.[3] "The peoples of Asia have long felt the pressure of poverty and hunger," it noted; the scale of the problem was such that "a new and more comprehensive approach" was essential. Since Asia played "an important part in the world economy as a major source of the food and raw materials consumed throughout the industrialized world," there could be no doubt that "external finance must continue to be made available if the constant pressure of population is not to depress living standards still further." To avoid this, "a fresh impetus should be given to economic development . . . in order to increase production, raise standards of living, and thus enlarge the volume of trade around the world from which all countries may benefit."

The program outlined by the Colombo Plan—an aggregate of the first development plans of the Commonwealth countries of Asia—was judged unlikely "to show spectacular results by 1957"; it would do "little more than hold the present position." Nevertheless, its drafters insisted, "it will be apparent to everyone [in the region] that progress is being made." Why mere lack of deterioration should be interpreted by the peoples concerned as progress seemed to be explained by the reiterated emphasis on the trading role of the countries in question. As the text pointed out, not even hinting at the problem of distribution, "The increase in incomes is likely, other things being equal, to contribute to the expansion of world trade."

Compared with the purity of intention of the United Nations Charter's aid prescription, the Colombo Plan—like the evolution of American thinking in the meantime

—already revealed significant shifts in emphasis. The principal preoccupation of the former colonial powers was the preservation of their long-established economic, political, and cultural ties. Their greater familiarity with local conditions perhaps helped them not to yield to excessive optimism. By the time Holland, France, and Belgium parted with their former dependencies, the pattern of bilateral aid practices was already firmly established. Later, when some North European countries, with Sweden in the forefront, entered the scene, the shortcomings of the emerging system had already become apparent enough to make them opt for greater humanitarian content in their policies. That they had no established interests to preserve in former colonies, and that by and large they were less pressed by urgent internal problems, no doubt facilitated their more altruistic stance. Finally, when Germany and Japan re-emerged as formidable economic and trading powers, both entered the assistance field with commercial and financial considerations heavily overshadowing the emancipating content of their action.

In a nutshell, these were the major stages the aid and development idea traversed in the two decades following the solemn undertakings of 1945. Though gradual, the descent from the lofty heights of idealism to the pedestrian practical level was nonetheless spectacular. And the drive, from the late 1940s, to fashion and to adapt aid programs so as to fit the industrialized powers' political, economic, and strategic interests in the cold war had several important consequences.

By the time decolonization was practically completed, most advanced countries had clarified their ideas as to how far their short-term interests could be allowed to trespass on their image of magnanimity, leaving the multilateral institutions to operate on the margins as mere keepers of their good conscience. Bilateral aid programs were to be concentrated on friends and associates, with occasional consideration to potential enemies. The objective need of the country for aid was to be superseded by the subjective economic and political requirements of those in a position to provide assistance.

Yet in the long run, doubts emerged even within this framework of constraints. As *The Economist* so candidly summed up several years later:

> . . . if aid is to mean anything, it should (1) involve nasty choices about where it is to go; and (2) enable the recipients to become more powerful enemies, as well as more powerful friends, of the donors. These two points are interrelated. On the one hand donors do not like giving money to countries that are patently hostile to them. On the other they try, if possible, to avoid having clear-cut criteria for giving aid, like presenting it all to the poorest, or alternatively to those most likely to succeed. There must be some doubt, in fact, whether donor countries really want to take responsibility for enabling developing countries to develop. . . .[4]

These basic doubts aside, the two trends of thought intertwined in the United Nations experts' report of 1951 clearly indicated the theoretical poles between which the aid debate has been oscillating ever since. On one side were those who considered that the only practical attitude was to try to graft the Western experience onto the economic and social heritage of the former colonial countries. On the other stood the protagonists of structural change, with their claim that this was a prerequisite of genuine development. Both approaches implied painful, costly, and immensely complicated processes. The "grafters" could at best expect slowly spreading results as the concentric circles of modernization affected larger and larger segments of the population. The "structuralists," on the other hand, could hardly have excluded the use of force to bring about the desired changes without at the same time being absolutely certain that the sequel would be rapid development. In the first case, success was a possibility, though it was probable that the structural deformations with which the underdeveloped countries emerged from colonial dependence would remain basically unaltered. In the second case, the structural changes to be brought about were likely to facilitate rational economic progress, but were far from certain to modify rapidly or fundamentally the sociological heritage which overshadowed all development efforts.

Indeed, irrespective of which of the two approaches was adopted, to bring about the admittedly desirable changes through orderly international action the convergence of purposeful action on both the giving and receiving sides would have been indispensable. This, as events have demonstrated, was too much to expect.

So, confronting the logic and the risks of the prescription for structural change, there was the temptation of comforting gradualism and profitable continuity or, in other words, of the status quo.

IV | *The Cost of Being Generous and of Being Aided*

Foreign aid is like an artichoke. When in flower it is fairly attractive in form and color. With time it becomes a prickly plant with merely a small part of it edible. Esteemed by specialists, it also has its enthusiasts. One of its ingredients is even believed to have curative effects against certain maladies.

But to judge its real worth, the innumerable leaves of the artichoke have to be plucked one by one. Many can be discarded as worthless. Others contain the nutritive substance responsible for its reputation. Inside, deep down, one comes upon its small heart, which, properly prepared and mixed with appropriate condiments, provides a tasty reward for the effort that went into the patient removal of the more or less worthless leaves which hid it.

To get to the heart of what is commonly referred to as "aid" to underdeveloped countries, it may be best to follow the same procedure. Before doing so, however, some clarification is required.

To begin with, there is probably no other activity in

the contemporary world on which statistical material is available in greater abundance than "aid." Yet there is certainly no subject about which such riches of data reveal so little that is really essential. To interpret their meaning, then, one is forced to choose between a comprehensive analysis of the immense, complex, and often contradictory documentation—which in itself would fill several volumes—and generalization, which involves the danger of inevitable but excessive simplification.

For specialists as for newspaper readers, "aid" has become a one-dimensional notion, quantified in monetary terms. Each donor country's "aid" is thus added up, and converted into its dollar value at official exchange rates, and the total so reached is presented as the "flow of financial resources" from donor to receiving countries. The expression "flow of financial resources" is employed loosely with words such as "effort," "assistance," and "aid" until even well-informed people are convinced that the "flow" is indeed synonymous with "aid" and so with their sacrifice as taxpayers.

More recently, this purely monetary expression of aid has acquired a new dimension through the attempted definition of its "quality." Such attempts have led to a distinction being drawn between the nominal and the real costs and benefits of aid. For the donor countries, the nominal cost means the bookkeeping value of what was "given," while in the case of the real cost a brave attempt has been made to estimate the *de facto* financial sacrifice involved. Conversely, for the receiving countries the nominal benefit denotes the bookkeeping value of aid received, whereas the real benefit implies the monetary evaluation of what the aid in question really offered at the receiving end.

To this it must be added that the real worth of aid varies with its composition: with the terms and conditions of the loans; with the proportion of grants (that is, nonrepayable gifts); with whether or not it has to be spent in the donor country (that is, whether it is tied or untied); not to speak of the variety of political and other nonquantifiable restrictions and obligations attached. Each donor, of course, applies its own mixture of these components. Also, each has its chosen policy, its own administrative practices and financial methods. As a result, whatever generalized figures emerge at the end can be scarcely more than reasonable approximations. Indeed, in exceptionally bad cases they amount to little more than an indication of the dexterity of the donor country's statisticians in dressing up questionable figures in the garments of generosity.

Several organizations produce these over-all statistical tables of "aid," including some within the United Nations. But the yearly catalogue which enjoys widest publicity is the one issued by the organization of the aid-giving countries themselves—more precisely, the yearly volume entitled *Development Assistance*, published by the Development Assistance Committee (DAC) of the Organization for Economic Cooperation and Development (OECD) in Paris. These yearly DAC tabulations divide the "flows" recorded and checked into three categories: *(a)* official development assistance, *(b)* other official flows, and *(c)* private flows.*

Although one could not quote any specific sentence stating that the three categories together constitute "aid," the continuing semantic ambiguity helps the world press to present their *total* as the donor countries' aggregate "effort" or sacrifice. Whether it is due to the convenient brevity of the word "aid" or to the soothing

* *(a)* consists of funds made available by individual governments on concessional terms primarily to promote economic development; *(b)* includes official export credits, part of which may have a concessional element, and net purchases by governments of bonds, loans, and participations of the multilateral agencies; *(c)* covers private investments (direct or portfolio), as well as private export credits with maturities of longer than one year.

effect it may have on bad consciences, the fact remains that even genuine protagonists of a greater and more sincere aid effort use the expression without any qualification.

The DAC's latest annual volume reported that total net flows from its sixteen member countries* increased in 1969 to $13,571 million.[1]

All this being said, one may begin the attempt to pluck some of the artichoke's leaves.

To begin with, of the $13,571 million of financial flows in 1969, nearly half—or $6,280 million—were private investments and export credits. The private investor, whether in advanced or in economically backward countries, risks his capital in expectation of satisfactory profits. There is no indication whatsoever that private investments in poor countries have been less lucrative than those in advanced ones; rather to the contrary. And this is especially true for private export credits. The fact that private investments could and ought to benefit the recipient countries no more justifies their classification as aid than, let us say, it would in the case of American investments in Europe. Indeed, publications really concerned with objective facts have given up the practice of including private investments in aid figures. The Pearson Commission's report, for example, insists that (using the DAC categories) "only Official Development Assistance should be designated as 'aid.' The flow of private capital and official credits (Other Official Flows) undertaken for commercial reasons have no more the character of 'aid' when they flow to developing countries than when they flow between industrialized countries."[2] According to the DAC figures, then, aid as understood by

*Australia, Austria, Belgium, Canada, Denmark, France, Germany, Italy, Japan, Netherlands, Norway, Portugal, Sweden, Switzerland, the United Kingdom, and the United States. Net flows are defined as gross disbursements minus amortization receipts on earlier lendings but not of interest payments.

the Pearson Report totaled in 1969 only $6,706 million. With the first leaf gone, as our point of departure we are left with less than $7 billion as the rich countries' aid effort.*

Next comes the thorny problem of measuring the *real* official aid flows.

Clearly, it is meaningless just to add up the dollar value of loans and grants. Loans have to be repaid with interest, and so their "cost" is less to the donor countries than that of grants. Equally different is their "worth" to the recipients. It is justifiable, then, to speak of nominal flows and of "adjusted" ones. The difference between the return on the loan extended to an underdeveloped country and what would have been earned by lending the same sum at home or at normal market conditions should yield the measure of the real sacrifice involved. Therefore the aid content of each loan has to be adjusted suitably according to its conditions. Which rate of discount should be applied (that is, how to estimate the "grant element" in a loan) is subject to debate. Individual economists apply different methods and so arrive at varying conclusions. They all agree, however, that the nominal total of aid considerably overestimates its real value. In fact, on the basis of these studies one would seem justified in concluding that, properly adjusted, the real cost of official bilateral aid is about 30 to 40 percent less for the DAC countries as a group than the published nominal figures would indicate.[3] If so, it would seem justifiable to reduce the less than $7 billion official bilateral aid total by about 30 percent. This leaves us with less than $4.7 billion of aid.

Another major reduction in the real value of aid is due to "tying." During the past decade the practice has been steadily spreading until "untied" aid has become

*$13,571 million minus $585 million of "Other Official Flows" minus $6,280 million of "Private Flows," leaving $6,706 million.

the exception (barely a fifth of the total flows). The essence of tying is that a country receiving such assistance, whether as grants or loans, has to spend it in the donor country and thus has to purchase the goods or services in question often at substantially above international market prices. In addition, increasingly narrow limits have been established on both goods and projects on which the aid so obtained may be spent. In fact, quite often such restrictions have been designed to make sure that the goods financed by tied aid are additional to "normal" imports. The only too frequent obligation to ship the goods bought in the boats of the donor country, or to have them insured by its companies, adds further to the real cost. Though less evident, a variety of indirect costs are also involved. Tying may force the recipient country to carry out importations and to undertake projects which normally would have had lower priority. The various administrative restrictions connected with tying in their turn obstruct rational planning, involve additional administrative and other expenses, and in the long run, divert trade from its economically desirable directions. Particularly in the case of food shipments, tying also diminishes the volume of trade between the underdeveloped countries themselves.

In actual practice, tied aid often amounts to little more than a subsidy to the donor country's exporters, though paid for by the recipient country. As such, aid-tying distorts the trade patterns of the donor country and, by bolstering its noncompetitive industries, tends to prolong and deepen their vulnerability. This is particularly pronounced when specific projects are so financed, though it is not much less onerous for the recipient countries even in the case of imports that are not tied to projects.

For all these reasons, the real cost of tied aid to the donor countries is considerably less than its nominal value. And here again, considerable research has been devoted to defining the difference. Such studies are necessarily approximate, but they justify the conclusion that, by and large, "the tying of aid entails significant direct costs for the recipient countries, and that these costs are likely to average at least 10–20 per cent."[4] Referring to the cost of aid-tying to the recipient countries, the Pearson Commission maintained that "they frequently exceed 20 per cent."[5] Given the fact that about 80 percent of all bilateral aid in 1969–1970 was tied, on a 20 percent basis, a further reduction of the real cost of aid by some $750 million would seem justified. Thus our grand total is down to barely more than $3 billion.[6]

A further factor which contributes to the systematic overstatement of the donor countries' real aid sacrifice is connected with surplus commodity sales.

Under the so-called Public Law 480 programs, such commodity sales, particularly of cereals, amounted to an important segment of United States aid during the past decade.[7] In DAC statistics these are included at their officially declared values. The worth of human lives saved in a famine cannot, of course, be estimated in monetary terms. Surplus-food distributions have saved and continue to save people from starvation just as, very probably, they have also helped to discourage higher production or overdue agrarian reforms. Nevertheless, the giving away of unsalable surpluses does not constitute a sacrifice to the donor country—chiefly the United States in this case—anything near their market price. It may even be argued that, by giving away unsalable surplus food, in some years the United States may actually have economized on storage costs. Some economists have attempted to estimate the real cost of such aid in terms of the price such surpluses would have fetched if released on an already saturated home market.[8] Commodity disposals having amounted to an annual average of about $1 billion during the past decade, on the basis of such estimates the real cost of aid flows from DAC countries ought to be diminished by another 5 to 15 percent of the net totals reported. In monetary terms again, this would call for a further cut of at least $500 million, bringing down our grand total to about $2.5 billion.

These adjustments—to account for the grant element in loans, for the tying of aid, and for commodity-surplus disposals—at least indicate to what extent the *real cost* of the combined aid effort of the DAC member states is overestimated. In actual fact, it is probably much less than half of what is listed as Official Development Assistance.

Nevertheless, the plucking of the artichoke's leaves is not completed.

For example, the net financial flow figures of the DAC include some countries of Southern Europe, such as Cyprus, Greece, Malta, Turkey, Yugoslavia, and even a colonial power like Spain.* Furthermore, the DAC's figures cover also financial flows to the overseas departments and territories of its members, and these usually account for an important share of their contributions.†

Surinam and the Netherlands Antilles, for example, obtained during the past few years well over a third of all of the Netherlands' official aid. Portugal's modest "official aid" of about $40 million a year went almost entirely to Angola and Mozambique, and some doubts may be entertained as to how much "aid" this really signified for the populations of those colonies or in what beneficial forms it reached them. As for France, one of the major aid-giving countries, in 1968 nearly 40 percent

*This may be compensated by the fact that they do not include donors like Finland, Iceland, Ireland, New Zealand, and South Africa, countries whose official aid programs, however, are of very modest proportions.

†With the exception of Greenland (Denmark). In the case of the United States only the Trust Territory of the Pacific Islands and the Ryukyu Islands are included.

of its public aid went to its overseas territories and departments. To determine how much of such aid to colonies and other overseas possessions really helps speed economic development and what proportion of it is devoted to other purposes would require more than mere statistical skills. Nor is it likely that figures alone could throw adequate light on the real value of the strategic, economic, and political advantages bestowed by the control of the overseas possessions so assisted.

Nor is this all. As one approaches the heart of the aid artichoke, there is a gradual shift from the more or less verifiable and quantifiable leaves to the much more vague, qualitative ones. Indeed, as one proceeds still further, any analytical attempt is bound to become more and more controversial.

At a given point, facts and figures give way to mere questions.

Take, for example, technical assistance. Nobody would dispute that to facilitate the acquisition of new knowledge and of appropriate specialized skills is the most urgent and most precious form of aid advanced countries can offer to economically backward ones. Quite rightly, technical assistance has been growing faster than aid as a whole. By now it accounts for nearly a quarter of the listed total of official aid. Moreover, much of it is offered in the form of grants and need not be repaid. In practice, it is made up of the cost of supplying teaching personnel, administrators, advisers, and volunteers, as well as of providing for students and trainees, mostly in the donor countries. Barely a tenth is dispensed through multinational institutions. The remaining 90 percent is bilateral, each donor country deciding for itself what kind of technical assistance to offer to whom.

By far the most important suppliers of technical assistance are the United States, France, Germany, and the

United Kingdom. In 1968 they spent on it, respectively, 657, 418, 146, and 99 million dollars.[9] Evidently, the major donor countries have accorded a very important role to technical assistance in their over-all aid policies. They have devoted to it from one-seventh (United States) to one-half (France) of all their official aid. Yet in each case the emphasis was very different when it came to choosing between offering technical advisers, teaching personnel, volunteers, or places for students and trainees. The United States and France were the leaders in offering advisers. Germany was far ahead in providing for students and trainees. The United States supplied three times more volunteers than all the other donor countries together. As for France, it sent out two-thirds of all the teaching personnel the DAC countries have put at the disposal of underdeveloped ones.

It is as tempting as it would be hazardous to try to draw conclusions from each country's preference for offering one or the other kind of technical assistance. But admitting the undoubted competence and devotion of the majority of experts and specialists in the field, what did these advisers advise, what did the teachers teach, and what did the paid volunteers do? Above all, to what extent did their advising, their teaching, and their volunteering help the development of the states where they were active—or did it rather promote the interests of their home countries? Obviously, no clear-cut answers are possible. Nevertheless, we come here to some of the questions.

Will it ever be possible to evaluate the cost of the wastage and of the ill-conceived decisions due to technical assistance based on the application of inappropriate techniques prompted either by the unimaginative transplantation of Western experience into vastly different sociological surroundings, by the inertia, inexperience, and rivalry of competing benefactors, or simply by choices occasioned by the barely concealed pressures of commercial interests? Who could define in precise economic terms the borderline between sales promotion and some forms of technical assistance? How can one determine beyond what degree of charlatanism the cost of innumerable projects, studies, and reports, or the products of consultants and fact-finding missions, begin to justify their inclusion within official aid figures? Again, how can it be decided what proportion of technical assistance has been pure waste for lack of follow-up action, without which it was foreseeable that the original contribution would be meaningless?

When it comes to aid in the field of education, once again the competence and often even the enthusiasm of most of the personnel is beyond doubt. What is much less certain is the motivation. Does this kind of aid procure advantages to underdeveloped countries comparable to the political, cultural, and trading influences it secures to the donors? Paid, as a rule, at least as well as they would be at home, do these teachers and professors dispense the kind of education the host countries really need? Teaching little Africans Racine or Shakespeare or the history and geography of the countries of their former colonizers may be a long-term investment on behalf of the donors, but how much does it contribute to local development? How can it be determined to what extent the teaching of metropolitan curricula has contributed to progress, or has rather helped to maintain or even broaden the cleavage between intellectually expatriate ruling groups and the majorities, a gap which is one of the recognized impediments to genuine, generalized development? Even in the field of technical education it often seems justifiable to question whether the knowledge and skills thus imparted really equipped the students and trainees for activities suited to their countries' needs and means, or rather created attitudes and demands calculated to produce predetermined import requirements. Last but not least, in the case of the students and trainees who have stayed on to work in the donor countries, what sum would have to be deducted from official aid figures to allow for the cost of their upbringing by the underdeveloped countries supposed to be the recipients?

But technical assistance is by no means the only field of aid activity where unanswerable questions abound.

No one would belittle, for example, the genuineness of the motivation of most young men and women who volunteer for work in economically backward countries. But, equipped with a Western education and unfamiliar with the sociological realities of the milieu in which they wish to act, all too often frustration takes the place of their initial enthusiasm. While it is easy to imagine that voluntary organizations like the Peace Corps offer valuable opportunities for citizens of opulent countries to familiarize themselves with the social and economic conditions of distant lands of poverty, it is much more difficult to believe that their contribution to local development corresponds to the sums included on their behalf in official aid figures.[10]

Or, for that matter, how can barely disguised political and budgetary subsidies which encourage countries, or at least their ruling groups, to live beyond their means, be distinguished from genuine assistance capable of speeding development? Can it be ascertained with any precision whether the economic interests of the recipients or the strategic ones of the donors have been more influential in the shaping of a given aid project? Is it possible to estimate the economic loss occasioned by the postponement of overdue agrarian reforms made possible by food aid which, when given, may have averted a politically dangerous local famine? Again, if an economically backward country is provided with television services which devote most of their programs to the entertainment of the rich urban minority and necessitate the subsequent import of all receivers and spare parts, by what criteria is such a commercially motivated and probably socially and economically harmful enterprise classified as aid?

In a wider context, how can one determine the real aid element involved when, as part of the alleged setting up of infrastructure, a road, a railroad, or a power station is built to enhance the profitability of the production and evacuation of local raw materials, without necessarily providing any proportionate advantage to any other sector of the country's productive apparatus? Or how could one estimate in realistic terms the ever-present endeavor to relate aid to foreign commercial interests in general, to influence the choice between alternative projects in favor of those likely to yield for the donor country the greatest and most lasting advantages in the form of follow-up orders and spare parts, to shape aid programs so as to maximize the donor country's invisible incomes (from shipping, insurance, or other services); or determine the cost to a recipient country occasioned by imposed projects which, though they may contribute to higher production in a given sector, may also cause disproportionate but foreseeable social damage?

It would be easy but also dangerous to lengthen the list of such and similar questions. Dangerous because, on the one hand, it would inevitably seem to exaggerate selfish or malicious motivation. On the other, it would risk understating the effect of unavoidable mistakes, usually helped by local complicity but most often due to inexperience, incomprehension, and the inert tendency to transplant the familiar rather than invent or adapt to local needs.

However, no further questions are needed in order to apply a certain sense of proportion to the current aid debate. As against the annual $13 billion of "aid" persistently referred to, only half that much would at best qualify for the definition. Its real worth in terms of purchasing power, as we have seen, halves that figure again. Disregarding for the moment the further reductions which might be justified if at least some of the answers to our questions were available, the $3 billion, roughly indicating the *real* yearly aid "sacrifice" of the world's sixteen wealthiest countries, could scarcely be called impressive. Ten times that much is spent in the rich countries each year on advertising alone. It equals about a fifth of 1 percent of their combined national product. For every ten dollars earned in the world's richest countries, it means two cents diverted in the name of international solidarity, though regularly, probably correctly, and publicly justified as serving the donors' self-interest.*

As a matter of fact, even this very moderate effort has been shrinking during the past few years. After expanding for over a decade, official development assistance has been declining since 1967, and the grant element within it has been shrinking even faster since 1964.[11] But all this relates to absolute figures, to totals in dollars. Measuring the real worth of aid and of the sacrifice involved in offering it, one would have to take account of inflation, which has been devouring 3 to 5 percent each year; of steadily hardening lending terms; as well as of the fast-growing national product of the donor countries.

Expressed as a percentage of the sixteen major donor countries' gross national product, official aid has been rapidly falling since 1961—ironically enough, as it was the opening year of the first so-called Development Decade. From over one-half of 1 percent in that year, it went down to one-third by 1969. In fact, the decline

*Long before the word "aid" was in vogue, between 1905 and 1913 the United Kingdom alone exported capital to the extent of a yearly average of £143 million, which represented 7 percent of its annual national income.

accelerated between 1967 and 1969 (from 0.43 to 0.36 percent), the very years which have seen spectacular growth in the wealth of the advanced industrial countries.

Over eight years the richest non-Communist countries doubled their national product to a total of $1,840 billion in 1969. During the same period their official aid advanced only from $5.5 billion to $6.7 billion, with the grant element declining and the terms of the loan part becoming more and more onerous. One of the reasons frequently invoked is the foreign-exchange cost of aid, that is, the balance-of-payment difficulties of the donor countries. In actual fact, however, countries with the most comfortable external balance-of-payments situations have been the poorest aid performers. Nonetheless, the burden of aid programs on balance of payments has become a favorite argument. In view of the complexity of any serious analysis, hard facts are of course difficult to come by. Yet with much of aid tied, with technical assistance accounting for a large slice, and with interest payments coming back in increasing volume—to mention only a few factors—the possibility of exaggeration is evident.[12]

Clearly, during the past few years the aid picture has been fast deteriorating. Increasingly, it is the will rather than the means that is lacking. Moreover, even if some smaller donor countries—such as Sweden, Denmark, Belgium, or Canada—have stepped up their official aid efforts, these are unlikely to become example-setting or long-term trends so long as the principal aid-givers, and the United States in particular, persist in the opposite direction.*

At this point it may be opportune to recall that the high-income countries have no contractual obligation whatsoever to aid the poorer ones and that an increas-

*For more detailed over-all aid figures and for explanatory notes, see Appendix II.

ingly vocal minority in each of them opposes even the modest efforts hitherto undertaken. In 1960 the United Nations General Assembly did in fact adopt a resolution calling on the rich countries to devote 1 percent of their national income to aid. This resolution was further elaborated at the first United Nations Conference on Trade and Development (UNCTAD) in 1964, and was later endorsed by the DAC. At the second UNCTAD conference in 1968, held in New Delhi, the goal—including official and private flows—was modified, to the extent that gross national product replaced national income. In practice, this would imply an increase of some 20 percent. The Pearson Commission went one step further. It recommended that the new 1 percent goal be reached not later than 1975, and in addition, that at least 70 percent of it should be official aid, and this before 1980. Considering that the DAC countries, during the eight years up to 1975, were expected to increase their combined gross national product from $1,700 billion to $2,300 billion, the Pearson Commission's prescription does not seem overambitious.

But very few of the donor countries which accepted the 1 percent goal have ever specified when they plan to reach it, least of all the richest ones. Instead, aid has been shrinking. Under these circumstances, then, the much-referred-to 1 percent target must be considered hardly more than a rhetorical device for international gatherings, a vague moral obligation which clearly involves no binding commitment. Indeed, if the postwar experiment in institutionalized aid-giving appeared to some as the first hesitant step towards the institution of a kind of international income tax, public opinion in the richest of the industrialized countries has clearly shown less and less enthusiasm for any such measure. Rightly or wrongly, the majority of taxpayers in the rich countries have become convinced that they are already making important sacrifices in favor of the poorer countries and that these have been recompensed neither by the gratitude they expected nor by convincingly constructive utilization of the assistance thus offered.

It is equally opportune to note at this point that, in the meantime, articulate minorities in most recipient countries have developed corresponding symptoms of frustration and disenchantment. They complain of contradictions and of alleged exploitation involved in foreign aid. They underline the disproportionate economic and political leverage that aid has procured for the donor countries over both the external relations and the internal structure of their countries. And in some exceptional cases, they are even calling for austerity and self-reliance as alternatives to continued acceptance of foreign aid.

To determine to what extent such and similar allegations are justified might keep a formidable team of economic and social research workers busy for a number of years. As with the donor countries, one can attempt here to examine only the quantifiable aspects of these complaints. And here, too, measurable facts will provide only part of the answer. Inevitably, they will deal mainly with the financial burden involved in receiving aid. In other terms, this means essentially the growing debt burden of the underdeveloped countries.

The total flow of official aid, as it is usually quoted from the DAC tabulations, is net of repayments on borrowed capital, that is, amortization. Interest payments are not deducted. In addition, the low-income countries also have to pay back private loans, so-called export or suppliers' credits and the interest on them, profits and dividends on private investments, plus whatever private capital is authorized to move back to its country of origin. The last two excepted, the rest is generally referred to as the developing country's debt burden.

Nearly all of these repayments have to be effected in

foreign, mostly convertible, currency.* But to procure the means to fulfill these obligations, an underdeveloped country has but five sources: its own (usually meager) foreign-exchange reserves, new grants, additional loans and credits, new private investment, and of course, whatever foreign exchange it can earn with its exports or with services rendered to foreigners.

What, then is the debt situation of the underdeveloped countries?

Not surprisingly, reliable data concerning their debts are much more rare and much less precise than data about the "aid" they receive. And whatever is known is given proportionately less publicity. Yet the basic facts are relatively simple.

According to World Bank figures, in 1967 the external public debt of the low-income countries stood at roughly $45 billion. In the same year their debt-service payments amounted to about $4 billion. But during the decade leading up to 1967, the external public debt had grown by 14 percent and the service payments by about 15.7 percent annually. The growth rate accelerated partly because repayments on some heavy borrowings started only after 1967 and partly because the terms of lending had steadily become harder. For all these reasons, it is likely that by 1970 the external public debt had approached the $55 billion mark, and the annual servicing burden surpassed $6 billion.[13]

But these figures do not include private borrowings not covered by government guarantees, nor short-term debts such as International Monetary Fund credits. According to an estimate, yearly repayments on these two categories alone may amount to an additional $2 billion.[14] This, then, would raise the underdeveloped coun-

*It frequently happens that export credits are made payable entirely in foreign currencies, even when much of the expenditure was incurred in the recipient country's own currency.

tries' current annual servicing burden to something like $8 billion.[15]

Behind these global figures, however, are concealed great individual differences. They cover countries still in a relatively comfortable situation to face their debts, as well as others where the magnitude of the problem is already alarming.

Let us imagine for a moment that we are in the imaginary bank of aid and that we are following the client who personifies the underdeveloped countries. At one window he will receive his aid and credits, and at another he will pay the capital and interest due that year. At the first window, then, he will get his share of governmental and private loans and suppliers' credits, as well as loans from international institutions like the World Bank or the International Development Association. With all this in hand, he will proceed to the other window to settle his debts on former borrowings. If he is from East Asia, he will pay in just over half of what he has received. Should he be an African, he will have to repay three-quarters. But if he represents Latin America, of every $100 received at the first window he will promptly repay $87, with barely $13 left to use for the acceleration of his continent's "development."[16]

But this is not the full story. Economists have been busy drawing up projections to see how the debt situation is likely to develop. Even if we suppose that up to 1977 the gross flow of new lending will remain unchanged—that is, that for ten years after 1967 our man in that bank will obtain at the first window the same sum each year—by that date he will have to repay more than he receives. By 1977, for every $100 received at the first window, our African will have to add $21 from his own pocket and repay $121. The Latin American will repay $130. As for the East Asian, he will have to search all his pockets to find an additional $34, and repay $134. In other words, at some moment between now and 1977 the "flow" will turn and the underdeveloped countries will pay back more than they receive. When, exactly, this historical turning point will arrive for any individual country or region, when the poor countries will in fact begin to "aid" the rich ones, depends of course on the contraction or possible expansion and on the terms of new lending. To postpone such a reversal of the flow of financial resources beyond 1977, new lending would have to increase annually by about 5 to 8 percent. During the past three years the trend has been rather in the opposite direction.*

Indeed, barring unforeseeable developments, the pressure will grow and will gather momentum. The Secretariat of the UNCTAD estimated that if the aid flow (net of service payments) remains constant at the 1966 level, by 1975 the yearly service payments of the underdeveloped countries will have doubled from about $5 billion to $10 billion.[17] Some economists have gone even further and have attempted to replace regional averages with more concrete definitions. One of these studies, taking seventeen of the most heavily indebted low-income countries, grouped them into three different categories according to the gravity of their debt situation.[18] It assumed that for ten years after 1967 capital flows (minus service payments) will not diminish and that lending terms will not become harder—both probably overoptimistic in the light of developments during the past three years. On this basis, the debt-service payments of the first group—composed of Argentina, Bolivia, Brazil, Mexico, and Turkey—already at the rather high level of $1.5 billion in 1967, will climb to almost $2 billion by 1977. Those of Chile, Colombia, Dominican Republic,

*If private credits as well as profits and dividends on private investments are included, for some countries or regions—and for Latin America as a whole, in particular—the reversal of the flow has already occurred.

Iran, Peru, and Tunisia, about $400 million in 1967, will have grown to nearly a billion. Finally, the 1967 debt service of $750 million of India, Indonesia, Israel, Korea, Nigeria, and Pakistan will have more than trebled by 1977, to reach $2,750 million.

So much for the prospects before our man in that imaginary aid bank. But the same problem may be viewed from a different angle if we move, as it were, from the bank to the docks. In other words, if we try to measure the debt burden, not in monetary terms, but rather as the proportion of a country's export income it absorbs.

Generally speaking, debt-servicing now eats up from a quarter to a third of the underdeveloped countries' earnings from their exports. Of every 100 bags of cocoa or every 100 tons of rubber loaded onto a cargo ship, 25 or 30 are being shipped out to pay for debts and interest. As usual, aggregates obscure individual differences. But here, too, projections are available about probable trends. On the double assumption that net aid flows will remain constant at their 1967 level and that exports will continue to expand at the same rate as during the fairly successful 1960–1967 period, the prospects of two groups of countries may be juxtaposed.[19] In the case of Bolivia, Iran, and Nigeria, instead of 5 percent of all their exports being shipped out for servicing public debts, 10 percent will have to go in 1977. But in the case of India, Indonesia, Pakistan, and Tunisia, as against just over 20 percent in 1967, more than 60 percent of all exports will have to go in 1977, merely to service their debts.*

So it is not surprising that several countries have already before them the painful choice of either slowing down their economic growth still further and seeing their already existing factories grind to a halt for lack of

*Once again, if private credits and profits and dividends on private investments were included, the proportions would be considerably higher.

imported raw materials and spare parts, or defaulting on their debt obligations. It has not been in the interests of either side to admit lack of foresight or bankruptcy. This would have constituted an inadmissibly dangerous precedent, particularly in view of the growth of and the growing dependence on private investments. The sinking countries had to be kept afloat. As a rule, the rescue operations amounted to a deferment of some of the payments due. Insolvency has thus been camouflaged behind such euphemisms as the "rearrangement," the "consolidation," or the "rescheduling" of debts.

Since 1957, at least eleven developing countries have asked for such relief from their creditors.[20] The debt service thus rescheduled during the past ten years amounted to over $3 billion. But in place of the consolidation of present short-term and medium-term debts into long-term obligations, usually only short-term postponements of a part of interest and principal was accorded. However, it is likely that very soon a growing number of low-income countries will face serious debt-servicing difficulties, and that unless the whole idea of at least moderate economic growth is given up, these rescheduling exercises will become regular features of the aid picture. And the repeated rescheduling of debts is likely to provide the donor countries with additional and powerful means of influencing if not guiding the debtor countries' economic policies.

Just as with aid, beyond these verifiable and measurable aspects of the debt problem we reach the much more controversial qualitative ones. And here too, figures will have to give way to mere questions.

Inevitably they will touch upon the very issues which feed disenchantment on both sides. For example, was the present impasse foreseeable, and if so, was it avoidable? Were inexperience and unrealistic expectations the main factors in bringing about the the present situation, or, as some of the more virulent critics in underdeveloped countries proclaim, was it all part of a conscious design? Have the architects of aid policies accepted the coming difficulties as the unwelcome but unavoidable price to pay for what they conceive as progress, or, as some detractors maintain, did their decisions fit into an economic strategy which aimed at the replacement of colonial dependence by new, this time essentially economic and financial controls?

That the debt crisis is proof of the wrong utilization of past credits is a tempting and popular argument. In the industrialized countries this kind of reasoning would certainly be valid. Effectively employed, capital should generate more additional wealth than its cost. Furthermore, with interest rates at almost unprecedented heights in the rich countries, lending at concessional terms implies an increasingly heavy burden on taxpayers. But was it realistic to suppose that countries without adequate infrastructure, with little entrepreneurial and managerial experience, and short of skilled personnel on all levels could use capital with an efficiency comparable to that of advanced industrial societies?

Alternatively, is it possible to ascertain what proportion of the aid provided came in forms which lent themselves at all to effective utilization? In the words of the Pearson Commission, "a considerable portion was allocated on essentially political criteria without regard to whether the recipient made effective use of it or not" and "even aid which was extended with the objective of promoting economic growth was given with little or no previous experience." Finally, "aid has often been directed at the promotion of financing of exports from developed countries with little relevance to development objectives in the receiving countries."[21] Yet even if recently there has been some concern about both methods and motivations, can this rapidly and fundamentally modify the political, social, and economic legacy of the last twenty years' practices?

Some maintain that the indebtedness of the low-income countries is merely a symptom of their trying to go too fast. Less ambitious development objectives would have meant fewer imports and fewer debts. But to what extent does such reasoning conflict with the donor countries' persistent advocacy of democratic institutions, the very parliamentary system which implies consideration and, as far as possible, satisfaction of the electorate's just aspirations for better living? Or, in view of the 2 to 3 percent annual growth of population, how can it be estimated how much a diminished rhythm of progress would frustrate the aid-giving countries' proclaimed purpose of improving living conditions so as to stave off growing discontent and the violence it engenders?

Finally, though present trends scarcely justify such hopes, it is not impossible that aid policies will be improved. If so, there may be more grants, a generalized and liberal "consolidation" of debts, greater prudence in recourse to expensive export credits, increasing contributions to multilateral soft-loan agencies, and all this simultaneously with more flexibility and with more concessional lending being introduced into bilateral aid programs. Needless to say, to expect such a constellation of real effort in the foreseeable future demands robust optimism. Nevertheless, changes of at least such magnitude would be required to ease the drain on the underdeveloped countries' foreign-exchange resources and so to provide them with just a modest margin of maneuver. But even if such improbably favorable changes occurred, who could say whether, without a simultaneous and rapid expansion in their export earnings, they would be adequate to push economic progress ahead of population growth? On the other hand, having thus stepped up their aid efforts, would the rich countries consent also to the wider opening of their markets to the exports of the low-income countries? In other words, would they be ready at last to face seriously the existing contradictions between their aid and their trade policies?

No one could venture to offer even tentative answers. In the meantime, there is growing disappointment with meager results, with the paucity of real sacrifices, as much as with the heavy burdens they have produced. Still, notwithstanding spreading disenchantment, both donor and recipient governments pursue their established policies. Giving and accepting continue as if the original premises needed no re-examination. Yet even if the accelerating effects of external aid on development were more convincingly demonstrable, it would still be timely to ask the real reason why aid in its present form is being offered. What is the validity of the ideas which have been shaping aid policies? And what kind of interaction of forces and interests keeps the enterprise with its discredited methods still going?

V | *Who Aids Whom and Why?*

TERMS LIKE "aid" and "development assistance" have humanitarian and charitable connotations. A naive logic would lead one to believe that aid is directed either where there is greatest poverty or, alternatively, where it can be best employed to put an end to an intolerable situation. Even a cursory examination of available data shows that this is not the case.

Verification and analysis are not easy, as global development assistance is fragmented into a bewildering variety of uncoordinated and often overlapping activities. Nor are reliable figures always available. Still, between 1967 and 1969 India and Pakistan, for instance, two of the poorest countries of the world, received respectively $2 and $3.70 of aid per capita of their population. Guinea, no better off, received less than $3. In contrast, Liberians obtained $21.50, Laotians $23.70, the citizens of Jordan $22.50, those of the Dominican Republic $13.20, and the people of South Vietnam (military "aid" apart) $26 each. As for the Egyptians, they received only $.50. Tanzanians got $2.80. On the other hand, the average Iranian, notwithstanding his country's enormous oil revenue, obtained nearly $3 in aid. The per capita share of the people of Venezuela, another large oil-producing country with an average income not much below that of Italy, was $6.30, or more than three times the sum the Indians received.[1] The degree of poverty of the recipient country, logic, or charitable sentiments, then, do not seem to have been decisive considerations in the allocation of aid.

Was it rather ideological affinity that mattered? We find a parliamentary democracy like the United States with unrepresentative and even tyrannical governments on three continents among its favorite aid recipients. Medieval sheikdoms are supported out of public funds voted in Westminster. French democracy keeps alive regimes in Africa which hold their political opponents in jail. For that matter, the centrally planned and authoritarian Soviet Union lavishes its aid in support of India, a liberal economy run by a parliamentary system. Even purist China aids landlord-ridden Pakistan, not to speak of some Middle Eastern countries little inclined to imitate Mao's austere ideological prescriptions.

Could it be, then, that George Woods, former president of the World Bank, was right when he remarked that "some countries have made it clear that they see development finance as nothing more than a disguised subsidy for their exports"?[2] Here, no doubt, we are getting closer to decisive motivations. Of every hundred pounds of British official aid eighty go to Commonwealth countries, and an official pamphlet, referring to the trading advantages they procure, states that "about two-thirds of all our aid is actually spent in Britain, thus providing orders and employment for British industry. It is already evident that countries satisfied with British products will continue to place orders with us outside the aid programme. . . ."[3] French official aid, apart from the more than one-third sent to overseas departments and territories, goes mostly to former French dependencies in Africa, and practically all of it comes back as remittances or in the form of export orders. Almost the same is true for Belgium. As for the United States, its interests and also its aid policies are more far-flung, but here too trade provides an important motivation. It was authoritatively estimated in 1960 that 90 percent of the military assistance funds and about half of the economic aid funds were spent in the United States, and that nearly half a million people were at that time employed in the United States producing goods and services generated by mutual security disbursements.[4] Eight years later, an official publication put it even more clearly:

> The biggest single misconception about the foreign aid program is that we send money abroad. We don't. Foreign aid consists of American equipment, raw materials, expert services, and food. . . . Ninety-three per cent of A.I.D. funds are spent directly in the United States to pay for these things. Just last year some 4,000 American firms in 50 states received $1.3 billion in A.I.D. funds for products supplied as part of the foreign aid program. . . .[5]

When we turn to Japan and Germany, both of which play increasingly important roles in the provision of official development assistance, once again commercial considerations appear to be important. About 80 percent of Japan's official bilateral loans are tied to purchase of Japanese goods or services, and repayment terms and interest rates are particularly severe. Much of Japan's aid program, in the words of the London *Times* (September 14, 1970), "is little more than trade promotion" and its performance "must be seen as part of a hyper-aggressive economic and trading policy." Germany, too, sees four-fifths if not more of its official aid come back in payment for German goods and services.

All this being said, the underdeveloped countries, even combined, play only a modest role in the over-all export picture of these major aid-giving countries. For specific industries, for shipping interests, and especially for farmers producing surpluses, the markets of the poor world may still be important. Yet the very fact that the United States, in total sums by far the largest provider of official assistance, directs only a fifth of it to Latin America while it allocates nearly two-thirds to South and East Asia—a far less important potential market—seems to underline the conclusion. Trade, at best, could be only one of the motives justifying the aid "sacrifice."

But if neither moral obligation nor ideological affinity nor export interests are decisive in determining who will select whom to benefit from his munificence, what other, more important considerations are at work?

Examining how development assistance could be more equitably distributed, the DAC itself confronted the question. "A striking feature is the virtual absence of change in the collective aid distribution to countries from one year to the other," it noted. "Donor-recipient relationships, once firmly established, are not likely to change rapidly." So the real question to be answered is how these relationships got "firmly established." More specifically, how did a given country originally get on someone's list of recipients and what, if ever, removed it from there?

"The allocation of [official] bilateral assistance . . . depends on decisions made by the donor countries" says the DAC. "These decisions have been influenced by the existence of historical, political, linguistic, monetary and commercial links . . ."[6] Implied between the lines is that one motive present in nearly all aid policies, the one by which their effectiveness is probably judged by the providers of aid, is the endeavor to establish or, where it already exists, to maintain and possibly expand the donor country's international influence. Foreign aid is the least onerous instrument for achieving this aim. Indeed, as an alternative to armed conflict in the pursuit of power and influence, it is an improvement over traditional, more destructive methods. It is being cheaper, and even if it risks embroiling unwilling partners in the antagonisms and conflicts of their benefactors, short of war it is still a relatively harmless diversion of the great nations' thirst for power, their bellicose competitive energies, and their perennial urge to dominate.

Those countries which have had to relinquish control over their empires have found in aid the most convenient instrument to prolong and strengthen their influence and power. Deprived of the means to participate decisively in the rivalry of the new superpowers, they found that these traditional links offered them the only conceivable way to maintain at least a diminished sphere of influence. Within this restricted area, they could maintain a preferential climate for the economic and financial activities of their citizens, or operate common-currency areas which would procure additional financial and commercial advantages. They have prolonged opportunities to influence or even to provide key personnel for the administrative, economic, and educational structures of the newly independent states. The same policies have ensured privileged access to raw-material resources as well as being decisive levers for determining their terms of trade. In some situations even military presence could be continued in politically and strategically sensitive areas. And in nearly all cases the new aid relationship also yielded reliable and valuable supporting votes in international assemblies. Indeed, aid policies have gradually revealed themselves as the most valuable innovation in the great contemporary mutation from costly colonial presence to more profitable indirect control.

Great Britain, France, Belgium, and to a lesser extent the Netherlands have all opted for this metamorphosis of relations. Even Italy's grant aid has been concentrated on Somalia, in view of its long-standing interests there.

Japan, deprived of its colonies, adopted the same method once its economic power was restored. Acting with its customary dynamism, it has already achieved greater ascendancy over East Asia than ever its armed might accomplished. Australia, for its part, while concentrating its attention on the defensive rampart of its trust territory of Papua and New Guinea, has gradually discovered through foreign aid how to extend its influence towards Indonesia and Southeast Asia, in the hope that this might offset animosities created by its racial exclusivity. As for Germany, unlike the other aid-dispensers, it entered the scene without special ties with former colonies. Thus being freer to select its recipients, Germany was better placed than the others to act upon its convictions and to place financial and commercial considerations above the need for grants.

The circumstances of the two superpowers have, of course, been quite different. Without inherited links, apart from the Philippines and Outer Mongolia, the clash of their world-wide ambitions automatically rendered global the scope of their aid policies. Their desire to gain influence translatable into political allegiance has been comparable. Their means, however, have been unequal. Therefore, Sukarno's Indonesia and Cuba excepted, Soviet aid policies have as a rule been employed in areas geographically not far removed from the Soviet Union's borders. For all these reasons, it is mainly in the aid policies of the United States that the decisive influence of power politics can most clearly be traced.

At the height of the cold war the principal purpose of foreign assistance was to help contain communism.[7] At the culmination of Stalin's threats against Tito, Communist Yugoslavia alone received more official American aid than all the republics of South America combined. With the focus of anticommunism shifting to Asia, at one time three antireform tyrants ruling over a bare 3 percent of Asians, but strategically located near the borders of China, received nearly half of all American foreign aid. During 1954–1958, Laos and South Vietnam obtained nearly as much in United States grants and loans as India and Pakistan. During the same period, South Korea alone was given more aid than India, Pakistan, Burma, Ceylon, and the Philippines put together. Although preoccupation with Asia did not lessen, Fidel Castro's victory led to the Alliance for Progress and so to a mild stepping up of allocations to Latin America. But as Castro grew less menacing and the Vietnam war continued to spread, China's periphery attracted even greater attention. In 1967, for instance, in addition to war costs, the United States spent three times as much on its Vietnam aid program as on aid to all thirty-eight nations on the African continent.[8]

Finally, as the intensity of the cold war diminished, the stagnation of the aid effort was its logical consequence. The United States Senate has been steadily cutting down on aid funds, but East Asia's share has not diminished proportionately. What has shrunk rapidly has been aid by the Western middle powers. And probably the main reason is that, their remaining spheres of influence being all in the Western Hemisphere where the subsiding of the cold war has indeed lessened tension, the aid instrument has become less indispensable for them.

In support of these generalizations, it is worth mentioning that some very poor countries indulge in the luxury of aid-giving. Though in view of their own often monumental problems one would hardly expect them to do so, other considerations appear to have convinced them not to forgo the advantages to be derived from such a potent instrument of foreign policy. China, for example, diverts some of its very scarce resources to aid, not only to strategically important, friendly neighbors but also to faraway countries in the Middle East and Africa, often without apparent ideological justification. Israel, a prominent aid-receiver, provides assistance in its turn. So do Yugoslavia, Egypt, and even India.

Even more revealing is the way countries are excluded or removed from the list of beneficiaries. If aid is to procure political allegiance, international alignment favoring the opponent implies disqualification. Sudden shifts in a country's political system or in its foreign-policy orientation tend to sever the aid tie. Guinea is one example, Cuba another. China, once it failed to follow Moscow's line, knew the same fate. Sukarno's Indonesia was struck off the list. But after his removal, and notwithstanding one of the greatest and most gruesome political massacres of modern times perpetrated on the occasion, Indonesia was quickly reinstated and literally flooded with offers of aid.

The objectives of aid-giving, however, are both political and economic. Economic insubordination is perhaps even more severely judged than political misbehavior. Unfriendliness to the donor country's investors, nationalization, or expropriation may provoke temporary or definite sanctions according to the severity of the case. But ideally, political and economic dependence are intertwined, as only together do they produce the complete client-state status. The threat of economic sanctions is an additional guarantee of political docility. For as economic ties tend to perpetuate most effectively the existing patterns of dependence, economic alignment accepting the donor countries' economic philosophy is perhaps of even greater importance. Mere political support may help the power status of *only one* donor country. Not to fit into the prevailing trading and financial system, not to abide by its rules—defined by and in the interest of the economically dominant Western powers—may open a breach in the very foundations on which the donor countries' *collective* supremacy rests. It would challenge the very world-wide division of labor inherited from the colonial era, that is, the fundamental status quo. If political infidelity is reprehensible, revolt against the global economic system is unpardonable. The first may provoke sanctions. The answer to the second is merciless retaliation: first, cessation of aid, and then economic dislocation through exclusion of recalcitrants from the "system" itself.[9]

It is in this connection that the question may be asked why the wealthy industrialized countries do not provide in other forms the advantages aid is supposed to confer. They have at their disposal a panoply of instruments which, utilized in appropriate combinations suited to each situation, might yield far greater material benefits than mere economic aid.

More careful consideration given to the economic consequences of their policies in a given underdeveloped country on the efforts of that state's neighbors would often help to avoid costly damage. Shifting their support from individuals and groups whose policies and interests demonstrably block development to those likely to help create its preconditions could be another form of potent assistance. Also, they could refrain from imposing materially damaging embargoes on trade with certain countries. Or they could forgo inducing poor states to enter political and military alliances which usually impose immediate financial burdens and often compromise long-term economic aims. They might also abstain from intervening in civil wars, thus limiting their length and the material damage they cause. With appropriate policies, they could help prevent, rather than encourage and profit from, the immensely costly competition in modern armaments in which some economically backward countries indulge. Or for that matter, they could hinder rather than facilitate the flight of capital from poor countries to secret refuges within their own borders. As a last example, the wealthy industrialized countries might easily adjust their immigration regulations so as to render it more difficult for trained specialists to abandon their countries, which paid for their education and badly need their skills. Such and similar measures, individually or combined, could contribute more to the low-income countries' well-being than any amount of financial assistance they are likely to be offered.

Or, it may be asked, why do not the rich countries translate their concern for progress into improved trading opportunities for the developing countries?

They could, for example, help rather than obstruct agreements aiming at the stabilization of the prices of commodities and raw materials, or pay prices for them which would increase at a rate comparable to those of the industrial goods they sell. They could stop subsidizing their farmers, whose energies might more profitably be employed in dynamic industrial sectors than in producing expensive commodities which take away the market from needy people only too ready to offer them at lower prices. Or they could modify their escalating tariff barriers and lower the other obstacles that discourage the low-income countries from processing their own basic materials for export.[10] As well as in thousands of books, articles, lectures, and resolutions, this was solemnly urged upon the rich countries by the 1964 United Nations Conference on Trade and Development (UNCTAD), invoking the enlightened self-interest of the industrial countries themselves. All this has repeatedly been recommended by resolutions of the Ecumenical Council, as well as by Pope Paul VI in 1967 in his encyclical *Populorum Progressio* appealing to the moral responsibilities of the opulent world.

Translated into practice, even if gradually, such and similar measures would offer constructive encouragement to productive potentialities now wasted in the preindustrial countries. They would render unnecessary the yearly struggle with public opinion and with legislators to get aid funds voted. They might even lighten the burden of the rich countries' taxpayers, for the slightly higher price of their imported basic commodities would be amply compensated by savings on cheaper imported consumer goods and by more exports to countries whose purchasing power was increasing. And mountains of well-documented literature proved that even modest progress in these directions would offer the underdeveloped countries far more important material benefits than all the real aid now put at their disposal.

No one, of course, has any illusions about the difficulties involved. Some maintain that most economically backward countries could not in any case benefit from such concessions for lack of suitable production techniques, skilled manpower, and market research. Others believe, and for similar reasons, that only a very few preindustrial countries could really take advantage of them and, in view of their lower wages, would do so in any case and in spite of the existing trade barriers. The contradiction, of course, is patent. Those already overcoming the obstacles, such as Hong Kong, India, Mexico, and a few others, could do so with enhanced success if the barriers were further lowered. As for the others, it would be worth trying in order to disprove the accusations, if for nothing else. Yet, insignificant and often apparent concessions apart, there is no sign of genuine progress in the direction which the world's economic assemblies and moral authorities have been recommending.

The practical reasons for this are manifold. Trade concessions tend to be irreversible. They cannot be suspended as easily as aid whenever sanctions are deemed appropriate. By creating mutually profitable new relationships, they may even bring into being their own pressure groups in the industrial countries themselves, likely to oppose politically motivated reversals of policy. Also, to make good use of modifications in prevailing trade rules and to mobilize their people for the purpose, many underdeveloped countries might be forced to grope toward structural changes. These in their turn might weaken the influence of groups in control, with whose collaboration alone the present rules of the game can be applied. Furthermore, as against the "addictive" nature of aid, changes in trade rules would be "curative." To that extent, they might enable at least some of the more energetic and more successful developing countries to embark on inward-oriented, nationally or regionally centered development policies in contrast to the now almost general internationally oriented ones which perpetuate their dependence on external economic circumstances. Last but not least, really serious improvement in trading opportunities by enhancing the prospects of self-reliant economic development might render aid less important or even unnecessary. Gradually it might produce basic modifications in the prevailing division of labor and thus lead to a loosening of the constraints of the "system." The first would deprive the richer countries of the power lever offered by aid. The second might menace the status quo.

Instinctively at least, this is understood as a threatening prospect. Equally instinctively, then, it is opposed. Notwithstanding endless negotiations and rhetorical fireworks, there is little progress towards any serious regulation of commodity prices and markets or towards the modification of the underdeveloped countries' terms of trade. Self-defeating policies of agricultural subsidization are prolonged. Changes in tariff structures and other obstacles remain symbolic. Instead, and notwithstanding fast-mounting debts and the very fact that no correlation between aid and development has yet been conclusively demonstrated, all ingenuity is deployed to rescue the aid instrument. This is not surprising. Aid is employed in the service of a variety of objectives. To accelerate development is one of them. Only very rarely, as in the case of the Scandinavian countries, is it among the most important. Much more often it is far down the list below other objectives. Those tempted to invoke philanthropy among nations might pause to look at available figures and note that for a very modest price, aid-giving assures the functioning of a far vaster mechanism, which in its turn is highly profitable.

On one side of the great imaginary balance sheet of the "system" is the foreign exchange the underdeveloped countries earn with their exports and services, what they obtain in the form of private investments, and what they receive in the form of aid. The three together determine how much they may spend abroad either wisely—to import essential goods, equipment, and services to improve their well-being—or foolishly, to import nonessentials and luxuries or armaments, which contribute nothing to the building of a better future, or to store away in secret accounts abroad the illicit earnings of insecure ruling groups. On the other side of the ledger are the obligations: the servicing of past loans and export credits, profit remittances by private investors, authorized or clandestine repatriation of capital, and various payments for indispensable services used, such as shipping, insurance, and banking, all connected with exports.

Even if statistics were uniformly reliable all over the world, it would be difficult to insert exact figures into such an imaginary balance sheet. But well-informed estimates are available. On this basis, in 1969, the total on the "income" side for all the underdeveloped countries together was $60,200 million. But to pay for imports, there remained only $47,600 million. The difference ($12,600 million) was absorbed by the servicing of debts, by profits on private investments, and by "other capital flows," which may mean anything from shipping and insurance charges to flight of capital.[11]

These, of course, are global figures. They ignore enormous differences between various countries or regions. For example, profit remittances from Asia between 1965 and 1967 absorbed only about a quarter of all new aid and foreign investments entering the region. In Africa, they absorbed nearly two-thirds. But in Latin America, they more than canceled out whatever came in. In fact, in certain countries, in spite of aid and additional private investments, even larger sums flowed out to service debts *and* to pay for profits. This was particularly true of countries which had started to borrow and to receive private investments earlier than others and had thus accumulated larger payment obligations. For example, Argentina, Brazil, Chile, Malaysia, Mexico, and Zambia, to mention only a few, in 1967 had already paid out more in interest *and* profits than they had received in the form of new investments or aid.[12] In a sense, ever since 1967 it is they who have been "aiding" their industrialized benefactors. And the list is growing longer each day. Nor is it an accident if the political upheavals in the underdeveloped world have been taking place mostly in the countries on this list or likely to join it soon.

Yet behind such figures is the daily existence of over two billion human beings—the exuberance of the bazaar, the chanting of verses in rural schools, the flowery religious festivals, the villagers' silent agony in time of famine. This medley of activity in all its variety is kept above the subsistence level and within sight of elusive hope by that $60,200 million which *might* be used to accelerate change.[13] Indeed, $47,600 million is being spent on things which, if well chosen, might do so. In the meantime, debts are paid, profits are repatriated, foreign shippers, banks, and insurance companies collect their fees, armament-makers have their bills settled, investment capital is repatriated, authorized, or unrecorded by officials, and illicitly earned money is smuggled abroad. The wheels keep on turning. Raw materials and basic commodities are purchased at prices determined mainly by the buyers. Terms of trade as much as the nature of exports are severely circumscribed by the rules of the game, designed to maintain the existing division of labor. The system continues to function. But it works only because the gap of $12,600 million is bridged by foreign investments and by official aid. This pays for debt-servicing, for the remittances of profits, and for capital flight. In 1969 the difference amounted to $13,571 million, which was made up by the donor countries' taxpayers and by their private investors, half and half. Indeed, if in 1969 the taxpayers contributed $6,707 million of official aid, the servicing of debts and the repatriation of profits on private investments amounted to about $7 billion. It was almost as if the first had paid for the second.[14]

One is cruelly reminded of the organization of the more efficient labor camps of recent history. The rules and the daily routine were established, and compliance with them was assured by bribes and the threat of force. But to maintain the system in working order, the inmates had to be administered the minimum quantity of nutritive intake so that their muscular performance should not fall below productive levels.

Logically, to keep the world-wide system functioning, official aid ought to increase if for no other reason than to keep pace with the growing volume of private investments and the resulting expansion of repatriable profits. But it has practically ceased to do so for several years. The growing opposition of public opinion in the major industrialized countries makes it less and less likely that legislators or governments will soon reverse the trend. Yet if in spite of this the volume of private investments in the underdeveloped countries continues to expand, one of two consequences seems inevitable. The first is that debts and profit remittances will eat up such proportions of export incomes that development efforts will slowly grind to a halt. The second is that one after the other, and more and more frequently, the underdeveloped countries will resort to demands to "reschedule" their debts as a prelude to ultimate default. This, no doubt, would endanger the very continuity of the system. It will have to be averted, even by unpalatable means.

In 1965 a group of United States economists and government officials, impressed by the low-income countries' growing dependence on imported food, came to envisage the possibility that larger quantities of manufactured products from those countries should be admitted to the American market. The alternative was either to let their people starve or simply to give away enormous quantities of cereals.[15] That was at a moment when India was beginning to face one of the worst famines in its history. Since then, for the time being at least, the food situation in India and in the underdeveloped countries in general has slightly improved. What, by contrast, has deteriorated since is the over-all balance sheet, owing mainly to the foreseeable but unforeseen debt problem.

The remedy envisaged is the same, though this time for a different purpose. Arguing that the nineteenth-century myth of equality and reciprocity among unequals—as enshrined in the "most favored nation" clause and in the rules of the General Agreement on Tariffs and Trade (GATT)—was in flagrant contradiction to the realities of the postcolonial world, the underdeveloped countries have been pressing the industrialized ones for generalized and nonreciprocal tariff preferences. This was to enable their new, inexperienced industries to sell on the rich countries' markets free of the same obstacles which guard them against the exports of old, established industrial powers. For several years, this idea was anathema. But with the expansion of both private investments and the debt burden, it has reappeared as a life-preserver.

The breach in the rules of the game, however, will not be general as requested. Each industrialized country has preferred to present its own selective list and thus determine how far to open its own door. A variety of escape clauses will permit the door to be shut again whenever it is judged necessary. Most of the processed agricultural products in which the underdeveloped countries are naturally most competitive, but which might hurt the interests of the rich countries' subsidized producers, will be excluded from the preferential lists. Yet even if the acceptance of the idea is subject to a variety of restrictions, to quantitative limitations and an insistence on its temporary nature, it still represents a new departure. Nevertheless, the size of the life-preserver has to be proportionate to the weight of the body to be kept afloat. This is calculable. At best, it is unlikely to amount to more than what is needed to improve slightly the underdeveloped countries' capacity to service their debts or to pay profits on private investments: in other words, to postpone the dreaded day of default.[16]

To marshal available data in this form will seem to many inadmissibly tendentious. It makes no mention of the low-income countries' often inconsistent economic policies, of their faulty priorities, of their inadequate efforts, or of their inefficiency and corruption, not to speak of the self-defeating whipping up of xenophobic passions, or the luxury of expensive imports of armaments. If the poor countries are unable to face up to their obligations, it will be objected, that is either because they have not employed money borrowed or received with the required productive efficiency, or simply because they aspire to a rate of economic progress beyond their means. If they do not sell more manufactured goods in the rich countries, that is due more to their overvalued currencies or their inability to produce the required quality and to explore markets with the necessary skill than to tariff barriers which are not really prohibitive for low-cost producers. If, rather than harassing foreign investors, they would assure them better reception, even more technical and managerial skills would come and bestow their cumulative benefits. More efficient production methods and diversification, it is maintained, would do more to stabilize raw material and commodity earnings than any international regulation. Better financial controls and improved investment opportunities would keep at home the capital that seeks refuge abroad. And more appropriate salaries and a congenial atmosphere of national solidarity, inspired by honest development policies, would help to retain most of the specialists who now prefer to work in richer lands.

There is a great deal of truth in such and similar strictures, though the generalizations take no account of the considerable diversity of given situations. Also, they invariably disregard inconvenient facts.

To begin with, they refuse to concede that if the histories of the preindustrial countries have failed to provide them with the indispensable mental attitudes, skills, and experience for modern production and organization, in that, to say the least, the now opulent countries have some responsibility. They overlook the fact that often the application of the suggested remedies would collide head-on with the real or alleged interests of the industrial powers and with the very motivation of their trade and aid policies. They transform the just disapproval of unthinking demographic expansion into indifference to its immediate and visible consequences. Even more often, the advice offered implies unquestioning acceptance of what qualifies as no more than a hypothesis, namely, that remedies taken from the industrial countries' own experience would yield comparable results in vastly different cultural, social, and racial contexts. Above all, arguments of this kind are symptomatic of obsessive preoccupation with the status quo and betray an almost cowardly philosophy in the face of the transformation of the contemporary world. They show unwillingness and perhaps even an inability to adopt a dynamic attitude, to take risks, or to face change.

Indeed, the marginal palliatives being discussed behind the smoke screen of good intentions are unlikely to bring about serious change. Very gradually they might lead to a slight reallocation of the world's resources so as to underpin even better the network of existing interests. But they will not be allowed to modify the basic division of labor or the other essential features of the system. Within such a framework, aid policies will be expected to continue to act as a catalyst. At the price of a very modest real sacrifice, they will continue to oil the mechanism of the descending escalator which the underdeveloped countries are supposed to climb, often only to find themselves stuck at the same spot. It is an ingenious but unedifying undertaking. It yields advantages out of proportion to the cost involved. Yet it could scarcely continue if, in most cases, it did not enlist the interests and rely on the collaboration of the very people and groups in the poor countries who are now in charge of the destinies of their own people.

VI | *The Mercenaries of the Status Quo*

THE POLITICAL ELITES which took over in most underdeveloped countries after independence were numerically small. In Africa they were usually a mere handful of intellectuals, officers, and civil servants. In Asia there existed a few broadly based political parties expressing the interests of emerging middle classes, but they were the exceptions. Latin America, of course, had had much more time to broaden both its professional and intellectual groups and its middle classes. Yet almost invariably, once the common denominator of antiforeign sentiment had faded, the failure of the ruling groups to rally popular support became apparent.

At the beginning, a fragile bridge existed. The overriding desire of the people who took over had invariably been to rid themselves of what they had most resented in colonialism: humiliation, exploitation, external control over important decisions, and in some cases, the misery and degradation usually associated with foreign rule. When independence came, a temporary union existed between the ruled and the new rulers in aspiring for these aims. It has been in the methods used to attain them that attitudes have never been synchronized. And the roots of this failure are found deep in history.

Its origins go right back to the establishment of the first trading posts on distant continents; to the displacement of traditional economic centers of gravity; and to the opening of those first coastal mercantile windows on a new, dynamic, and increasingly interdependent world. The alert, the ambitious, and the adaptable had opted for alliance with the inevitable. They learned the intruders' language, assimilated their culture, their methods, their ways of living and thinking, and sometimes even their religion. The jacket, the tie, and the Western education have become symbols of their acceptance as successful auxiliaries of the alien innovators' new world, as much as of their severance from the traditional societies from which they came.

But the encounter with Western imperialism and with the economic system into which the colonized areas were fitted provided no more than a thin veneer of modernization. It produced a few big cities, usually the ports in which the export-import pattern imposed by the new economy took shape, the small beginnings of a middle class, and communications geared either to the conquerors strategic interests or to the evacuation of natural wealth. It gave birth to capital-intensive industrial enclaves incapable of providing a bridge between the artisan and the new production techniques, as well as to tiny groups of intellectual elites reared on classical Western education. What it failed to do was transform food-farming methods in the vast hinterlands. These were abandoned to neglect and stagnation, left to grow inward-looking in their traditions and in their sullen refusal of the ways of both the aliens and their compatriots who had chosen to serve the foreigners' designs.

Once gone, colonialism left behind a mere façade of ambition. For the vast majorities independence was synonymous with the end of imposed constraints, with the return to traditional patterns of living, or at best, with the vague endeavor to harmonize desirable modernization with the inherited skills and attitudes of an indigenous society long since deprived of its liberty to choose its own way. But for the minorities that inherited power, the change had a different meaning. It offered greater scope to imitate the manners and methods of the departed rulers, or in other words, to hasten westernization. Such were the origins of the cleavage.

It was with this additional burden that the practical problems of running new states had to be confronted. Listening to the words of the solemn international declarations of the immediate postwar years, the new rulers were only too ready to believe that these promised reparations for past exploitation. Idealism, naiveté, and opportunism, in varying mixtures, helped to convince them that the hour of the welfare world had come. Modernization and westernization were to be accelerated by assistance provided by the former imperial powers. Some genuine charity helped to prolong the illusions. But as aid policies gradually took institutional shape, the recipients were soon forced to judge their worth in practical terms. They could do so either from the viewpoint of statesmen or from that of mere tacticians. In the first case, they had to measure both the dangers and the advantages. In the second, it was enough to see what benefits aid would confer on their power, their influence, or their prosperity.

Since aid was inextricably bound up with other elements in the donor countries' policies, its acceptance nearly always implied compliance with the aims of those policies as a whole. Insofar as aid was meant to be the catalyst to make the whole package more easily acceptable, its role became crucial. The statesmen had to determine to what extent the presumed positive features of the aid component counterbalanced what the rest of the package contained. They either had to pretend to believe in its advertised virtues, or to hope to benefit from what seemed promising while attempting to neutralize the harmful.

To play off one donor against another seemed the ideal solution. It demanded a suitable geographical situation and considerable political skill. But few were the Nehrus, the Sukarnos, or the Nassers who could attempt it with any chance of success. And in any case, the scope of the game was limited. The impact of the non-Communist industrial powers was world-wide. They controlled capital, communications, and markets. The means of the Communist powers were relatively modest in comparison and could be mobilized in selected areas only. Thus, a few exceptional situations apart, the chances that Communist aid policies would offset the other side's massive presence were rather modest. So, in most cases, the balancing act was short-lived or was not a real, practical alternative. Almost always, the scrutiny of aid policies had to take place within the context of the former imperial powers' individual or collective relations with the territories they had ruled. It remained a confrontation between the mighty and the vulnerable. And there was little if any bargaining power on the weaker side.

Yet if Nehru or Nasser could play the balancing game longest or stand up to the confrontation with at least relative success, this was due mainly to the popular support, from town *and* village, that they commanded at home. Most of the other leaders in the underdeveloped countries have been handicapped by lack of such communion with their masses. As a rule, they have lacked popular roots in culture and tradition, and there has been nothing solid on which to build a power basis. Political life in their new states took the shape of coalition or rivalry between small competing groups of intellectuals, civil servants, officers, or spokesmen of economic interests. They clung to power, helped by the military, or occasionally by foreign intervention or the threat of it. With the exception of countries like Chile, Mexico, and Costa Rica, or those with traditional rulers like Thailand or Ethiopia, all over Latin America, Africa, and those parts of Asia where Western parliamentary institutions had already disappeared the usual method of change of government became the *coup d'état*. By definition, this precludes mass participation. It is merely a shift in the balance of forces among rival factions and cannot even pretend to alter fundamental issues or structures affecting society.

Yet against this inherent fragility of most governments in the economically backward states, there is the pressing urgency to improve living conditions. Economic development, however, depends on three principal factors. By far the most important is the mobilization of internal resources, both material and human. Another one, far less decisive, is exports, to provide the bulk of the foreign currency needed to buy those indispensable instruments of modernization which cannot be produced at home. Though unequal in importance, both involve effort and sacrifice. The third tool of economic development is aid. It demands no sacrifice on the part of the recipient, and it is presumed to be offered precisely in order to lighten the effort and sacrifice that either the mobilization of internal resources or the stepping up of exports would entail. In monetary terms it is marginal, but it can be decisive in influencing priorities. Above all, according to what the whole package contains, it may seriously influence the effectiveness or even the utilization of the first two tools.

The development process is normally hindered in a thousand ways by both internal and external causes. The external ones are inherent in the very functioning of the world-wide economic and financial system sponsored by the dominant powers. As for the internal obstacles, they may be constituted by a wide variety of causes ranging from inappropriate institutions to personal attitudes to inherited values. But the system which contains the external brakes of development also exerts power over the internal obstacles. It may help lessen their obstructive influence, or conversely, it may prolong or even aggravate them. It is here, then, that the historical cleavage acquires its importance. For the external forces that benefit from existing blockages in the underdeveloped countries are related to those internal ones that have a direct interest in the prolongation of the prevailing situation. The two tend to become mutually reinforcing. Indeed, the result is frequently a veritable alliance between the external impact and the internal forces geared to conservation. Their common denominator is the mutual desire to maintain the status quo.

It is against such a background that the interaction of the two sides within the aid relationship become apparent. The sponsors of the system are motivated by their desire to satisfy their political, economic, or strategic interests. And the same is true of their indigenous collaborators. Some among them may genuinely believe that such cooperation is the best if not the only method of achieving personal or even national goals. For most of them, however, mental predilection may be more decisive than the mere desire for material gain.

Their personalities have been shaped by foreign associations, tastes, and values. Their emoluments and other material benefits are based on "metropolitan" scales. By mental habit, they are more at ease in the comfort and life-styles of the rich countries than in the inherited setting of their own societies. Their imported sophistication has become incompatible with traditional ways. Their contempt for their uneducated and non-westernized compatriots is no less than was that of the colonial rulers. The inferiority complex they acquired while aping their former rulers is compensated by an exaggerated preoccupation with dignity and social prestige, and from there, it is only one step to self-deluding arrogance, condescension, or rapacity, all justified by the presumed inability of the exploited to aspire to the same intellectually expatriate status they themselves have reached. Cut off thus from the majorities, they transmute their resulting sense of insecurity and fear into the conviction that any change that threatens existing privileges would also be against the interests of the community as a whole. And since as a rule they lack any ideology, their only commitments are to self-interest and to those who help satisfy it. Such is the stairway descending to the level of the internal colonizer.

The consequences of the gulf thus having become unbridgeable are significant. The new ruling groups represent only small urban elites and lack the means of communicating with the masses. They cannot mobilize their people. Yet to do so is an indispensable prerequisite of the mobilization of internal resources. Unable to do this, they are deprived of the major instrument of development and so become proportionately more dependent on the other, far less important components: exports and aid.

To illustrate the process, there is the so-called green revolution. It is the most spectacular example to date of what can be accomplished by the application of scientific and technological progress in suitable social settings. New high-yielding varieties of wheat, rice, and maize can now double or triple harvests even in countries perpetually on the edge of famine. But the proper utilization of those magic seeds demands carefully controlled irrigation, large quantities of chemical fertilizers and pesticides, and, to obtain optimum results, education. Moreover, to maintain the momentum of transformation, land distribution and credit facilities would be needed to provide incentives, and purchasing power distributed to create markets for surpluses. All this, of course, signifies a revolutionary upheaval in the very countryside with which the urban elites have scarcely any contact. The usual result is that only small, already prosperous agrarian minorities benefit from the new techniques and the masses are bypassed by the new developments. The problem which might be solved remains unremedied. Nutritional needs continue to be satisfied either through expensive imports or through external assistance in the form of food, which in its turn tends to discourage higher production. In this way, the urban elites' natural tendency to neglect agriculture is compounded by their inability to communicate to the masses the means whereby the problem might be solved. Simplified, like all examples, this becomes a perfect model of the social short circuit darkening the prospects of development.

Some maintain that democratic institutions ought to provide the alternative. But a very few exceptions apart, no suitable context for the functioning of parliamentary institutions exists in the economically backward countries. Before the arrival of the colonizers there had been examples of peaceful persuasion or dialogue between rulers and ruled, but very few instances of satisfactory experiments in government by mass consent. Then, for two or three centuries, all was hidden behind the colonial curtain. It was based on authoritarian command backed by military might, and its impact produced lasting economic and social distortions. To imagine that, imposed on such a background, the fragile, North Atlantic type of parliamentary institutions could yield satisfactory results is about as realistic as to expect a hunchback with a wooden leg to triumph in a class of ballet dancers. Whenever parliamentary government has seemed to succeed for a while, it has been owing to an exceptional and usually temporary constellation of circumstances in its favor. In Chile and Uruguay, geography, racial composition, or prosperity have provided temporary shelter. In the former British territories of Asia, it has functioned so long as the arithmetical superiority of the dominant party was invulnerable to opposition. In the world of Islam and in Africa, it was a non-starter. In 1971, of the 127 member states of the United Nations, only less than a third permitted organized opposition. Among the over 90 underdeveloped countries taken alone, the proportion was even more modest. The stark reality in most economically backward states consists of small urban elites surrounded by a sea of primeval rural misery, with the first unwilling or unable to communicate with the second. The urban ruling groups —whether the anglicized minorities in India, Ceylon, or Malaya, the oligarchies of Latin America, or the military–intellectual–civil-servant trinities in Africa—may have marginal political decisions in their hands. But they have less than full command of the economic levers, and more often than not, can have no recourse to the only alternative, owing to their lack of dialogue with their own masses.

Whether the result of cupidity and shortsightedness or the legacy of history, whether mistaken or intentional, the outcome enhances the disproportionate influence of external forces in the form of trade or aid. Yet broadly speaking, the few exceptional countries which have seriously attempted to remove structural impediments to their development have nearly always found themselves penalized either by discriminatory trade measures or by the reduction or even the cessation of aid. In contrast, ruling groups which have refrained from disturbing inherited structures have usually been generously rewarded with improved trading opportunities and expanded aid. Exhortations to urge reforms have not, of course, been lacking. Implicit in their wording, however, has been the warning that these should be palliatives likely to improve performance within the system rather than structural changes that might endanger their fitting into it.

The rich countries' formidable arsenal of instruments of pressure is hardly ever put into service for fear that marginal reforms might snowball into fundamental changes likely to affect the status quo. The roles are politely played out on the stage of international organizations, each side respecting the rules and maneuvering within self-imposed limits. There are endless rhetorical fiestas to work out grandiose aid and development strategies. The rich pretend to wish that the poor would carry out structural reforms. The self-appointed spokesmen of the poor, for their part, resist the demands, claiming that this pressure is but a cheap substitute for a more generous volume of aid. The rich try to appear careful in their urgings, justifying their caution by respect for the sovereignty of new states. The negotiators of the economically backward countries, in their turn, grow indignant at any hint that the constructive utilization of the larger volume of aid they clamor for ought to be verified. It all resembles Chinese opera: titanic and noisy battles fought with mimed passion while the well-rehearsed movements inflict no real damage on the actors. The few on either side who are really sincere in their demands are overruled or ignored in the midst of the artificial heat of the confrontation. The tacit community of interest of the rest is camouflaged by diplomatic verbiage. And on both sides, the upholders of the status quo find their hypocrisy provided with a respectable alibi, thanks to the sacred principle of nonintervention. Yet, even walking peacefully in the jungle, the elephant inevitably intervenes in the world of fragile branches and of small and vulnerable animals on or among which it advances.

In the words of an American specialist on aid administration:

> Whether there is a legal basis for it or not, the fact remains that economic relations between nations generally lead to a mutual involvement that subtly crosses national boundaries; and foreign aid is in many ways the most promising means of influence. . . . Circumstances in each country will determine the point at which "involvement" through foreign aid becomes "intervention." American insistence on using U.S. shipping, offering bids to small businessmen, or withholding aid from producers of certain agricultural commodities will be resented more in some countries than the suggestion that the host government take note of certain previously unrecognized needs among its own people. . . . Most governments will object to an attempt to influence an election outcome, but it will accept open efforts by Americans to persuade elected officials to take certain courses of action. . . . Indeed, through foreign aid, the American politics of the 1950s touched virtually every country in the underdeveloped world.[1]

Observations by specialists from other donor countries are not necessarily very different. But how could it be otherwise? In 1967, for example, official aid for India and Pakistan amounted to the equivalent of 39 and 35 percent of the sums those two countries spent on their imports. It was almost the same proportion for Tunisia and Indonesia, nearly a third for Turkey and South Korea, and over a fifth for Bolivia.[2]

Nonintervention in aid relationships is barely more than a fiction. As for the fear of intervention, it could be genuine only if rulers wanted to carry out changes going beyond what the aid-providers admitted as serving their designs. To press ahead with such changes would require both ideals and courage. Even so, they would inevitably conjure up dangers ranging from inertia and internal opposition to change, to external sanctions including the cessation of aid. Under these circumstances it is scarcely surprising that the dominant inclination is to comply with the rules of the status quo with recourse to self-delusion when necessary. And in varying mixtures in each case, the chain of consequences is manifest practically all over the underdeveloped world.

Still, when contemplating the bleak reality of poverty and backwardness of the poor countries, one also has to be aware of their immense potential. We are told that at present not more than 20 percent of the natural resources and only 10 percent of the human productive capabilities of the underdeveloped countries are being fully utilized.[3] Yet any genuine policy to put these wasted resources to productive use must also determine who should bear the burden of the developmental effort and how its limited, short-term fruits should be distributed. Indeed, to do so is a prerequisite. Otherwise it will be impossible to inspire the sense of participation indispensable for integrating national consciousness and sustaining effort. But for the westernized upper classes, the answer is predetermined. Reluctant to carry their due share of the burden, they are also incapable of providing the motivation for mobilizing the masses. Instead, they take inadequate response to their westernization efforts as a justification for the prolongation of the prevailing, manifestly inegalitarian social and economic situation.

The means of doing so at their disposal are manifold, ranging from physical coercion to more subtle, almost instinctive attitudes, all serving the same central purpose. And either directly or through the accessories wrapped up in the "package," aid administrations tend almost invariably to render their task less difficult.

The ruling elites may manifest sudden enthusiasm for some of the donors' economic projects, even when these are not directly connected with activities benefitting from foreign assistance. Political or planning priorities may be adapted to more or less discreetly conveyed requirements. Treatment of private foreign investors or even the choice of imported equipment may be influenced by considerations explained by the role of aid in other fields. Harmful political and economic consequences of the donors' activities in neighboring countries may be accepted with passive silence for fear of retaliation in aided sectors of direct interest to the ruling groups.

There may be an inexplicable lack of interest in practical measures likely to lead to urgent and highly desirable economic integration and regional cooperation with neighbors. One of the causes may be the awareness that the donor countries prefer the present vertical relationships within which they can deal with small and vulnerable individual partners rather than with regional entities of greater economic weight. Or fateful choices may be made between rival philosophies determining development strategies. The ruling elites' faith in the sovereign, regulatory role of market forces—that is, the free-enterprise system—for instance, merits some sympathy. In the now developed countries, it has certainly produced spectacular results. Also, it has assured greater freedom for larger numbers than any of the alternative systems. But all this, of course, does not prove that it would perform with equally beneficial results in the economically backward states. To take this for granted requires either ideological blinkers or self-delusion fueled by self-interest. Yet this is precisely the kind of effect the aid relationship tends to bring about. If necessary at all, intimations or pressures convey what is desirable and what would provoke displeasure. Gradually, a subtle parallelism of interests emerges. As a result, in the sequence of predetermined situations, the ruling elites deprive themselves of any means likely to improve their countries' potential bargaining positions, and do so in favor of attitudes more likely to benefit their class or individual interests.

The cumulative effect of such and similar options is far-reaching. They can help either to remedy or to prolong prevailing injustices. They may facilitate the removal of impediments to development, or accentuate their obstructing effects. But perhaps none of them have more decisive and more lasting impact on the future than attitudes toward the existing educational system.

This is by far the most powerful instrument for perpetuating the concepts, the outlook, and the values on which the privileged classes' power is built. In most poor countries it is still a continuation of the system erected by the colonial regime. It had not been among its tasks to put an end to illiteracy or to lessen the ignorance of the masses. Primarily, it had been designed either for the education of clerks to assist the colonial bureaucracy, or for the cultural assimilation of tiny, selected minorities.

In practice, the original system was built on memorization and on preparation for examinations which, in their turn, opened the door to subaltern posts in the colonial administration. It was not meant to encourage analytical or critical faculties, nor as a rule did it provide opportunities to train specialists for the remedying of pressing local problems. Also, as a whole it powerfully accentuated the traditional disdain for physical labor.

Primary education was usually limited and of inferior quality. Often it was left mainly in the hands of religious organizations, whether Christian, Moslem, Hindu, or Buddhist. Notwithstanding their efforts—particularly on the part of Buddhist institutions dispensing basic literacy—only small segments of the population were touched by formal education or could acquire the arts of writing, reading, and reckoning. Secondary education, almost invariably on the Western model and in the language of the imperial power, was already a costly privilege accessible only to the children of the well-to-do. To attend a university meant either study abroad or involved mental and financial preconditions at the disposal of only the upper classes. Facilities for training professionals and specialists capable of confronting urgent social ills were rare or nonexistent. As for legal and literary education, it often provided an entry to the governor-general's cocktail parties. By contrast, agronomists, doctors, and engineers commanded far less esteem.

In the more prosperous Latin American countries, particularly those with populations of predominantly European extraction, the situation is quite different. But in most of the other underdeveloped countries the system prevails without any fundamental modification, and the present ruling elites are its product. The connection between the existing educational facilities and the increasingly inegalitarian social and economic structures has been abundantly analyzed and documented. In the words of Gunnar Myrdal, "Monopoly of education is—together with monopoly of ownership of land—the most fundamental basis of inequality, and it retains its hold more strongly in the poorer countries."[4] Nevertheless, neither the ruling groups themselves nor their foreign supporters can really be expected to modify or to undermine the very system which so effectively bolsters their existing power base.

Yet the need for change is obvious enough to command at least lip service. It takes the form either of distorting statistics which conceal rather than reveal the true situation, or of marginal modifications which do not touch basic issues. Frequently, the authorities in underdeveloped countries, echoed by uncritical international organizations, give publicity to their greater educational effort in the form of undoubtedly growing but often inflated school-enrollment figures. In doing so, they may feel intellectually backed up by the fashionable quantitative approach to development problems in Western intellectual circles. Enrollment figures, however, reveal little about the geographical, class, or sex distribution of this expanding education, and even less about its quality or content. Even today, "in most African and Latin American countries over half the primary school pupils never return to school after the second year, and this phenomenon is especially true in rural areas. Even fewer go on to any programme of secondary studies. In addition, those who do manage to complete the primary level tend to receive an inadequate and badly oriented schooling, given the demands of their rural community life—especially from the economic point of view."[5] According to the president of the World Bank, "In many countries of Africa the dropout rate during the six years of primary school is over 70 per cent; in large parts of Asia the rate is over 80 per cent. . . ."[6] As for programs for secondary schools, these "are rarely designed to equip their graduates to meet the requirements of industry, agriculture or government. Training is often purely academic and detached, without regard for practical application."[7]

As a matter of fact, much of the education now dispensed in poor countries is not only irrelevant to the solution of the problems they face but tends to be positively harmful. It perpetuates contempt for menial tasks, and widens the gulf between the privileged minorities and the uneducated or illiterate masses. Sometimes, with substantial foreign help in the form of technical assistance, it stamps alien attitudes and values on minorities who, because of their foreign education, are destined to become members of the ruling groups. It fails to provide any vocational training, elements of modern science, useful technology, or knowledge about modern agriculture to confront real problems impeding material progress. And while it usually produces a few highly qualified scientists and specialists likely to flatter national pride, it almost universally fails to provide the required number of foremen or even of trained mechanics capable of repairing and maintaining valuable imported equipment in proper condition.[8]

How little university education is geared to the real needs of the communities it is meant to serve can be shown by a few random illustrations. Of the 600,000 professionals at university level in Latin America, for example, only 3 percent are employed in agriculture, which absorbs 46 percent of the total labor force. A quarter of the total are in "production." Altogether, only 350,000 are in scientific, engineering, medical, and allied fields. But as in other underdeveloped regions, many even of those trained in medical or technical fields turn to trade or politics.[9]

In India, according to the National Sample Survey of 1960–1961, there were 1,192,000 professionals on or above graduate level, but 90 percent of them had diplomas in law, arts, and commerce. Only 4.9 percent were in engineering and technology, 3.4 percent in medicine, and a mere 1.2 percent in agronomy, in a country where over two-thirds of the population works in agriculture.[10]

In Nigeria during recent years, nearly two-thirds of all undergraduates studied at faculties of arts, humanities, and social sciences.[11] Indeed, the inordinately high concentration in humanities seems to be a general feature in underdeveloped countries. In Ghana in 1963, 96 percent of all university students followed courses in humanities, law, social sciences, education, and fine arts, and only 4 percent courses in engineering, medicine, or agricultural science. In Senegal in 1965, the same proportions were 78 and 5 percent; in Cameroon (1964), 93 and 7 percent; in Brazil (1964), 63 and 33 percent; in Ceylon (1963), 82 and 9 percent; in Pakistan (1964), 75 and 6 percent; and in India (1962), for every 10 students preparing for diplomas in engineering, medicine, or agriculture, there were 90 in law and humanities.[12]

The difficulties, of course, should not be underestimated. Not even a country as ready to use harsh and revolutionary methods as China has yet been able to find conclusive answers to the challenge. Much of the upheaval of the Cultural Revolution was indeed connected with the attempt, and it has produced some interesting experiments. However, all over the underdeveloped world, poverty, the sheer paucity of means, is itself the basic stumbling block. The lack of purpose, or of clear ideas about what kind of change would suit local conditions, is comparably important, as without clearly defined aims, half-measures might defeat even the best intentions.

The Indian *Report of the Education Commission* of 1966 succinctly summed up the dilemma: "Indian education needs a drastic reconstruction, almost a revolution. . . . Tinkering with the existing situation . . . can make things worse than before." Its prescriptions were clearly spelled out:

> We need to bring about major improvement in the effectiveness of primary education; to vocationalize secondary education; to improve the quality of teachers at all levels and to provide teachers in sufficient strength; to liquidate illiteracy; to strengthen centers of advanced study and strive to attain, in some of our universities at least, higher international standards; to lay special emphasis on the combination of teaching and research in agriculture and allied sciences. All this calls for determined and large-scale action. . . .

And, with commendable honesty, the report warned that its recommendations were no substitute for action, and that "the future of the country depends largely upon what is done about education during the next ten years or so."

But India is not the worst case. The situation is more acute in most of the other underdeveloped countries. For that reason, even to determine what ought to be done becomes more complex. With mainly the African situation in mind, a British observer summed it up the following way:

> To build into one and the same school system an education with a strong element of cultural continuity and a real relevance to the conditions of a slowly modernizing rural life, and a curriculum designed to produce the small but vital technical and administrative leadership with which to replace expatriates, has proved beyond the wit of politicians and planners and of their foreign advisers; it remains an unsolved and even more pressing problem today.

According to the same observer, however:

> After the decline of the fashion for high-level manpower studies aimed exclusively at the modern sector, the pendulum has swung back to a revived concern for an education more related to environment, to national cultural tradition and to economic and educational needs at the lower and middle levels of society. It has proved hard to translate this new approach into practice, whether in syllabus or in structure. For one thing, the association of education with superior employment has had time to be deeply engraved in the minds of parents and pupils alike. But above all, an education really suited to the rural environment in which the great majority of Africans and Asians live can become both acceptable and genuinely functional only when that environment begins to offer real opportunity and to require skills and knowledge on a large scale, which an education revised both in content and structure could provide.

And he draws the conclusion: "It is useless to dream of a revolution in education without a revolution in the economy."[13]

His conclusion, of course, helps to explain much of the inconclusive and frustrating "tinkering with the existing situation." The need for change is stated and restated all over the world. According to the president of the World Bank, "There is little dispute in the developing countries about the importance of education, but the problems of advancing it are so inextricably tangled that it is likely that many of the scarce resources devoted to it are in fact being wasted."[14] Nevertheless, some limited and halfhearted experiments are being launched. There are endless feasibility studies and a few pilot projects. But nothing even remotely proportionate to the urgency and importance of the change is taking place. Countless children in Asia and Africa still study the geography, the history, and the literature of the countries of their former colonizers. They are still shaped by an alien culture and continue to leave their schools ignorant of their own countries' real problems. The lucid analysis and recommendations of the Indian *Report of the Education Commission* of 1966 have up to this day produced no real change. Though a series of examples—from the Soviet Union to Turkey, Mexico, and Cuba—demonstrate that rapid and effective action to reduce or eliminate illiteracy is possible, the number of those still deprived of the basic element of human dignity constituted by the ability to read and write is still growing.* It is significant that the only really meaningful experiments in the basic transformation of inherited educational systems in the non-Communist underdeveloped world have taken place almost exclusively in those countries which have also attempted structural reforms in their economies and, by doing so, have tried to lessen their political and economic dependence on the industrial powers. The switching of stress

*More than a third of adults in the contemporary world remain illiterate. In fact, their over-all number is increasing. There are today some 800 million illiterates, or about 100 million more than there were in 1950.

from formal academic to vocational and agricultural training and the familiarization of pupils with work in the fields are features of serious attempts, among others, in countries such as Tanzania, Zambia, and Kenya. And in those countries they are part of a wider reconsideration of the concepts and values underlying inherited socio-economic realities.

Even of these three countries, only Tanzania has been trying a really radical new strategy. Notwithstanding the modesty of the country's resources, a fifth of the national budget is spent on education. All primary schools have been reorganized and all have set up a farm or workshop in order to foster in pupils the concept of self-reliance through socially useful manual work. The same pattern is gradually being tried in secondary schools. As for university education, it is being expanded according to estimates of requirements, with the great majority of undergraduates training to become general civil engineers, mechanical engineers, or science and mathematics teachers. In practice, admission both to secondary and university education, and therefore the output of graduates, is strictly related to the manpower projections of the current five-year plan. Moreover, those educated at the state's expense have to serve it (mostly as teachers) for five years after graduation. As Dr. Nyerere declared:

> Those who receive this privilege of university education have a duty to repay the sacrifice which others have made. They are like the man who has been given all the food in a starving village in order that he might have strength to bring back supplies from a distant place. If he takes his food and does not bring help to his brothers, he is a traitor. Similarly, if any of the young men and women who are given an education by the people of this republic adopt attitudes of superiority, or fail to use their knowledge to help the development of this country, they are betraying

> our union. . . . Publicly provided "education for education's sake" must be the general education for the masses. Further education for the selected few must be education for service to the many. There can be no other justification for taxing the many to give education to only a few.[15]

And in practice, university students too have to join the so-called self-reliance schemes either to teach in literacy classes or to help build primary schools, involving work with their hands.

How far, in the long run, the system will succeed in translating its high ideals into practice, it is too early to say. But a beginning is there, something that could not be said of most other underdeveloped countries no less urgently in need of a completely new departure in educational policy.[16] Shirking the issue will continue to obstruct the path of those who are sincerely seeking new political and economic formulas for a better future. By the very nature of cultural decolonization, foreign aid has scarcely anything positive to offer in this domain. Even more than with economic decolonization in general, the underdeveloped countries will have to confront the educational task by relying on their own will and methods. But as is the case with other practices and institutions which conflict with development requirements, the success of any new approach will largely depend on the mentality and interests of the ruling elites and on the support their options can find in the motivations of foreign aid.

Another telling example is corruption.

It is equally easy to underestimate or to exaggerate its ravages, as its extent and incidence are not measurable. Social, economic, or historical factors strengthen or weaken its hold. National characteristics themselves are not entirely dissociable from it. Sudden riches accruing from the exploitation of natural resources such as oil may incite small groups to appropriate their benefits. In some countries where one would expect corruption to be endemic, it may exist to a mild degree only. On the other hand, sometimes not even strong reformist regimes can entirely extirpate the practice. Moreover, experience seems to suggest that some correlation could be established between abundance of foreign aid and the degree of corruption in the recipient country. In certain situations, this is manifestly not the case; in many more, it is.

In varying degrees, however, corruption is an almost universal phenomenon in the economically backward countries. In its most benign forms, the lowering of public morals may be expressed merely as patronage. The civil service is grotesquely inflated, or an absurdly numerous and luxurious diplomatic apparatus is built up. These serve to accommodate relatives, friends, and potential political clients, or to offer an agreeable exile to rivals. Others may be recompensed by cars, villas, and all the other symbols of social desertion, or by expensive missions and study trips whose cost is usually out of proportion to any benefits they might procure.

But more often, nepotism and venality are twins. The dilapidation of public funds in many countries becomes rampant, and substantial proportions of export and aid receipts are misappropriated before they could ever be put to constructive use. Only too frequently, the steepness of the ascent to power becomes proportionate to its abuse for personal gain. The power position of the rulers is shamelessly exploited for veritable orgies of rapacious profiteering, with consequences degrading for all concerned. Integrity becomes a luxury and is put under heavy strain by almost irresistible temptations. Whatever confidence in the rulers' intentions may have existed is dissipated in spreading cynicism. And the gap between rulers and ruled fatally widens.

Curiously enough, development specialists usually

avoid the subject in their inquiries and research. This may be due both to the fact that it does not lend itself to easy quantification and to an understandable lack of encouragement from the authorities in rich and poor countries alike. In fact, on the official level in the industrialized countries there is hardly ever any public censure of corruption. Instead, in conformity with their humiliating practice of not telling the underdeveloped countries about their failings, there is amused compliance. How far this is in self-defense, it is difficult to tell. Not surprisingly, no data are available to show to what extent foreign governments or businesses have been active in promoting corruption. But private conversations soon reveal that, for comprehensible reasons of expediency, they have not deprived themselves of recourse to it. And so the tacit alliance of aid-providers and aid-receivers envelops the scandal in diplomatic silence bordering on connivance, presumably all in the name of nonintervention.[17]

Certain observers maintain that in some societies corruption, though it denotes the corrosion of traditional values and the disintegration of standards of proper behavior, nevertheless performs a useful service. It fulfills "positive functions which are at the time not adequately fulfilled by other existing patterns and structures."[18] Security, incentives, respect, or reciprocity of obligations have different connotations in varying cultural settings. Accordingly, some sociologists believe, the clash of an imposed and dehumanizing market system with the indigenous balance of forces aiming at the humanization of the economy may be at the root of the problem.[19] In such a perspective, the addition to the indigenous system of the habit of corruption has, in a sense, facilitated that system's "linkage" with the international economy.[20] If this is so, corruption may in some cases even help to maintain stability and continuity by harmonizing traditional morality that is under strain with new patterns of behavior produced by confrontation with a different culture. In such a context, corruption is but the price of change, "the outcome of the opposition of entrenched values to changing institutions."[21]

Be that as it may, corruption on the scale that exists in the majority of the underdeveloped countries not only helps to discredit authority but also renders its manipulation by external forces much easier. Moreover, it seriously contradicts the very idea of planned progress. It deflects from the task indispensable factors and essential forces. It creates and maintains an atmosphere of uncertainty and insecurity or even fear of inevitable and violent change. The consequence is preoccupation with quick profits and the regular and large-scale flight of capital to safer pastures.

No figures are available from the industrialized countries to shed light on the volume of clandestine capital reaching their banks from low-income countries. Yet hypotheses built on admittedly inadequate data seem to indicate that sums amounting to an important proportion of the total flow of real aid reaching the underdeveloped countries may be involved. For example, according to serious estimates, the secret transfer of funds from underdeveloped countries "may have accounted recently for as much as 80 per cent of the total flow of resources into the Euro-bond market" alone, "which amounted in 1969 to about $3,500 million." In addition, the "developing countries accounted directly for 22 per cent or less of the funds flowing into the Euro-dollar market in 1967, but it is likely that part of the funds flowing from the developed countries may have originated in developing countries in the first instance. In that year the size of the Euro-dollar market was $16,000 million."[22] The total alluded to, then, must have been above $3 billion.

For Latin America alone, it was estimated that "the net outflow of private domestic capital," registered but mostly unauthorized, "can be roughly estimated at an aggregate of 5,000 million dollars (1946–62). . . . It has represented approximately 30 per cent of the total inflow of all forms of foreign capital into the region for the post-war period" (that is, equally for the years 1946–1962).[23] Over the same period, official aid to Latin American governments reached only $1 billion, or only one-fifth of the private domestic capital leaving the region.[24]

Though no satisfactory data are available, it is quite likely that flight capital leaves the other underdeveloped regions of the world in comparable proportions. Indeed, the conclusion is inescapable that the aid-providing countries could make a more significant contribution to the backward countries' capacity to import their tools of progress by controlling, and when possible, by discouraging this illegal drain on their resources, than by increasing their much-advertised assistance efforts.

This massive smuggling of the poor countries' resources to the rich ones, however, is accompanied by another drain of comparable importance, though even less often mentioned at official levels. It is in the form of the underdeveloped countries' increasing participation in the armaments race.

International trade in weapons in 1970 totaled about $6 billion. A third of this was sold to underdeveloped countries.[25] The sum of their purchases, then, amounted to more than half the real worth of the aid they received in that same year. Furthermore, 95 percent of these lethal goods were sold to them by four major aid-providing countries: the United States, France, Great Britain, and the Soviet Union.

It would be unjust, of course, to say that the industrialized countries force the poorer ones into this ruinous diversion of their limited resources. The leaders of the underdeveloped countries too are exposed to the temptations of grandeur. Their generals also are inclined to desire expensive status symbols in the shape of more and more complicated arms. In any case, wherever they could not be manufactured locally, a certain amount of light arms would have to be imported simply to maintain internal order. Some low-income countries like Thailand and Cuba may indeed be forced to arm in view of genuine fears for their security. Others, like India and Pakistan or Egypt and Israel, may have legitimate grievances sufficient to persuade their peoples to face heavy sacrifices. Nevertheless, the real question is whether the powers which supply both aid—intended to speed development—and weapons—the payment for which hinders economic progress—do or do not discourage or at least try to slow down the process.

To do so, they would have practically unlimited and irresistible means at their disposal. In fact, insofar as they alone produce the more advanced weapons, by common agreement they could stop traffic in them entirely. Political rivalry among the powers is invoked to explain why this is impossible. Neither side can afford to forgo the advantages that the sale of arms procures. In some cases, the export of arms may even be a prerequisite to production on a scale permitting technological innovation. Yet all this would be perfectly compatible either with refusal to sell sophisticated arms to countries manifestly not in need of them, or with restraint in the nature and the quantity of sales to underdeveloped countries that are not merely unable to shoulder the burden but are also receiving assistance to speed their economic advancement. In practice, just the opposite is happening.

Evidently, the underdeveloped countries would import arms even if all their leaders and their articulate public were austere, logical, and devoted to a superhuman degree. The crux of the question is to what extent the inevitable absence of such qualities is being exploited by the suppliers of weapons. In practical terms, this is the difference between real and invented needs. Under what kind of influences, then, are real or imaginary threats assessed? To what extent do the actions of the donor countries accentuate the genuine need to possess defensive or offensive arms? And how can it be determined whether the need is due primarily to external danger or rather to the desire of unrepresentative ruling groups, often bolstered by foreign aid, to protect themselves against internal threats generated by their own policies?

Such and similar questions involve a chain of imponderables. None can be answered unequivocally. Nevertheless, at least three decisive components of the possible answers are held together by the common denominator of the direct or indirect impact of the aid-giving countries' policies. They are, first, the international context shaped by their own maneuvers to broaden their spheres of influence; second, the growing insecurity of the ruling elites in most low-income countries; and, finally, the interaction of the industrial countries' commercial interests with corruption throughout most of the underdeveloped world.

"The arms competition in the Third World would be very different if it were not for the fact that the great powers are seeking influence there"—in the words of the Stockholm International Peace Research Institute (SIPRI). "They may be looking for strategically placed allies, they may be anxious to support regimes friendly to them against internal armed opposition, or they may wish to protect their economic interest, or to gain general support for foreign policy (in the form of votes in the United Nations, for example). One of the main methods of exerting influence is by supplying arms. . . ." Thus, a study of arms trade "throws light on the effects of the interests of the major powers on the arms competition in the Third World." In fact, the types of weapons supplied sometimes indicate "whether the recipient country's military preparations are mainly concerned with an external or internal threat—a decision often influenced by the supplier country."[26]

Available figures seem to suggest that "the number of industrial countries that are willing and able to supply arms is increasing. Several European countries justify their sales of arms . . . as a means of keeping their own industries alive"—according to a study sponsored by the Carnegie Endowment for International Peace. "The United States, the Soviet Union, and Communist China all regard arms aid as an important adjunct to their over-all foreign policies. None of the major supplier countries seems willing to curtail this traffic."[27]

As for the actual volume of the trade in major weapons sold to the underdeveloped countries, it has grown in value faster than the over-all military expenditures of the purchasing countries.* Between 1950 and 1968, while their military budgets grew by a yearly average of 7 percent, their arms imports went up by 9 percent. And the acceleration in imports has been particularly noticeable since 1962.

The two main areas receiving imported arms have been the Middle East and Indochina. During the past three years these two areas alone accounted for about two-thirds of the total major-arms deliveries. But in the Middle East, apart from the re-equipment needs following the Six-Day War, there have been massive purchases of modern arms also by Saudi Arabia, Kuwait, and Iran. The latter, with a yearly oil income approaching $1,300 million, diverts a sizable proportion of it to the acquisition of both supersonic aircraft and anti-aircraft missile systems from both the United States and the Soviet Un-

*"Major weapons," as defined by the *SIPRI Yearbook of World Armaments and Disarmament 1969/70* (p. 12), include aircraft, ships, missiles, and tanks.

ion. When the United States Agency for International Development objected to the American sales on the ground that they harmed development prospects, the deal was defended during hearings before the Senate Foreign Relations Committee in 1967 and 1968 with recourse to the argument that Iran needed a strong defense capacity to protect its oil installations against possible threats by the radical Arab states.[28]

Even more tragic is the ruinous arms competition between the two states of the Indian subcontinent. Though India and Pakistan are among the poorest countries in the world, the proportion of their budgets devoted to military preparations is among the highest. Following the war with China and, later on, between Pakistan and India, both military budgets and arms imports have grown still faster and practically all the major industrial powers have participated in hastening the build-up. Several of them have been supplying both sides, with the Soviet Union and the United States in the lead. India has been importing supersonic aircraft since 1958, and Pakistan from 1962 onwards. Though even some sophisticated arms are now produced locally under license, particularly in India, both countries still receive large quantities of major arms either in the form of grants or by buying them new or secondhand. India and Pakistan together imported major arms in 1959 for about $90 million. During the next decade that annual figure continued to climb until, in 1969, it doubled and absorbed the equivalent of more than a quarter of the development aid the two countries received.

Although it has known no serious external threat to its security and its main border disputes have been for the most part dormant, Latin America too has been indulging in an accelerating arms race. Its sudden urge to acquire more and more modern armaments is probably not unconnected with the multiplication of military regimes in the area. In fact, during these past few years Latin America has been the theater of bitter competition between American and European arms salesmen, with the latter scoring a lucrative victory over their transatlantic rivals.

Since 1968 the United States has considerably reduced its sales to the Latin American republics. This was due in part to the Symington Amendment to the 1968 Foreign Assistance Act, which curtailed United States aid to countries which buy sophisticated weapons they cannot afford and do not need. But it was caused also by the United States concentration on less costly but more relevant counterinsurgency equipment, helicopters in particular. As a matter of fact, during the presidential campaign of 1968, former Vice-President Hubert Humphrey called for strict control of arms sales to Latin America, asked for European cooperation to see that it was obeyed, and expressed the view that "predatory colonels" were as much a threat to democracy as "armed terrorists." But neither the predatory colonels nor the European sellers of arms were disposed to listen to his advice. Led by the military governments of Peru, Brazil, and Argentina, there followed a veritable escalation of South American orders for European naval vessels, supersonic aircraft, missiles, and even for secondhand aircraft carriers. Finally, concerned at being left out of the Latin American arms bonanza, the United States too reappeared as a supplier of supersonic jet planes. Between 1965 and 1970 alone, it is believed that Western Europe and Canada sold over $500 million worth of major arms to Latin America.[29] By now, the region imports these advanced weapons to the tune of about a yearly $100 million, a figure probably over a quarter of all aid reaching it. The principal importer, Argentina, is the least exposed to any conceivable external threat, is no nearer to Havana than Paris is to Karachi, but has an apparently inexhaustible supply of predatory colonels and higher ranks to man her successive governments. As for Central America, the sober example of Costa Rica apart, it too has caught the malady. Indeed, the air force of El Salvador, consisting of six Mustang planes and lost in the brief so-called Football War with Honduras, was replaced within a month.

Although in the days following the celebration of independence several African leaders dreamed of their continent as a disarmed area, Africa too has been irresistibly drawn into the deadly and costly competition it can so ill afford. At one end of the continent there occurred an arms race of their own between the four North African states, with oil-rich Libya in the lead. The others have either been obtaining weapons as aid or have been buying them for cash or in exchange for their exportable primary products. At the other end, South Africa's arming is being speeded and both Rhodesia and the Portuguese colonies are being equipped with more and more advanced weapons. In between the two, black Africa as a whole is still a relatively small spender. But owing to a combination of factors, ranging from civil wars, the proliferation of military regimes, racial tensions connected with the policies of Portugal and South Africa, and support of liberation and counterinsurgency forces, to Sino-Soviet rivalry for the allegiance of Africans, a steadily accelerating diversion of resources from development to armaments is unfolding.

The civil war left Nigeria, for example, with a vastly increased military establishment. Between 1967 and 1970 the Nigerian army grew from 10,000 to 120,000 men, and British weapons sold to the country, amounting to less than a sixth of total arms imports, increased from £80,000 in 1966 to £2.8 million in 1968.[30] The Sudan, for its part, has purchased £100 million worth of arms from the Soviet Union, and the Congo (Kinshasa) too is importing major arms on a considerable scale. How difficult it would be to arrest the growing arms traffic to Black Africa is best illustrated by the fact that relatively moderate and liberal governments like those of Zambia and Tanzania now feel themselves compelled to join the race and have decided to purchase jet planes and air-defense missile systems to prevent Portuguese and Rhodesian air incursions over their territory.

With modern armaments piling up at the two extremities of the continent, with racial and tribal tensions and the Sino-Soviet rivalry intensifying, and with growing instability within small and often unviable states with artificial borders leading to the establishment of military regimes, the probability is that Africa too will go the Latin American way and will divert a fast-growing proportion of its scanty resources to the acquisition of advanced instruments of war. And it is unlikely that the almost inevitable spread of military governments will help to reverse the trend.[31]

Viewing the underdeveloped world as a whole, the expansion of trade in major arms is not likely to slow down in the foreseeable future. To begin with, fear of real or imaginary external dangers and of internal threats to the existing regimes will not abate. Secondly, with major war within the northern industrial belt of the world less and less likely, the people of the Southern Hemisphere are becoming the natural guinea pigs on whom the lethal effects of new weapons can be tested. In the third place, technological innovation brings with it accelerating obsolescence. The faster progress the advanced countries make towards more sophisticated and therefore more expensive weapons, the more eager they will be to find buyers for what they wish to discard. Thus the momentum of technological advance in armaments sweeps both rich and poor countries towards higher arms spending. Moreover, population growth combined with inadequate social and political adjustments is bound to multiply military regimes, bringing in their wake situations in which arms purchases will bear no relation either to genuine defense needs or to economic resources. Finally, with their characteristically unsentimental approach, arms dealers will increasingly invoke sharpening competition and even their countries' balance-of-payments difficulties to cover with respectability their indiscriminate use of objectionable sales techniques.

As a matter of fact, the day has passed when the blame could be put mainly on more or less anonymous private traders, important and prosperous as they still may be. By now most industrial countries have developed their official or semiofficial but highly complex and impressive apparatus for the sale of arms. The four countries responsible for most of the trade—the United States, France, Great Britain, and the Soviet Union—publicly congratulate themselves upon the victories they score in the arms business. In company with the lesser exporting countries, they have an almost unlimited keyboard to play on in order to produce the desired material and psychological pressures. These range from gifts to sales for cash or in exchange for raw materials; from supplies in payment for military facilities to guaranteed and long-term arms-export credits; or from orchestrated rumors to the manipulation of armed forces by means of bribes or instructors, or by the choice between the supply of defensive or offensive equipment—all designed to encourage and satisfy demand or, whenever necessary, to revive it through the judicious injection of offensive weapons into areas where even reluctant governments are left with no alternative but to arm themselves for fear of their oversupplied neighbors.

As for the suppliers, the United States and the Soviet Union are by far the most important over-all exporters.

Since 1961 the United States official arms sales to all countries have run at a yearly average of about $2,300 million. Those of the Soviet Union (together with Czechoslovakia and other associates) have probably amounted to a similar figure. Their exports to non-Communist countries have reached an annual average of about $600 million, the rest being made up by sales to partners within the Soviet military bloc. France, in the meantime, has fast moved up to third place, reaching a yearly level of about $1,500 million. She has overtaken Great Britain, now in the fourth place with something like $800 million. So, the slice of the world market left to the smaller suppliers is relatively modest. It is filled in mainly by Canada, Italy, Sweden, Belgium, and Switzerland, with a number of industrial countries in the wings either as suppliers of small arms or as exporters of secondhand wares. China too is in the running, and she may account for a yearly average of about $40 million, directed chiefly to the African countries and the Arab Middle East.[32]

But the most significant feature of that part of the international arms trade which concerns the underdeveloped countries is that the major supplying powers have steadily been drawn deeper and deeper into local conflicts between the underdeveloped countries they have been equipping. Most of the armed clashes since the end of the Second World War have occurred in the Southern Hemisphere, and the great powers have been participating in them, as it were, by proxy. Their military bases in conflict areas, their camouflaged direct interventions, or their arms transfers to tense areas have been recurring features of such involvement. Nor was it rare for both sides in a conflict to be sold arms by the same supplier. The Soviet Union sold weapons both to India and Pakistan. The United States did the same with Jordan and Israel. Other industrial countries followed the good example, though on a smaller scale. Racial, political, or ideological sympathies have not noticeably trespassed on the workings of the profit motive. But in all these armed conflicts, from the Middle East to Indochina and from Biafra to the equipment of liberation armies and counterinsurgency forces, the one constant feature has been the fact that the presence of the big powers, as suppliers of indispensable arms, has invariably altered the nature of the conflict. This has been the case not merely because the wars have been fought with the weapons they supplied, but also "because the weapons are supplied for political influence, thus subsuming the local issues under world-wide issues—the issues between the supplying countries themselves."[33]

That the providers of arms do not impose restrictions on themselves or fail to extract the most advantageous terms is not surprising. But that so few of the underdeveloped countries have taken initiatives to curtail the traffic can only be less charitably interpreted. In fact, the two attempts of recent years, in 1965 and 1968, to urge the United Nations to have the arms trade registered and publicized in order to mitigate its dangers encountered particularly strong opposition from the representatives of the poorest underdeveloped countries.[34]

And so, the armaments race of the poor continues. The Galbraithian assertion that the consumer has no choice but to endure even greater indoctrination to consume more seems certainly applicable to trade in weapons with the underdeveloped countries. The more their ruling elites come to equate prolongation of their privileges with compliance with the industrial world's interests, the better buyers they become. And the more they squander their nations' resources on the purchase of sophisticated weapons, the more they will be in need of protective integration. If aid is just one of the instruments to hasten the process and thus promote the industrial powers' interests, so is the supplying of arms.

Though in economic terms the two may be contradictory, they are complementary on the political plane. Indeed, if aid is only the tip of the iceberg, the sale of armaments is just another, and probably the most profitable, part of the whole package floating invisibly below the rhetorical surface of generosity.

But perhaps neither the educational system, nor corruption, nor the armaments trade illustrates more tellingly the interplay of disparate interests of aid-giving countries and of the ruling groups of the aided ones than the relatively recent phenomenon known as the brain drain.

This is another of the uncomfortable subjects hardly ever mentioned in the flow of spoken and written official eloquence devoted to aid. As with corruption and the arms trade, there are few dependable data. And in this case, too, the relative silence is symptomatic of embarrassment on both sides.

Owing at least partly to the difficulty of finding exact and comparable definitions, the real extent of the brain drain is not known. Fragmentary facts, however, give an idea of its probable dimensions. One estimate claims, for example, that almost 50 percent of the graduate engineers of Latin America work in the United States, and that two-thirds of the health services in Britain are manned by Pakistani and Indian doctors.[35]

According to another claim, between 1949 and 1961 no less than 43,000 scientists and engineers came to the United States from abroad, a large number among them from the underdeveloped countries. In 1964–1965 some 11,000 interns and residents in American hospitals—out of a total of 41,000—were graduates of foreign medical schools, and more than 8,000 of them came from low-income countries. It is believed that more than 90 percent of Asian students who arrive for training in the United States never return to their home countries.[36]

The World Health Organization, for its part, claimed that about 4,000 foreign doctors were practicing in Great Britain, most of whom came from India, Pakistan, and other Commonwealth countries, and that there were as many Togolese doctors and professors working in France as there were French technical assistants in these two fields in Togo. Cameroon finds itself in a similar situation in that there are as many Cameroonian doctors working in France as in their own country.[37] Even more striking, there are more Iranian doctors in New York City alone than in the whole of Iran.[38]

Another study reported that 80 percent of Jordanian students in the West never go back to work in their country, and that of about 120 students attending Western universities each year from Saudi Arabia, only some 30 or 40 return.[39] Thus a former deputy director-general of UNESCO could declare that "top-level emigration is a new dimension in the life of the Arab elite. The brain drain is putting off by decades the development of Arab universities as centres of scientific excellence."[40]

The industrially advanced countries themselves are not immune from the damages of the brain drain. There is a regular movement of trained talent from Eastern to Western Europe, and from there especially to Canada and the United States. But with the highest technological level attracting most of the specialists, the United States inevitably emerges as the ultimate magnet of highly trained personnel.[41] The major importers of trained specialists are the United States, the United Kingdom, Australia, and France, although in proportion to its population, Canada's intake appears to be the most massive in the world. The underdeveloped countries most affected by the drain seem to be the United Arab Republic and Nigeria in Africa; Argentina, Mexico, and Colombia in Latin America; and India, Pakistan, Iran, the Philippines, South Korea, and Taiwan in Asia. In some cases, such as Argentina, South Korea, India, the Philippines, or the United Arab Republic, important proportions of the annual crop of doctors and engineers leave the country for work abroad. It is certain that a large number of underdeveloped countries allow their own specialists to leave in equal or superior numbers to those in the same fields who come from abroad to help them. Equally clearly, in several of the countries in question health services are grossly undermanned while large numbers of doctors (and nurses) trained in the country prefer to emigrate.

Wandering scholars were not unknown in previous centuries. Furthermore, it is clear that not even the most stringent restrictions could prevent individuals of exceptional capabilities from seeking more congenial intellectual, political, or material surroundings in order to satisfy their justifiable ambitions. Nevertheless, the brain drain in its contemporary composition and dimensions is something quite different and has no parallel in history.

It signifies the loss, without compensation, of a vital resource. It is involuntary technical assistance in reverse. It causes shortages in critical skills. Moreover, it implies a general lowering of professional levels, as it is the most talented, the most enterprising, and the best equipped who emigrate. In another sense, it is the result of the newly independent countries' discovery that education is an article of consumption difficult to deny on political grounds, and that the demand for it, in one form or another, often exceeds what would seem justifiable solely on the grounds of productivity. It follows that some unemployment among the educated is almost inevitable in the underdeveloped countries unless economic expansion generates the required absorptive capacity for the type of specialists produced. This, however, would demand exceptionally well balanced growth and perfect planning, as well as the precise harmonization of required human and material resources. Such a near-perfect combination being more than rare, the world has become a vast marketplace for human talent, an entirely new development. But with free-trade principles applied to people with higher education, and with grossly unequal forces competing to the inevitable advantage of the richer, the result is the draining away of tens of thousands of highly trained specialists whose education, in the case of the underdeveloped countries, has been financed at great sacrifice and who quite often will have to be replaced by foreign technical assistants.

Whatever the causes, the loss is considerable. To estimate it in monetary terms is almost impossible owing to inadequate data, to the wide differences in educational expenses in individual countries, not to speak of the difficulty of calculating forgone earnings, interest, or quality levels. Nevertheless, the rough calculation was made for Colombia, one of the most affected countries, that its average yearly loss in educational expenses for its emigrating high-level manpower from 1955 to 1968 was on the order of $25 million, plus nearly $5 million for "intermediate personnel."[42] A specialized study on Turkey reckoned the present value of future gross earnings forgone at nearly five times the value of the educational investment in the country. It is believed that the equivalent would be less for Africa. But it would be an even heavier loss in most of Latin America, where higher education is more expensive. Anyway, the study assesses the present value of future earnings forgone for Turkey's annual exodus of about 575 professionals at $54 million. This, it is noted, is the equivalent in value to one month of Turkey's commodity exports.[43]

In 1968 alone, 22,590 "professionals, technical and kindred" from the low-income countries went to the United States, and their steadily increasing numbers have raised some questions about American immigration policy. A House of Representatives committee noted that the United States spent $75 million in that same fiscal year "toward providing some 5,400 trained (including U.S.) persons to the very countries engaged in 'exporting' some 5,200 of their scientific professionals" to America. The countries concerned were India, Korea, Turkey, Formosa, Brazil, Pakistan, Philippines, Iran, Chile, Israel, and Colombia, which accounts for most of the countries outside Europe that have received $1 billion or more United States aid in the postwar period (with Colombia just under $1 billion). These countries provided two-thirds of the scientists entering the United States from the developing world. The 5,400 trained persons provided by the United States, on the other hand, included 1,500 American technicians working in all these eleven countries (except Israel) and 3,900 nationals of these countries whose study and training in the United States, and occasionally in a third country, was financed by the American aid program.[44]

Over-all estimates of the loss to the underdeveloped countries are both rare and inevitably very approximate. A study sponsored in 1970 by the United Nations Institute for Training and Research estimated that, assuming "an average educational cost, based on Colombia figures of some $10,000 per professional . . . the educational value contributed by the developing nations to the 75,000-odd scientists, engineers and medical personnel entering the United States from 1953–69 would be in the order of $750 million." In 1968 alone, the study noted, the cost would be $132 million.[45] The value of those going to other developed countries considered, the study suggests that the $750 million would at least have to be doubled, which would give $1,500 million. Any such simple multiplication, however, takes no account of the long-term economic and social effects of the drain: the inflated educational expenses caused by the departures; forgone earnings and interest; the loss in creativity, leadership, and other social consequences; or the compounding of the economic, social, and educational gap left behind. Indeed, it was asserted not long ago that "foreign aid to the United States in the form of skilled manpower [between 1949 and 1967] is estimated to be as great as, or greater than, the total of American aid to countries abroad in the same period."[46]

There seems to be no rapid or easy remedy. As a matter of fact, new immigration regulations in the United States, Canada, the United Kingdom, and to a lesser extent in Australia promise rather to step up the inflow. Nor are there any signs of effective countermeasures or changes in educational policies in the underdeveloped countries likely to modify the trend. Indeed, the educational systems of most underdeveloped countries are still those imported from the West, and quite frequently their products cannot be utilized in the non-Western sociocultural framework within which they seek employment. The situation is further aggravated either by inappropriate interpretations of academic freedom or by overambitious educational aims dictated more by considerations of nationalist pride and prestige than by sober and practical appraisal of genuine needs.

Thus one encounters underdeveloped countries that are training aerodynamicists but are without an aerospace industry, that are preparing people for advanced research but lack suitable equipment and laboratories, that have scores of atomic scientists but no technology to construct an atomic reactor. Abstract scientific experiments may be carried on at great expense while new agricultural methods have to be imported for want of funds and interest in research relating to a field of such vital importance to the national economy. Last but not least, in the social and political climate prevailing in most underdeveloped countries, it is very exceptional indeed for doctors, engineers, agronomists, or other scientists to enjoy incomes or social prestige comparable to those accorded politicians, the military, or other members of the ruling elites.

So long as social and material opportunity lies almost exclusively in the westernized slice of fragmented economies, education, and higher education in particular, will be subordinated to the needs, the values and the rewards of that small sector only. The prevailing educational system will pump in enough trained men to satisfy those needs. Beyond that, inevitably, unemployment will occur. Under such circumstances, despair among the educated is deepening and the situation is unlikely to change radically in the foreseeable future. The more enterprising and the more talented will succumb to the temptation to seek satisfaction abroad. The frustration of those who remain will continue to pile up, a potential detonator of grave troubles to come.[47]

Nevertheless, if they wanted to, the advanced countries could take appropriate steps to prevent or at least slow down such a depletion of the poorer countries' trained professionals. They have efficient means at their disposal when they wish to control the entry of foreign laborers. With not much greater difficulty, they might also modify their immigration regulations so as to harmonize them with the proclaimed purposes of their aid policies. They could rethink the educational programs they provide under technical assistance so that these would cease to encourage emigration or failure to return. Above all, the rich countries could afford to expand their own higher education in order not to be dependent on imported skills.

As for the poor countries themselves, they too would have effective means at their disposal if they really wished to prevent this regular nullification of their financial sacrifices. Aside from the possibility of instituting—for a limited period at least—obligatory service for those whose training has been assisted by the state, they might see to it that the education they cannot refuse their citizens is adapted to genuine needs. They could create conditions under which the material and social rewards offered to indispensable personnel would become proportionate to the economic benefits their specialization can bestow. Above all, whenever feasible, they might train their own available talent for the tasks they now let be performed by foreign technical assistants. All this may be too much to expect under prevailing economic and sociocultural conditions over most of Latin America, Asia, or Africa. Yet given time and the will to do it, it could be done. And the need to begin becomes each day more urgent.

In the meantime the brain drain, like the persistence of nonadapted educational systems, the toleration of corruption, or the contradictions implicit in the arms trade with low-income countries, is but an arbitrarily selected illustration of what amounts to collusion between external and internal interests developing within a context which the aid relationship tends to bring about. The complementarity of interests in the status quo of both the aid-givers and the recipient governing groups dictates tolerance of each other's shortcomings. Yet even so, in the face of mounting criticism by their own compatriots, the acquiescence and the collaboration of the ruling elites would be deprived of all pretense to respectability if they could not invoke the intellectual backing and the theoretical justifications of the *clerks* of the international aid establishment.

VII | *Trahison des Clercs— North-South Version*

The commendable endeavor to assist development in the economically backward half of the world has brought into being an administrative-academic complex of unsuspected dimensions. Sprawling across rich and poor countries, within two decades it has become one of the largest industries in the world. It provides a livelihood and a career to more people than do any of the giant international corporations, yet it turns out no goods. Moreover, it is the sole industry in the world which, though in decline, continues to expand its personnel.

The employees of this enormous apparatus fall into three main categories. First, there are those working for their own governments: in aid-giving or aid-receiving organizations; as planning officials or technical assistants; as members of appraising or verifying missions, or of delegations at intergovernmental meetings concerned with aid and development problems. Secondly, there are those in the service of international organizations: economists, planners, and the personnel of technical assistance schemes; statisticians as well as bureaucrats and administrators of all kinds. Finally, there is the academic community: the theoreticians of development, model-builders and econometricians, university teachers and researchers, or authors and consultants. To these three main categories would have to be added what might be described as the auxiliaries of the development establishment. On the one hand there are the full-time workers in voluntary and charitable organizations and in pressure groups, or the organizers of public manifestations, from marches to meetings. On the other are the publishers and printers of the avalanche of books, periodicals, and articles dealing with aid and development; the organizers of the yearly hundreds of lectures, seminars, meetings, symposia, congresses, and round-table conferences devoted to the subject, their interpreters and translators, the editors and condensers of their texts, and all those who service these occasions down to the distributors of sharpened pencils, not to speak of the hotels and the airlines, a sizable proportion of whose clientele such events provide.

Like all good civil servants, those who work for their own government can believe, or at least pretend to believe, that they serve their country's interests. But as in all other fields of governmental activity in both rich and poor countries, the daily confrontation of the desirable and the possible is bound to reduce the enthusiasm of all but those who never had any or those who are incurably naive. Beyond that, the stage is filled either by opportunists dreaming of their pensions, by professional negotiators hoping to score prestige-building victories, or by mere functionaries fully aware and dutifully respectful of the ultimate motivations of the game.

The picture is not very different in the international organizations. Within those representing the interests of well-defined groups on the side of either rich or poor, there may be skirmishes between traditionalists and liberals or moderates and extremists, but few really basic differences about ultimate aims. The lot of those working in world-wide intergovernmental organizations—as, for example, the two-thirds of the combined personnel of all United Nations agencies who are occupied with questions related to aid and development—is less simple. Individually, they may have their own convictions. Collectively, they find themselves in the impossible situation of having to act in the name of compromises between diametrically opposed views and interests. In practice, they are reduced to hoping that by sheer repetition they can render respectable and acceptable notions hitherto considered inadmissible by one side or the other. In order to live and work in the shadow of such paralyzing imperatives without succumbing to utter disillusionment, they have to develop the defensive conviction that what they may achieve is more than just marginal. Yet if compromise in politics may produce temporarily workable solutions, compromise in ideas and theories inevitably breeds hypocrisy, and as a result, for those not yet cynical, tormenting frustrations. Thus the international civil servant is condemned to an existence between emasculated projects and semiutopian sentimentalism. To make it bearable, such an existence is filled in with artificially built-up passions connected with synthetic or irrelevant issues. And behind them all there is the reality of immutable interests and the soothing daily routine, with corridor-loads of disillusioned accountants of quantified fantasies hurrying between confidential consultations, long-distance telephone calls, and preparatory committees.

These are but the executants. Their liberty of action is severely circumscribed by identifiable interests and pressures emanating both from the rich countries and from the recipient governments. What helps to articulate and occasionally even to modify such interests and pressures is ideas. And the ideas are usually provided by the academic wing of the aid and development establishment.

Development economics is a post-decolonization phenomenon, and has in turn conditioned the shape of aid policies. Notwithstanding their short history, however, development doctrines have produced rival schools of thought and their respective high priests of either respectable or controversial ideas. Indeed, development theories, like ladies' garments, are subject to fashion. Some show surprising resistance to change. A few soon look worn. Others are too obviously unreal to survive confrontation with reality. So, swings in theory are usually followed by periods of critical reappraisal, the discarding of some old beliefs, and the emergence of new doctrines presumably better adapted to mounting empirical evidence supplied by research.

Once decolonization unveiled the problem, the development economists went to work like the men in the Oriental tale who were ordered blindfolded into a dark room to touch an elephant and to attempt a description of the animal they had never seen. As they touched its trunk, its tail, or its legs, the imagination of each produced its own associations, comparisons, and conclusions. As a matter of fact, the metaphor is not so far-fetched as it would seem at first sight. Most of the development economists had little knowledge of underdeveloped countries, or knew only one or two in a given region with specific problems not present in other parts of the world. A good many of them, including the fathers of some of the most popular and influential doctrines, had never lived in a low-income country, or at best, their knowledge of them did not go beyond the main avenues of the capital city connecting the airport with the luxury hotel which hosted the symposium to which they had been invited. Thus the temptation was almost irresistible to explain the shapes touched by conceiving the elephant in the form of some familiar animal. That, of course, meant the one best known to all of them: the experience of the West.

In fact, a minority went even further. Convinced that they had correctly conceived the shape and the nature of the animal, they embarked on predicting its behavior and even its future reactions to manipulated changes. Thus, in addition to the shaping of theories and doctrines, a distinct branch of development economics has unfolded. Applying mathematical reasoning to arbitrarily selected facts, statisticians and econometricians have begun to produce for each other's enjoyment algebraic presentations of imaginary circumstances. By doing so, they have been claiming quantitative respectability for vulnerable hypotheses in the form of abstract mathematical growth-models and econometric forecasts, convincing perhaps under aseptic laboratory conditions but quite often without any relevance to observable, concrete situations.

As for the theory itself which, with greater or lesser refinements and modifications, has been behind most Western (and Communist) analysis, it resembles indeed the Western (or Communist) animal. Simplified to the extreme, its central hypothesis is that rapid investments in industries will employ an increasing amount of surplus labor from agriculture; that output on the land will not suffer because those who remain in agriculture will be able to produce the same quantities with harder labor; that the resulting emergence of middle classes and an industrial proletariat will gradually provide a more progressive social framework; and that, like concentric circles, prosperity will gradually cover more and more people prepared for it by social and political change and by the income-spreading role of either market forces or (in the Communist view) the planner's intervention. This, in a nutshell, was the first phase.

Implicit in it were a number of assumptions and consequences. At least four of them turned out to be of capital importance in shaping the aid policies built on this doctrinal base.

To begin with, development seen in this way meant a unilinear movement towards an ideal, which happened to be the West's material achievement. Within such a framework it became feasible to define distinct phases along the road leading to such fulfillment. Equally implied was that development in the West had disposed of poverty, the progress of the underdeveloped countries being considered synonymous with measurable increase in the per capita share of the national income. Moreover, based on the Western norm, and having economic growth as its central aim, the theory offered justification for the practice of quantifying the process in order to measure retardation, deviation, or progress.

The second major consequence was the admission that inequality was the price of progress. During the West's industrial revolutions, resources were allocated by the market mechanism and the savings of the rich provided the first entrepreneurs' investment capital. Dickens and the social historians of the nineteenth century described the price of deferred demand. But the prosperity of the twentieth century has demonstrated its fruits for the coming generations.

The next important consequence followed from the supposition that increased well-being brings in its wake reforms and structural changes likely to attenuate and eventually to dispose of the more acute social and political tensions. Agricultural, educational, and fiscal reforms, together with complex distributive mechanisms aiming at the equalization of opportunity, have demonstrated this in one Western country after the other.

Finally, accomplished in due time and in the proper sequence, all these changes have enabled the mature

Western economies to become reasonably resistant to outside influences and to see their productivity acquire its own momentum, or in other words, to reach the stage of self-sustaining growth. And the implication was clear that the same reward would also recompense those of the underdeveloped countries that were willing to pay the price and to pass through the successive phases traced by the West's experience.

Thus, aid philosophies derived from such ideas not only admitted but even expected their consequences. Indeed, foreign assistance was presumed to help hasten the process and to lighten the human price paid for economic progress. Its role was to enable a higher proportion of the national income to go into investments than would have been the case without aid. And to this end, more specifically, foreign aid was to provide capital in the form of gifts, loans, or private investments, either to supplement inadequate local savings or to fill the gap in foreign-exchange earnings so as to permit the importation of a larger volume of the indispensable tools of progress.

Such were the broad outlines of the first, optimistic phase of development economics and of the resulting aid policies. Still, right from the beginning it was felt that such an approach did not take adequate account of the immense complexity of the problem and that it almost entirely ignored its human dimensions. And with growing evidence of difficulties provoking more and more articulate doubts, two protest movements, as it were, developed.

On one side, it was claimed that foreign aid tended to distort the natural workings of market forces. To re-establish their sovereignty, the reduction or even the cessation of external assistance was called for. In its place, whenever necessary, reliance on private investments was recommended, and this on the assumption that it would fulfill more effectively the tasks expected from aid, and in addition, would stimulate performance with the same rigor it had shown in the West's own experience.

The other side, too, had misgivings about the role of foreign aid. But these were merely projections of a much broader reappraisal of the neoclassical doctrines' basic assumptions, particularly of their belief that Western methods could be transplanted.

Putting an end to the tendency to turn analysis into prescription, these new approaches betrayed an increased preoccupation with the human and psychological aspects of development, and by doing so, proceeded with greater modesty and without the concealed arrogance of belief in the established supremacy of Western methods and values. Historical perspectives at last became tools of economic comprehension. Attention was paid to the differences in initial conditions for development as compared with those which had characterized the West's industrial revolutions. Moreover, it was no longer taken for granted that the underdeveloped countries' social and political structures could be considered automatically adaptable so as to permit the manipulation of economic variables. Above all, there was growing consciousness of the interrelation of internal and external structures: of the interdependence of sociopolitical realities within underdeveloped countries and the worldwide economic, trading, and power systems surrounding them.

This new phase of development economics is still unfolding. It shows the way towards a more complex but probably more realistic assessment of contemporary realities. How fast or to what extent it will modify or replace the analyses and ideas of the neoclassical schools is still uncertain. Much research is still needed before its hypotheses are provided with all the factual backing they merit. Clearly, the new approach has already demonstrated the vulnerability if not the untenability of many of the basic assumptions of the first phase. Yet equally clearly, it has failed so far to have any serious impact on the aid policies inspired by those contested and now largely discredited views.

What could better illustrate this resistance to change than the tenacious predilection for quantification?

Economists, of course, have had a decisive influence upon the formulation of aid philosophies, and they have an understandable bias in favor of the measurable. They were bound to find a ready audience among all those who, anxious to see the alleviation of extreme poverty, wished to have measurable proof of it. Expressed in dollars, the effort of the poor to catch up with the rich becomes dramatic.

Although mere mechanical indicators convey far less than the full story, they certainly have their role to play. In the words of Simon Kuznets, "Modern economic growth implies major structural changes and correspondingly large modifications in social and institutional conditions under which the greatly increased product *per capita* is attained. . . . Yet for the purpose of measurement the changing components of the structure must be reduced to a common denominator."[1]

This is obviously true, but only on condition that per capita income is utilized as merely one among many possible indicators of a country's real development. However, in current development literature, and in the publications put out by the international institutions in particular, it tends to become not only the sole aggregative yardstick of progress but even an index of the effectiveness of external assistance. "The record of development is mixed, but it is far better than generally realized. The average rate of increase in the G.N.P. of the developing countries has reached 5 percent per annum in the

1960's," the Pearson Report proudly stated, providing a perfect illustration both of the identification of development with the per capita share of the national product, and of the uncritical utilization of the aggregative approach. That "the global average conceals great contrasts" was admitted a few lines later. But, exuding optimism, the report quickly rectified its doubts by declaring that the results have still demonstrated that "underdevelopment can be overcome."[2]

The aggregates generally referred to cover some ninety low-income countries. They include quite a number where the per capita share of the national product has actually declined, even more where it has increased only modestly, as well as a few where—thanks to oil revenues, to particularly heavy foreign investments, or to other exceptional circumstances—it has grown much faster than the population. At best, this would justify the statement that a small proportion of the underdeveloped countries have increased their gross national product considerably during the past few years, that many more have achieved growth rates barely higher than the expansion of their populations, and that in the case of a fair number there has been rather a decline. It would not justify even an implied generalization about how the increment was distributed, and of course it would say nothing about the numerous other factors characterizing "underdevelopment"—such as unemployment, bad health and housing, illiteracy, indebtedness, or transfer from owned land to shantytown—all of which, in concrete situations, may be of far greater importance to the individuals concerned than their hypothetical share in the growth of the gross national product.

Nonetheless, one-sided emphasis on quantified indicators has become the dominant feature of current development literature. In fact, they are presented as meaningful criteria not merely of development but even of aid. The percentage share of a donor country's national income devoted to grants, to profitable private investments, to high-interest loans, or to aid projects of varying usefulness is lumped together and carefully tabulated in monetary terms as a measure of its virtue. This again is integrated into grand totals of the virtue-coefficients of all the donor countries combined. And so "performance" in both aid-giving and aid utilization is distilled into the fashionable global and quantified Esperanto of Development Documentalese.

The addicts of the game maintain that such common denominators, though simplified, are helpful either for reassuring flagging public opinion about results or as instruments of pressure to obtain more aid. But a diametrically opposite interpretation may be no less convincing. It is perfectly conceivable that the aid-providing countries find it convenient to encourage reliance on averages and global generalizations about "growth" because these tend to produce more flattering evidence of the effectiveness of their assistance. And for understandable reasons, the benefitting ruling elites raise no objections. But the same applies also to aggregates relating to aid. The combination of disparate aid components in a single percentage figure helps to camouflage its often dubious ingredients and to divert attention both from its profitability and from the very modest real sacrifice involved in the sum total. All this is fairly obvious. What is more regrettable is that the United Nations and its specialized agencies should not merely echo such data but bestow respectability upon them by issuing statistics based on the same approach.

The constitutional constraints of the United Nations are known. They apply also to its widespread activities in the economic and social fields. The only alternative to compromise is triumph by numerical majorities who lack the means to force any change in the attitudes of the dominant economic powers. Yet even so, it may be asked whether any consensus is worth the damage the United Nations suffers by associating itself with the interested practice of identifying Western concepts and value systems with what the underdeveloped countries ought to desire. Indeed, the one-sided approach implied by grandiose plans and global strategies built on aggregate per capita GNP growth rates of some ninety low-income countries, with only cursory reference to the social and political aspects of development, cannot be entirely fortuitous. It signifies either the majority's inability or its unwillingness to admit the complexity of development, or perhaps even its preference for diverting attention from or avoiding the real problems.

But the tenacity of the aggregative methodology is intimately connected with another heritage of the neoclassical school's assumptions: the problem of equality.

Averages and aggregates reveal little about the enormous inequality of monetary incomes prevalent in most poor countries. And in spite of the constant references to per capita shares, they reveal even less about how the growth of the GNP is shared out.

In fact, a simple arithmetical exercise quickly exposes the irrelevance of the much-publicized growth figures. Let us imagine a country with a population of 1,000 and with a gross national product of $1,000 which grows annually by 5 percent, and whose population expands each year by 2.5 percent. Let us also assume that 5 percent of the country's population is "privileged" and can assure for itself six times the average share of the annual growth of the GNP. In addition, let us suppose that another 15 percent of the population, because they are city-dwellers, industrial workers, or trade unionists, can protect their interests and secure for themselves twice their proportionate share of the increase—that is, 10 cents instead of 5 cents. This would correspond to the existing situation in an "average" underdeveloped country, though in a good many cases growth is slower and the privileged minorities appropriate far more than six times their per capita share of growth. Moreover, in most cases the "organized" minority makes up much less than 15 percent of the population. But keeping to our example, what happens to the revenues of the remaining 80 percent?[3]

While the prosperous group's members increase their revenue from one dollar to $1.277, the organized 15 percent see theirs go up to $1.078. Simultaneously, the per capita share of the remaining 80 percent will decline to 99.9 cents.

But if one supposes everything unchanged except that the 5 percent privileged minority appropriates not six but ten times its due share—probably nearer to what is really happening in the majority of the poorer countries—their one dollar will grow next year to $1.473, and that of the organized 15 percent ot $1.078. In this case, the per capita share of the remaining 80 percent of the population will be in still faster decline, down to 98.6 cents.

Thus even a 5 percent annual growth in the GNP, so triumphantly announced in development statistics, is perfectly compatible with a steady decline in the incomes of the overwhelming majority. And this is precisely what is happening in dozens of poor countries, including several regularly held up as the most successful examples of rapid "development."

Available estimates show that the proportions given in this example are understatements rather than exaggerations. Statistics in this field are, of course, notoriously vague. Yet owing to widespread tax evasion and to other circumstances of the same nature, they underestimate rather than overstate existing inequalities. A recent study of Colombia reported, for example, that "people included in the 5 per cent of the population with the largest incomes receive between one-third and somewhat more than two-fifths of total income," and added that the "concentration of income has not lessened during the last fifteen years; it might even have increased."[4] Yet between 1961 and 1968, Colombia's GNP per capita grew by 1.4 percent.[5] In Brazil, the 5 percent of the population with highest revenues received 40 percent of total income; in Argentina, 31 percent; and in Mexico, 29 percent.[6] In Turkey, where the GNP per capita was growing by 3.2 percent annually (1961–1968), about two-thirds of the population earn per capita only about a fifth of the amount those belonging to the more fortunate one-third receive.[7] In Ceylon, 1.5 percent at the top earn one-fifth of the nation's income; at the same time, the per capita annual growth of the island's GNP has been 2.3 percent.[8] Figures from most other underdeveloped countries would tell a similar tale.

It would seem, however, that there is no cause for surprise. For it is an article of faith among development economists of the old school that distributive economic justice is a luxury that developing countries cannot afford.[9] This is based on the assumption that a more egalitarian sharing out of incomes would dampen incentives and lower savings, and thus would slow down growth.

That not even higher wages or profits will induce peasants in traditional societies to produce more was a popular feature of the economic folklore of colonial times. Usually it disregarded the socio-economic constraints which influenced the producers' behavior. Though still inadequate, recent research seems to produce evidence rather to the contrary. Observers from India and Pakistan to Thailand and Africa have found that, under appropriate conditions and when they can demonstrably benefit from their increased effort, peasants respond to incentives and experiment with new crops and methods in expectation of higher incomes.[10] Wherever providing the cultivators with suitable credit and marketing facilities was tried out, the so-called green revolution invariably provoked fast-growing demand for the inputs needed to increase production. And the more peasants are freed from the colonial type of socio-economic relationships, the more the original assertion is likely to be disproved by empirical evidence.

Unfortunately, there is a comparable scarcity of information about the saving habits of peasants in underdeveloped countries. Yet in this case too, recent research casts some doubt upon the belief that only capitalists and the urban commercial classes are savers and that peasants, being too poor, are unlikely to save voluntarily. As a matter of fact, there appears to be no positive correlation between inequality and higher savings. In Chile, Colombia, Guatemala, and India, for example, the upper 10 percent of income earners receive respectively 47–49, 48, 44, and 33–37 percent of total income, and the savings ratios in the same countries are about 3, 6, 4, and 10 percent respectively. Thus India, though the poorest and the least inegalitarian among the four, has the highest savings ratio.[11] Indeed, the few studies relating to individual countries seem to confirm that it is far from obvious that the rich save more than the poor.[12]

But the case for more equal distribution of income in order to speed development has a much broader logical base. Clearly, it affects both a country's pattern of consumption and, as a consequence, its level of employment.[13]

A few years ago Ragnar Nurske put forward the theory that the influence of the consumption patterns of rich countries tended to constitute an "impediment to domestic saving and capital formation in the poorer countries."[14] But in actuality the low-income majorities have only limited means to imitate the foreign consumption patterns they see in motion pictures or hear about on their transistors. It is rather the high-income minorities who model their consumption patterns on those of the rich countries. And their demand for modern luxuries will be supplied either by local, protected industries or by imports.

The well-to-do in the underdeveloped countries naturally tend to consume more imported articles than do people with modest incomes. If one refers to locally produced goods only, the proportion of imported ingredients is very different in the case of articles consumed by the wealthy and of those consumed by the poor. The import content in the production of manufactured basic necessities such as clothing, shoes, kitchen utensils, toys, or furniture is very low. It becomes much higher when it comes to refrigerators, television sets, or cars.[15] In fact, not only do parts have to be imported but very often such articles are produced by foreign-owned companies, or with the use of foreign licenses. This again involves the transfer abroad of profits, interest payments, or royalties. And the more sophisticated the articles in question are, the higher will be such costs incurred in foreign currency. Thus the greater the income inequality, the heavier will be the demand for imported goods or for locally produced articles with a high import content, and the less foreign exchange will be left to purchase abroad indispensable equipment likely to provide additional employment opportunities.

Moreover, there is a comparable difference in the labor content of the articles consumed by the prosperous minority and of those consumed by the majority with modest revenues. The import-substitution industries, which cater mainly for the needs of the minority, are usually modern and employ relatively few people. Consumer goods accessible to the public as a whole, on the other hand, can more easily be produced with simple, labor-intensive techniques, and as a consequence offer employment to larger numbers. It follows, then, that a given amount of income spent on essentials the poor can afford will generate more employment than if it were spent on the sophisticated goods only the rich minority consumes.

It may be objected that, at least in those low-income countries where import substitution has already produced an industrial base, the volume of imported consumer goods is rather modest, and that change in the distribution of income could therefore have marginal effects only. This, of course, takes it for granted that import controls are effectively enforced, which is not uniformly the case. But the conclusion would seem doubtful in any event, in view of the very high import content of precisely the type of articles the richest group buys, because of important quantities of luxury items entering the country as contraband, and finally, because of the very high tourist expenditure by the same minority, implying also the introduction of luxury goods purchased abroad. In the case of Colombia, for example, of the country's total export revenue of $510 million in 1967, only $34 million was spent on imported consumer goods but $51 million paid for expenditure by Colombian tourists abroad.[16]

It would be difficult to say how far such figures are typical of other underdeveloped countries. Though there are surely some countries where imports, contraband, and tourist expenditure are effectively controlled, it would be rash to conclude that Colombia must be an exceptional case.

A variety of further arguments may be invoked in favor of more equitable income distribution as an accelerator of development. To begin with, it would help to create that sense of participation which is a precondition of incentives to innovate or, eventually, to develop entrepreneurial talents. Also, the attenuation of the high concentration of incomes, which now tends to encourage capital flight, luxury housing, and other investments irrelevant to development, would help control tax evasion and, because of the broader tax base, could lead to higher rates of public savings. Moreover, if their efforts were accompanied by desirable fiscal reforms and the progressive elimination of ostentatious wealth, governments might more easily obtain the cooperation of the population in wage restraint and thus in the taming of inflation. Above all, income redistribution would produce new consumption patterns and, given the fact that the poorer classes spend a high proportion of their revenue on food, would lead to increased demand for agricultural products. This in turn would have direct effects on health, on morale, and ultimately on productivity. It might also help check the exodus of villagers and the resulting uncontrolled urbanization. And in view of accumulating evidence produced by research that small farms often show higher yields than large holdings, reforms of land tenure might in the long run lead also to increased agricultural output.[17]

At this point, however, one comes upon another major assumption of Western aid policies: that following the Western European and North American pattern, fast economic growth will usher in reforms and structural changes likely to relieve social and political tensions. Once again, there is little evidence to support the abstractions of the theorists.

In the Western experience, reforms and structural changes followed in the wake of economic adjustments effected by newly emerging classes. That the investment rate had to go up to a point where the growth in output outstripped the rate of population increase was self-evident. But to reach that point, appropriate production techniques had to be developed and accumulated knowledge, experience, and inventions had to be integrated into the productive process. A few had to take risks and provide leadership; many more had to acquire the technical and organizational skills and adopt the appropriate attitudes to fit into the emerging new social framework. In the West, it was the bourgeois revolution which liberated the forces of commercial and industrial capitalism and inspired the social and structural reforms which were its prerequisites. And with greater economic equality on its way, inequality in political power also began to diminish.

In most of the underdeveloped countries, this process could not be repeated. The deformations caused by their encounter with the West have blocked the mechanism, and the impact of international market forces has certainly not helped to unblock it. Whatever economic progress or industrialization has occurred has been brought about either by the state, by foreign capitalism, or by local entrepreneurs allied to foreign interests and dependent on their support. Either no indigenous bourgeoisie has emerged, or it has remained small, ineffectual, and wedded to inappropriate foreign attitudes and methods. Its hypothetical inclinations to reform being circumscribed by dominant foreign interests, it has been condemned to become a mere auxiliary of the international status quo. For attitudes, methods, policies, and institutions to change, the link between the two would have to be broken. Without that, political power in the underdeveloped countries will tend to remain associated with the present extreme inequality of incomes. And in such a context, certain types of quantifiable growth are more likely to produce and to exacerbate social and political tensions than to attenuate them.

In the few exceptional cases where governments came to power disposed to effect the required changes, their energies have usually been diverted towards battling the opposition of powerful local groups in control of decisive economic levers, groups that rely on the moral and propaganda backing and, whenever necessary, the immense commercial, political, and occasionally even military sanctions of their foreign protectors.

In practice, the temptation to identify growth with development encourages the equation of progress with the short-term goal of economic stability. Moreover, the resulting continuity without structural change is often further aggravated by international advice given in the name of rigid financial orthodoxy, which is likely to lead to declining real wages and to growing unemployment. Interpreted in this narrow sense, growth may very well leave major social problems not only unremedied but on the way to becoming explosive.

The contemporary variant of Aristotle's dictum that "in human society extremes of wealth and poverty are the main sources of evil" is that social upheavals are not about the aggregate value of the national income but about how it is distributed. Yet clearly, a country that leaves its social problems unsolved is unlikely to be strong enough to complete and to maintain its real independence.

This, then, would seem to challenge the Western aid policies' supreme promise, that the underdeveloped countries which have passed through the successive phases traced by the West's own experience will ultimately reach the stage of self-sustaining growth.

In this case it would be unjust to claim that evidence contradicts theoretical assumptions, as the term "self-sustaining growth" itself has never been clearly defined. The development establishment uses it with the barely concealed aim of reassuring impatient legislators and public opinion alike. In underdeveloped countries it usually figures in optimistic preambles to five-year plans, its purpose being to calm the critics who maintain that foreign aid is nothing but a shoehorn to fit their countries into perpetual dependence.

The Pearson Commission employed the term to imply the end of dependence on external assistance. "But can the majority of the developing countries achieve self-sustaining growth by the end of the century?" it asked, only to give its own encouraging reply: "For us the answer is clearly yes." What this achievement within the next thirty years ought to be was made clear in the paragraph preceding the question: "The goal of the international development effort is to put the less developed countries as soon as possible in a position where they can realize their aspirations with regard to economic progress without relying on foreign aid."[18] In a later chapter the report returned to the question, claiming that as well as being rapid, growth "must also eventually be *self-sustaining*, wherever this is consistent with the other objectives of development and the mutual desires of donors and recipients. This means that developing countries should generally become independent of the need for aid on concessional terms as soon as they can do so without reducing their rates of growth below the 6 per cent level. . . ."[19]

What those "aspirations" and "other objectives" might be, or when the mutual desires of donors and recipients might cease to coincide, was not made clear. Nevertheless, deviating on a single occasion from its standard identification of development with economic growth, the report mentioned that by development it understood "a much broader process for which economic growth is a necessary but by no means the only condition."[20]

All this is far from unequivocal. Could it be, then, that the real meaning of self-sustaining economic growth is nearer to what W. W. Rostow defined as the "maturity" following the "take-off" by about forty years? According to him, it is

> the stage in which an economy demonstrates the capacity to move beyond the original industries which powered its take-off and to absorb and to apply efficiently over a wide range of its resources—if not the whole range—the most advanced fruits of . . . modern technology. This is the stage in which an economy demonstrates that it has the technological and entrepreneurial skills to produce not everything, but anything that it chooses to produce. It may lack (like contemporary Sweden and Switzerland, for example) the raw materials or other supply conditions required to produce a given type of output economically; but its dependence is a matter of economic choice or political priority rather than a technological or institutional necessity.[21]

If we agree that the 1960s were the take-off period for the currently fastest-growing underdeveloped economies, Rostow's time-lag of forty years would correspond to the Pearson Commission's promise of self-sustaining growth at the end of this century. But whether we accept the Rostow or Pearson interpretation, many questions remain unanswered. For example, will the efficient application "over a wide range of its resources—if not the whole range" of "the most advanced fruits of . . . modern technology" ever be possible without more evenly distributed purchasing power? And would this help to solve the underdeveloped countries' enormous problem of unemployment? Or did not Japan lay the foundations of its astonishing development by relying first on simple technology requiring modest amounts of capital, and on borrowable and by no means "the most advanced" technology for a long time after? Turning to the Pearson version, on the other hand, is it not likely that between now and the year 2000 the aspirations of those whose labor is to produce the annual 6 percent growth will also include social and political changes likely to provide them with benefits of greater relevance to their daily existence than the mere increase of an ill-distributed national product? Or if such measures aiming at greater social justice slow down economic growth, threaten the power of the ruling elites, and menace the influence and interests of the present donors, would the "mutual desires" of both still converge towards the satisfaction of "the other objectives of development"? And is it realistic at all to assume that concessional loans will become available in so large a volume or that the international trading rules will be modified to such an extent as to render supportable the burdens thirty or more years of continual borrowings and private investments would impose?

So much for the assumptions. As for the results, the emerging social and economic panorama of the Southern Hemisphere could scarcely be more different from what the theoreticians promised or from what was the aid-givers' professed aim.

Wherever there has been growth, its expected diffusion has failed to occur. Instead of there being generalized development based on rapid growth, economic and social inequalities have increased rather than lessened. Educational systems and nutritional and health conditions have continued to be divisive factors, and huge majorities remain deprived of any sense of participation in their country's transformation. The contrast between urban affluence and medieval conditions in the countryside has grown more acute. In place of industrialization adapted to prevailing needs, protected industries relying on advanced, imported technologies have been established primarily to provide for the requirements of the prosperous minorities. The introduction of modern production processes has been accomplished without much increase in industrial employment, and in most underdeveloped countries a dangerously growing proportion of the labor force is partly or totally unemployed. Population growth combined with neglect of agriculture has stimulated the exodus from rural areas and deprives the villages of their youngest and most dynamic elements. In the cities, to live in shantytowns, *ranchos, bustees, barriadas, bidonvilles,* or *favelas* is slowly becoming the rule rather than the exception. And the passions stoked by the degradation of this way of life surround the pathologically swelling cities like a noose.

Meanwhile, the well-to-do of Bombay, Abidjan, or Bogotá have grown more closely linked in attitudes and habits of consumption to the inhabitants of London, Paris, or New York than to the majority of their own compatriots. Rather than acquiring their own economic momentum, barring a few exceptions, most underdeveloped countries have merely created modern sectors dependent on foreign equipment and materials, with much of the benefit resulting from economic growth flowing abroad in the form of profits, interests, and royalties, in payment for luxury imports and tourism, or as the fleeing capital of insecure privileged classes. Most of the commanding heights of the economy have been taken over by foreign companies. Instead of spreading well-being, the structural orientations imposed by foreign influence allied to local interests have prevented rather than encouraged the serious confrontation of the new problems. And in the meantime, the mechanism and rules of the world economic system transform, one after the other, the underdeveloped areas of the world from recipients of assistance into suppliers of resources to the rich world.

Clearly, something has gone wrong. The pattern of development suggested by the West's experience has failed to materialize. Instead, from hungry villages to festering slums, there are warning signals of historic forces moving into position to contest the very system that helped to produce the present predicament.

There is plenty of room for honest differences of opinion about causes, failings, and responsibilities. Yet an awareness that degrading poverty was not inevitable, or a concern to put an end to it, did not necessarily imply that foreigners could do anything really effective about it. Perhaps the very nature of the challenge was misconceived. And maybe by its very nature external assistance could never have performed what was expected of it.

Although written with the specific intention of justifying and encouraging foreign aid, even the Pearson Report had to admit that "the correlation between the amounts of aid received in the past decades and the growth performance is very weak."[22] Following years of close study of the development attempts in one of the world's most afflicted regions, Gunnar Myrdal came to the conclusion that "the participation of outsiders through research, provision of financial aid, and other means is a sideshow of rather small importance to the final outcome."[23]

A few years earlier, Joan Robinson had recognized only two situations in which foreign aid is indispensable: when a country is unable to pay for indispensable equipment it is incapable of producing, or alternatively, when it lacks adequate food to feed those who leave the land to work elsewhere. Such rare cases apart, she held that "foreign aid is not, strictly speaking, indispensable, but it is politically helpful, since it removes the need to cut luxury consumption. When foreign aid is applied to reduction of taxes or takes the form of salaries, commissions and bribes, which are spent on imports that would not have been made without it, it contributes nothing at all to development."[24]

Still others point to the outward-oriented nature of

the underdeveloped economies, to their being captives of international market forces. Without structural changes, they claim, the inherited dislocations and the sectoral disparities in production will continue and mere growth will be only "development of underdevelopment."[25]

But some recent academic thinking probes even beyond such doubts and claims that capital imports, instead of accelerating development, have in some cases retarded it.[26]

The basic assumption that the larger the proportion of the national income going into investments, the faster development will be, inspired the conviction that capital imports would help to step up investments. Aid, in this sense, was expected to supplement either savings or foreign-exchange earnings. By providing foreign exchange, it was maintained, aid would in fact help to make available equipment the lack of which might restrict production and thus lower savings. But foreign and domestic resources are often interchangeable, and so the only real constraint remaining is shortage of savings. The basic issue, then, is the relationship between aid and savings.

Beyond these considerations, however, there is also the possibility that an increase in aid might reduce the capital-output ratio, that is, contravene the most productive utilization of funds available.* This, it is claimed, might occur for a number of reasons. To begin with, in search of political benefits, aid donors tend to spend on showy and dramatic projects likely to hit the headlines of the local press. Speedways, congress halls, ultramodern university campuses, or experimental atomic installations will have priority over unspectacular small works capable of producing simple agricultural machinery, modest irrigation schemes, or pumping stations, even

*Capital-output ratio is the amount by which a given increase in investment increases the volume of output: a rough measure of the productivity of capital investment.

though the potential contribution of the latter to development may be demonstrably greater. This tendency is reinforced by the methods of the aid agencies, which also tend to favor larger, more easily administered schemes. Though a combination of smaller projects might be more productive, they would involve higher administrative costs, organizational headaches, and additional personnel for supervision, as well as the possibility of a numerically higher proportion of failures. The resulting systematic preference for large projects is an additional factor likely to lower the capital-output ratio.

Moreover, aid agencies or bilateral aid programs tend to discourage government ownership, and so foreign aid goes more often into infrastructure, such as dams, roads, transport, or power stations, than into immediately productive fields. This ever-present endeavor to prepare the ground for private investments is in turn closely related to the practice of aid-tying. Not only will the recipient be obliged to buy his equipment at above world market prices but, almost invariably, it will involve continued dependence on equally overpriced spare parts and other supplies, lowering the productivity of the initial investment and, in the long run, rendering its products internationally less competitive. Furthermore, aid attached to specific projects normally provides financing for their foreign-exchange cost only, which encourages recipient governments to select them on the basis of their high import content rather than according to their real urgency; or to maximize in any given project the components which have to be bought abroad.

Yet even if all such influences and practices combine to lower the productivity of investments, still they might be helpful in encouraging greater consumption and perhaps even in raising the growth rate. But this would occur only if, in the meantime, domestic savings rates remained constant, uninfluenced by the inflow of the savings of foreigners. Evidence seems to prove that usually this is not the case.

The real question, then, is whether aid is entirely devoted to helping capital accumulation, or to what extent it becomes a mere substitute to permit higher consumption. Figures are not lacking to show that the second case is much more frequent. In Colombia, for example, from 1950 to 1963, "for every dollar of foreign aid received, domestic savings declined by about eighty-four cents."[27] In fact not even aid provided for specific projects excludes such substitution.

In actual practice, increased inflow of foreign capital may lead to a decline in public savings because governments will feel less pressed to collect taxes or, perhaps because they will use part of the aid received to expand government expenditure in ways calculated to procure political support. The military assistance that accompanies aid will invariably demand complementary local military expenditure. And food aid can discourage local production of food grains by reducing demand and thus depressing prices. But an increased flow of foreign capital may cause decline also in private domestic savings, either because money may become cheaper, so that there is less incentive for local investors to save, or because the growing competition of foreign private investments is likely to curtail the indigenous entrepreneurs' opportunities. Finally, capital imports may have a depressing effect on domestic savings by stimulating the consumption either of imported articles or of locally produced ones which otherwise might have been exported.

For all these reasons, no amount of foreign aid is likely to help an underdeveloped country achieve a given growth objective. In such a perspective, it is even conceivable that a reduction of capital imports might improve the growth rate whereas an increase might retard it. In other words, the protagonists of such an approach claim, under certain conditions a reduction in the availability of foreign capital might lead to a rise in domestic savings and to greater effectiveness in the utilization of available funds.* Indeed, these two effects might more than compensate for the reduction in total available resources, and as a result, the rate of economic development might actually accelerate.

The cost of self-reliance and of greater economic independence, then, is not necessarily slower growth but less current consumption. And the implication is clear that the sacrifice should not have to be borne mainly by those belonging to the majority whose consumption is already severely limited by the modesty of their means.

And so we come to the end of the journey across two decades of experiments, myths, and lessons.

Paradoxically, the original justification and purpose of aid, to lighten the human and social cost of the development effort, is called into question for its alleged role in achieving just the opposite. Human nature and human institutions being what they are, even magic carpets tend to be teleguided. Thus there seems to be no shortcut consistent with dignity which bypasses frugality today as a necessary condition for self-reliance and real progress tomorrow.

*In technical terms, a rise in the incremental capital-output ratio.

VIII | *A New Phase*

THE MOOD has clearly changed. The role of aid, as hitherto conceived and dispensed, has to be reconsidered in the light of new thinking about development. After the initial period of excessive optimism and simplification, followed by the phase of empirical research and of the growing acceptance of the diversity of situations, a new stage has now been reached.

It will probably be characterized by an increased turning away from the goal of quantifiable growth in favor of social, cultural, and economic restructuring. Both nationally and internationally, this will demand greater institutional emphasis in place of market-oriented inducements. The change has become necessary in order both to heal the blocking deformations caused by the impact of the West and to help the emergence of sociocultural frameworks built on indigenous foundations and likely to provide more congenial settings for values and ways of living not shaped by imported norms.

But interests, opinions, and routine will not easily yield even in the face of concrete evidence. Discredited ways of thinking will persist in self-justification. Outdated methods will linger on through organizational inertia. And the hypocrisy that can arise from trying to combine a concern for development with the preservation of vested interests will not disappear. Yet the gap between the development establishment's rhetoric and reality in the Southern Hemisphere will grow each day more glaring.

Though it may be doing so for the wrong reasons, the general public may not be mistaken in withdrawing its support from the government's current aid policies. Even if the selfish motivations of such attitudes are to be condemned, the erosion of confidence may be due to the instinctive realization that in its present forms aid has not only failed to mitigate but has even accentuated great social evils, and that quite often it has helped to debilitate rather than stimulate potential productive energies. Such conclusions cannot be ascribed to selfishness or ignorance alone. Even the activist minorities, the idealist young, the liberal internationalists, and the enlightened academics are affected by them. Even they are losing confidence in a system which they now see as favoring the privileged rather than helping the needy, and as instrumental in strengthening local and foreign interests already deeply entrenched in the underdeveloped world.

Indeed, the evidence is becoming irrefutable that the simple belief that the gross national product measures human welfare has been causing extensive damage to the very people who were to be assisted. Through the mercenary role of ruling oligarchies and with the catalytic effect of aid, the underdeveloped countries have become even more firmly knit into the pattern of the international market economy with its rules so heavily weighted against their interests. Gradually they have become captives of the vicious circle of unmanageable debts, distorted social values and patterns, and the alienation of majorities, until aid has grown almost indistinguishable from a subsidy to keep them within the prevailing system.

Left free from external obstructions, and given

honesty of purpose, the will, and the ability, policies which really promote development are, apart from a few hard-core cases, usually possible without reliance on foreign favors. And experience seems to prove that where these qualities are lacking, foreign aid seldom helps to stimulate or to replace them. In place of aid to speed up the growth rate, then, emphasis will shift to changing the developmental process itself. Preoccupation with average standards of living will inevitably yield place to concern with ways of living.

But wherever it can be accomplished, the transition will be slow, often confused, and nearly always painful. Inevitably, it will also involve international strains. For all these reasons, it is probable that the easiest period of postcolonial relations is coming to an end.

One after the other the former colonial countries will grow less and less inclined to live submissively under the degrading, perpetual tutelage of the industrial powers. Barring unexpected major initiatives, the burden of debts, inequality, and unemployment will lead to explosive crises. Social problems will grow still more acute. And while the agronomists and the demographers will expect miracles from each other, the drift towards despair and anarchy will continue. Gradually, the guerrilla may command greater respect than the legislator who comes with his promises in order to be re-elected.

The man in the paddy fields of Asia or the mines of the Andes has never heard of the gross national product. But he can compare his shack with the landlord's mansion, or the dispensary where his child died with the city hospital where the rich are treated. And he knows what unemployment is. He will easily be convinced by those who refuse to equate development with growth in the narrowest sense of the expanding aggregate production. He will listen with sympathy to arguments calling for an end to foreign aid on the grounds that it serves primarily the interests of the wealthy and that it is used to subvert rather than to promote social progress. So far as he is concerned, he will certainly accept the view that a country may be making perfectly satisfactory progress by effecting social changes or by opening up employment or educational opportunities in order to create the preconditions of genuine development, even if its national income remains stationary, or even if it declines for some time.

But if, as is likely, such attitutes become more prevalent in the coming years, this will demand corresponding mental adjustments within the industrial world and within the international agencies particularly concerned with problems of development. Such adjustments have become urgent not so much because thinking in the underdeveloped countries about their own future is changing fast, but rather because the misinterpretations on which our own assumptions about their aims were built are becoming untenable.

Even so, the belief that the immediate and central objection of development policies is the acceleration of economic growth will not quickly disappear. But as a measuring rod of achievement it is fast turning into a dangerous instrument. It may serve to belittle the efforts and so encourage criticism of the growing number of countries that will be more and more occupied with the redefinition of their economic and social objectives as a prelude to their real development. The criticism thus leveled against them may not only become a powerful factor of discouragement, but may also be a means at the disposal of interests determined to discredit such endeavors or even to prevent their success.

Likewise, there is need for change of an even more delicate nature in another field. It concerns the small but dedicated minorities in the industrialized countries who, in the name of human solidarity, have been tirelessly working to fight indifference to avoidable suffering. They have been, in a sense, missionaries of the assumptions about the central role of economic growth and about the accelerating benefits of external aid. Their devotion and personal commitment has helped to create at least a nucleus of opinion concerned with world poverty and development. It is a painful responsibility, when they are already battling against indifference, protectionism, and the mood of introversion, to divert their attention and enthusiasm from what has so magnificently commanded their energies and idealism. The coming change of focus may discourage some of them. But the enthusiasm of the others will have to be sustained so that it can advance towards a higher level of awareness of contemporary realities.

In place of the relatively simple view of injected capital and technical assistance leading to greater well-being, they will have to assimilate the more complex image of both indigenous societies and their international framework needing to be reordered and restructured. An already difficult task must become even more so if it is to remain constructive. The compassionate rationalism of Western humanism will have to make its compromise with the reality of diversity. It will have to be recognized that if it is morally inadmissible to be against aid, it is immoral to prolong it when it implies acquiescence in the price it exacts in its present forms. It will be no easy task for the activists of international justice to apply their zeal to the conveyance of such a complex message. Nor will the task be rendered easier by the probability that the coming mutations will often seem to take, or will be forced to take, forms opposed to the short-term interests of the Western industrial powers.

To remain apologists or even advocates of such changes might indeed demand nothing less than a new dimension of tolerance. It will involve basic questions about the real possibilities of aid and about the aims of development itself. Moreover, it will have to place the diversity of approaches above short-term national, cultural, or racial interests.

These will be no easy adjustments for people so far removed from the sociological roots of the grim realities calling for change. There will be no escape from the political and moral nature of the choices and priorities involved. In the meantime, indifference and isolationism will remain tempting alternatives. Yet the longer the task is postponed, the heavier will grow the shadow over the hope of a peaceful transition towards a more viable world order.

Part TWO

IX In Search of the Favorable Wind

THE RAPID WORLD-WIDE CURRENCY achieved by the abbreviation "third world" is symptomatic of the rich world's thinking about the underdeveloped countries. Its extraordinary success implies that it has satisfied a deeply felt psychological need.

In the beginning at least, it was probably a helpful device for focusing people's attention on a complex problem thay had to live with. An understandable predilection for brevity doubtless played its role. To dissolve the uneasy conscience of former individual colonial powers within a global notion embracing traditions, cultures, and climates, combined with the more quantifiable consequences of foreign rule, was also helpful. Much more important, however, was the desire to gloss over the immense variety of problems and situations in order to be able to generalize about them in a simple and comforting fashion. Moreover, within the prevailing world political context, it was tempting to imagine that the underdeveloped countries, just freed from colonial control, were faced with the choice of opting for the methods of the "second world" or simply for westernization.

The very concept of the threefold division is, of

course, debatable. Economic and sociocultural differences between the United States, Europe and Japan on the one hand, or between the Soviet Union, Cuba, and China on the other, are probably greater than the differences between some developed and underdeveloped countries. Yet the threefold division of the world aside, the lumping together of all the underdeveloped countries under a single common denominator could not fail to do a great deal of harm.

It helped to fix the image of the low-income countries as a homogeneous group and, as a consequence, to render plausible the belief that a common therapeutic was conceivable to remedy their ills. Though in practice a certain degree of differentiation has been unavoidable, prescriptions believed to be valid for all economically backward countries have remained the rule. Moreover, this tendency was reinforced as the problem of the low-income countries became one of the principal themes of the newly emerging international organizations. Their constitutional preoccupation with nondiscrimination and with fictitious equality was only accentuated by the oratorical prominence of the spokesmen of a few relatively advanced underdeveloped countries, each understandably anxious to improve its bargaining strength by pretending to speak in the name of the "third world" as a whole.

But the abbreviation has never fitted any recognizable reality.

The so-called third world includes countries which have been independent for well over a century and others which have had no more than a few years of experience in self-government. Some are vast territorial entities with a broad diversity of natural resources. Many more have smaller populations than a metropolitan suburb and are devoid of either human or material resources on which a viable economy might be built. Next to states with huge reserves of untilled but fertile land are others that have no alternative left but to try to increase yields from already cultivated surfaces. There are those with natural borders that correspond to ethnic, linguistic, or cultural realities, and much more numerous ones with grotesquely artificial frontiers drawn for the administrative convenience of colonial rulers and in complete disregard of the organic factors that make a nation.

Latin America's basic sociocultural pattern is European, received through the Ibero-Catholic filter. It has produced credible variants of Mediterranean societies wherever the Indian or Negro element did not constitute a majority. Behind South Asia's thin façade of modernity, on the other hand, there are the sociocultural realities of civilizations older than Europe's and still sufficiently alive to thwart the foreign impact. And between Islam in the north and European colonialism in the south, carved up into artificial entities corresponding to no logic, a mosaic of more or less viable African states attempts to build technicoadministrative structures on a barely recognizable sociocultural base.

Some newly independent countries possess a high degree of ethnic and cultural homogeneity, though far more numerous are the largely artificial ones whose unity may be purely formal. Consequently, a certain number among them have an adequately articulated national consciousness. More numerous, however, are those which have inherited ethnic and racial diversities produced by the requirements of mines and plantations, or simply by the limits of foreign conquest, but which now constitute obstacles to even a modest degree of administrative or national coherence.

A few underdeveloped countries are already overpopulated to such a degree that only miracles of production could transform their resources into adequate means of livelihood. Others are still so short of people that all their endeavors are frustrated by distance or by the enormity of tasks which only ultramodern technology could perform. A handful have industries capable of supplying more consumer goods or even capital equipment than purchasing power within their borders could buy. Many more still lack even elementary mechanical tools, as well as the men to handle them satisfactorily.

Rare are the former colonial countries which could bring about the changes necessary to establish some relation between reward and economic performance. Much more often, large minorities benefit from nonfunctional privileges unrelated to any economically or socially useful role. Education may be needed where it is nonexistent, or it may be overabundant but almost useless. In some countries, there may be a lack of mechanics to repair imported tractors. In others, large numbers of highly trained professionals may have to emigrate for want of opportunities at home. If in some cases historical circumstances have contributed to the emergence of administrative traditions, in many more a complete absense of public ethics short-circuits even an elementary degree of social discipline and political stability. And if some underdeveloped countries, because of conscious effort or geographical proximity, have managed to maintain at least some familiarity with the thinking and activities of the economically advanced world, a number of others are mentally unprepared to assimilate even what would be indispensable to satisfy their most urgent needs.

Assumption of development theories notwithstanding, in real life there exists an infinite variety of situations. No two countries are alike. No single country faces exactly the same situation tomorrow as it had to confront today. In each of them there exists a specific combination of obstacles to development. And the diversity between states is compounded by the variety of circumstances within each one, rendering general prescriptions even less realistic.

The base itself, the nature of the peasant and of village life, changes from area to area. The mentality of the Mexican cultivator in an isolated valley of the Sierra Madre is very different from that of the peasant planter in the rich flat delta land of the Irrawaddy near the port of Rangoon. In fact, the attitudes and interests of the Mexican peasant locked in the folds of the mountain are not comparable to those of his compatriot working in the hot lowlands along the Pacific Ocean. Similarly, the Southern Burmese rice-grower's worries and reactions have little in common with the preoccupations of his compatriot working in the interior, south of Mandalay. And the differences are there even when the distance separating them is much smaller.

Specific conditions and varying stages of development, then, require local discretion as to which approach to a given problem will be most effective. A unique mixture is demanded for each province, for each valley, for each village. To be effective, even a national plan has to be the sum total of a variety of local ones, each totally different in methods and emphasis, each relying on different incentives and attempting to harness enthusiasm for specific ends. Thus, over-all policy must arise from a synthesis of local analyses, conceived as a whole but executed with appropriate elasticity and improvisation.

Tempting though it may be as an intellectual exercise, categorization concerning underdevelopment rarely yields really practical results. For example, in absolute terms, a large part of Africa may be underpopulated, but so are Brazil, Thailand, Iran, and hosts of other countries with nothing else in common. East Pakistan may be grossly overpopulated, but so are Java, most of North Africa, and the Caribbean islands, each with its own set of problems. Latin America has large middle classes and numerous professionals and administrators, just like India, Ceylon, Jamaica, or Nigeria, without much else to provide a common basis for action. Brazil, Argentina, and Mexico, like India and Turkey, have important industrial installations, abundant natural resources, and sizable internal markets, yet tiny Hong Kong, without any other resource than the diligence and talent of its inhabitants, exports more industrial goods than 650 million Indians and Pakistanis combined.

It is unlikely that results would be more satisfactory if an analysis were attempted on the basis of selected historical or sociological indicators. As after shaking up a kaleidoscope, the same elements might regroup themselves into new, unsuspected patterns. But once again, no meaningful common denominator for action would emerge.

Different, more or less decisive criteria might be tried. Which are the countries, for example, where the essential link of craftsmanship between precolonial handicrafts and contemporary industry has been irrevocably destroyed? Per capita, India has taken in more foreign machine-made goods than China, and its precolonial crafts have withered. They have practically disappeared also in most of Black Africa; in those parts of Latin America where Indians or Negroes are in the majority; and within Indonesia, on Java, though not on Bali and the other larger islands of the archipelago. But what conclusions are justified when it comes to prospects for industrialization? Or one might try to discern countries where traditional values might be enlisted as components of contemporary incentives. Alternatively, an attempt might be made to group together states where the very persistence of such values tends to block the effectiveness of economic stimulants. But does Africa's tribal tradition fall into the first or the second category?

And to what extent are the Koranic concepts of social relations compatible with modern economic organization in Morocco, on Sumatra, in the Islamized areas of Sinkiang, or in Soviet Asia? Do such comparisons yield any guidelines as to where, how, and under what circumstances traditional values can be enlisted as propellents of productive enthusiasm?

Or again, who could determine what kind of stimuli would induce citizens of overpopulated countries to respond to birth-control propaganda in Catholic and industrializing Puerto Rico, in magic-ridden Moslem Java, in the villages of the Nile valley, or in fertility-respecting Hindu villages? What kind of internal or external challenge, or nutritional change, in comparably well endowed but backward states would galvanize their populations for more disciplined, better coordinated, and more sustained physical exertion? What statistical common denominators in terms of teachers, thinkers, classrooms, or economic opportunities would indicate which of the underdeveloped countries is likely to appreciate the urgency of serious efforts to conceive an educational system related to its means and requirements? How can it be determined which are the countries where personnel, leadership, material needs, and the challenge of foreign example exist, or where they might combine to produce a spirit of innovation among people hitherto content with traditional responses?

Clearly, none of such or similar attempts at classification are likely to yield helpful results. The manifest lack of any homogeneity makes all comparisons artificial. Nor, for that matter, is it certain that we are better equipped even to spot unmistakable symptoms heralding change.

Two decades of thinking about development problems have merely underlined the fact that projections are hazardous, that all generalization is inevitably distorting, and that an element of unpredictability will continue to overshadow even the most systematic and rational approach. What may be foreseen with some degree of probability is modest in scope, offers no concrete indicators, and might be summed up in two rather general propositions.

First, that the underdeveloped countries of tomorrow will be built on the foundation existing today. More or less revolutionary changes may cause greater or lesser discontinuity, but the structures which emerge will still bear more resemblance to the original base than to any utopian projections. Second, that the international system of power, trade, and finance will not suddenly dissolve, that its modifications will be limited by the need and capacity of its dominant members for adaptations only to the extent that it can wring the concessions it desires. Reality, in the foreseeable future, will evolve within the perimeters of these two inflexible determinants.

This is, of course, a disappointingly inadequate guide for action. Yet according to Seneca, there is no favorable wind for the one who does not know where he is going. In the midst of the present disarray, however, any attempt to discern such a direction ought to begin with a return to basic factors: to the satisfaction of essential needs, to material constraints, and to the aims of those with power over both.

X | *The Pillar of Fundamental Needs*

WHICH ARE the underdeveloped countries where the industrial civilization originally developed in the West, with its value system, its social attitudes, and its organizational techniques, has really penetrated in depth?

As we look for an answer among the more than one hundred low-income or formerly colonial countries on the world map, a somewhat surprising conclusion emerges: in the overwhelming majority, Western industrial civilization has affected only small minorities. In very few cases has it changed society as a whole. Where it has done so—in Chile, Argentina, Uruguay, and the south of Brazil—nearly the whole population was of European origin.

In all the remaining cases, whether in Africa, Asia, or Latin America, the Western industrial system was superimposed on totally different cultural backgrounds, on other social systems and values—that is, on non-Western civilizations. In all these situations a small minority was integrated into the alien system. It adopted the foreigners' way of living and thinking, but the majorities remained aloof. Indeed, in most cases their noncooperation and resistance gradually turned into passivity and, quite often, even into apathy. The alleged benefits of the new productive apparatus not only failed to trickle down to their villages but aroused instinctive opposition and a refusal to accept the values or to respond to the incentives of the imposed civilization. This, so it seems, is the essence of what we now refer to as the problem of underdevelopment.

Before asking what went wrong, it might be better to attempt to see why the same phenomenon did not occur in the non-Western parts of the North Temperate Zone, where successful industrial civilizations, affecting all society, have emerged.* These extraoccidental success stories in the transformation of preindustrial societies are, in chronological order, that of Japan, that of the Soviet Union, and now that of China.

To begin with, there is the highly controversial issue of climate. What seems more concrete, however, is the fact that none of these countries were colonized by the West and so their sociocultural heritage did not have to confront directly the physical coercion which came with the West's industrial civilization. In the second place, at the time of the territorial expansion of the West, all three of them were lively sociocultural entities, not free of internal crises—particularly in the case of China—but still with faith in their own values, if not in their own superiority. Their self-confidence was unimpaired, and they were aware of the existence of innovating and adaptive forces at work within their own borders. Finally, either before the West's full impact reached them, or

*They have also emerged, of course, in the South Temperate Zone. But in all those cases, whether in the south of Latin America, in the South African Union, or in Australia and New Zealand, whatever indigenous civilizations existed were either liquidated by brute force or relegated to a marginal existence, their scope circumscribed, as it were, outside society. In all those cases, then, white immigrants built their outposts based on imported values, technology, and organizational methods.

soon after its domestication began, all three of them deliberately cut themselves off from external influences and saw to it that their own work of selection, adaptation, and harmonization was achieved free of external economic and physical pressures. Moreover, all three achieved their transformation without external aid. There was almost no direct foreign investment, and even foreign credits played only an insignificant role. And Japan, at least, developed with practically no natural resources of its own.

In all three cases the result was not the wholesale transposition of the Western system, nor was it just selective assimilation. It rather took the form of conscious harmonization with an original sociocultural base preserved almost intact, and within traditional structures which may have changed but have never been deformed by external forces. Whatever foreign influences did penetrate, in terms of crucial decision-making the center of gravity of these nations remained within their own borders. Though China faced that danger at a given moment, none of them were "colonizable" at the time the overwhelming material force of the West reached them. And in none of the three cases did a minority take over an alien pattern which it was, subsequently, unable to communicate to the majority. In a nutshell, though all three were exposed to external influences, neither Japan nor Russia nor China found itself in a situation where it had to endure the imposition of an alien civilization upon its own.

As a matter of fact, Japan preserved much of its preindustrial social structure and its cultural traditions, and indeed utilized them to the full in order to provide the social discipline needed for the country's modernization. This outstanding example of symbiosis was certainly one of the decisive components in Japan's subsequent remarkable success. The Soviet experiment in creating its own variant of Western industrial society has been less smooth. After half a century it has not yet made its peace with the country's sociocultural past, and the problem of suitable incentives is still far from being settled. In China's case, a greater willingness to build on the country's sociological heritage promises more satisfactory results. Yet a series of upheavals, from the Hundred Flowers experiment, through the Great Leap Forward, to the Cultural Revolution, have punctuated the difficult process of the sinization of the Communist variant of the Western impact. But in neither case has any need arisen for culturally expatriate minorities to act as a transmission belt, since the majorities have not been left out of the process of transformation. No alien civilization has been imposed. No majorities have been forced onto a sullen defensive in the face of an alien new order unconnected with their own past, one whose motivations they could neither comprehend nor accept. And so none of these experiments bred passivity or apathy.

What, then, went wrong outside the North Temperate Zone where the industrial civilization of the West was imposed on non-Western peoples? Why does one find, throughout those huge regions, rural stagnation and an almost total absence of generalized development?

One has to turn to history for possible answers. The West's eruption over the rest of the world had multiple motivations, ranging from economic and the military to the religious and the cultural. But in view of the West's unchallengeable military and industrial might, economic interests backed by superior arms turned out to be most decisive in their immediate effects on the daily existence of people in the colonized areas. To speak merely of exploitation would oversimplify the issue. The great religious persecutions the West has known, for example, far from implying a lack of interest in their victims, arose rather from a blind commitment to their salvation. Though fully conscious of their own interests, Western traders and conquerors, no less than missionaries, were fully convinced also of their emancipatory role. They could the more easily believe in the superiority of what they were forcing on others in that they rarely troubled to inform themselves about what they were trying to replace. And if the presumed economic advantages manifestly failed to spread, they never entertained any doubts as to its being only a question of time.

It would have required a truly exceptional degree of detachment and objectivity to pause and to appreciate the dehumanizing moral, spiritual, and political consequences of what was happening. Instead, like protective vaccines, there emerged theories of racial superiority, of the intrinsic virtues of the market mechanism, as well as ancillary convictions concerning the superiority of Western thinking, morals, and institutions. Nevertheless, the resulting devaluation of all noneconomic realities became the starting point of a lasting misunderstanding which has evolved into a decisive barrier to any development meaningful in human terms.

The transformation of whole societies, the destruction of time-honored traditions or their forcing into the service of purely material aims of Western inspiration, became a legitimate end and have gradually even become identified with economic progress. Since all noneconomic considerations were treated with impatient contempt, it was easy to overlook the price that was imposed —cultural suicide.

Success, of course, remained only partial. For it is questionable whether the basic Western concepts of economics are applicable at all without tying the mind to the Western pattern of living, the one from which they are abstracted. When such interdependence was lacking, only minorities could respond, and they were usually incapable of attempting the required adaptation in depth, or else unwilling to do so.

Thus, the majorities were bypassed and forced to retread into their psychological defenses. The old social solidarity began to break up without anything viable to replace it. The new structural determinisms clashed increasingly with moral convictions and spiritual beliefs. Familiar institutions decayed for want of acceptable inspiration to adapt them to contemporary realities.

Savings, capital formation, and investment remain, of course, the essence of the problem. But their primary source is labor, that is, the work of the indigenous population. Its interest, collaboration, and enthusiasm, however, can be obtained only in exchange for the hope that these will serve desired ends. Effective mobilization of savings and the successful application of investments, then, involve the mobilization of savings and utilization of labor in forms which are not merely useful in terms of economic analysis but appear desirable and acceptable to the people involved because capable of fulfilling their own needs. To effect the mobilization of indigenous effort on the required scale and with the inevitably modest material rewards possible, there must be recourse to methods the people are familiar with. These methods will need improvement, and may gradually undergo modification through the addition of foreign experience. Perhaps constraints will even have to be increased if innovations are to be applied with the desired speed. But the process cannot be dissociated from the familiar. And under no circumstances ought it to confirm the humiliating fear that everything that does not imitate what is foreign is to be regarded as inferior, that is, that the people's traditional approach is worthless and deserves only contempt.

Although this is what would seem desirable, it is very far from what is really happening. A few exceptions apart, the attitudes of the industrial powers, as much as those of the private investigators and even of the international organizations, lack such patience and tolerance. Economic development is considered an end in itself, with moral, cultural, and psychological considerations as auxiliary luxuries, at best. The westernized ruling groups have no difficulty in joining the foreigners in belittling traditional attitudes and in considering efficiency in only economic terms rather than in those of the satisfaction it procures. The inefficiency is no doubt there. The question is merely whether it is contempt and impatient dismissal which, in the long run, will accomplish the desired change, or rather a different time-perspective making allowances for gradual improvement and for adaptation built on familiar foundations.

Notwithstanding its apparent naiveté, this is a basic question any humanist observer of the aid and development experiment is obliged to ask. After all, what do we see all around us?

In one underdeveloped country after the other, beyond the enclaves of modernity in big cities or around industrial installations, in the attitudes of that three-quarters of the population that lives in rural areas, there is a sense of drifting and resignation. Of course, there are some exceptions, but often the impression is inescapable that the masses remain maladjusted to the modern world and have not even made up their minds whether they really want it. In some cases this may seem to be contradicted by migration towards the nonexistent opportunities of the big cities. But the enormous majority who remain sink into a mood of helplessness, often ending in an almost unconquerable apathy. What used to be mere quantifiable lack of necessities is turning into the much more tormenting impossibility of satisfying intangible needs such as dignity or not feeling futile. Poverty, in short, is degenerating into misery.

The experience of many technical assistants seems to confirm this impression. Examples are set, but they fail to spread. Taboos are fought, but obstinately they persist. A lack of flair for mechanics often looks ominously like a disbelief in mechanics. There is a lack of sense of maintenance. When a machine breaks down it is often discarded like a dead body—more out of apathy, it would seem, than out of lack of skill to repair it. Promising pilot projects fail to take root, make little impact on indifferent neighbors, and slide downhill as soon as the expertise of their initiators has to be replaced by local interest, energy, or funds. The impression is widespread that the foreigner is fighting against the tide; that the pilot projects do not fit into a wider program of education, of transformation, or of the changing of mentalities; that all that is done is on too small a scale to produce any lasting impact; and that the people thus aided are not firmly committed to making use of the expertise the Westerners are trying to instill in them. Beyond occasional limited success, goodwill, and even transitory cooperation, there is the almost palpable presence of instinctive and deep suspicion. For the real, the almost immutable obstacle is not economic but psychological. Somewhere in the course of the encounter with industrial civilization, as has happened in some battles against numerically vastly inferior but frighteningly armed colonial conquerors, there occurred a tragic breakdown in self-confidence. With the passage of time, it has turned into self-tormenting humiliation, into loss of self-respect and sullen introversion. Ultimately, and in economic terms, it has led to the present paralysis and to the almost universal inability to respond to the signals of the alien system.

Demonstrably, there has been no development wherever the attitudes assimilated by westernized minorities failed to be communicated in suitable form to the majorities. This was not for lack of desire for change and progress, but rather because the kind of change offered and the form in which it was presented did not correspond to felt needs. The situation might indeed be succinctly summed up by the answers attributed to two returning technical assistants when questioned about their achievements. The first reported no success. "But," he added, "at least I managed to make them unhappy with their present ways and with their refusal to change." The second, probably with more experience in the proper approach, advised, "Find out what the people are trying to do and help them do it better."

The struggle against the past is daunting in any economically backward country. Moreover, it can scarcely be successful unless it concentrates on accelerating and channeling change already in motion. The question is whether, behind the façade of apparent immobility and aimless drifting, there are not already evolving new aspirations and new forces shaped by them. With population pressure, the transistor radio, and motion pictures, it would be surprising indeed if these were completely absent. But our economic seismographs, equipped to record tremors measurable only in Western economic terms, may fail to note them. Perhaps investigation and research to facilitate their detection might yield unexpected results and might even help to avoid surprises. Who would have expected the Chinese, only half a century after the disappearance of their barefoot, umbrella-carrying army, to produce nuclear bombs and long-range missiles? Or for that matter, who among their contemporaries ever appreciated the series of social, cultural, psychological, and institutional changes throughout the century preceding the Meiji Restoration as preliminaries to Japan's astonishing development? And in 1949, only twenty years before Japan's gross national product became the third largest in the world, did not a specialist on the staff of the American occupation authorities express the view that, if assured of financial assistance for an indefinite period, Japan might reach its 1930–1934 level of living, but that if it had to be self-supporting it would gradually sink to the bare-subsistence level?[1]

It is only through a rigorously disinterested assessment, free of deforming comparisons, that the aims of a society's development may be defined. Inevitably they will include material progress, but only in the light of the cultural and structural heritages of each society in question. And so it happens that both are different wherever still-vigorous civilizations prevailed at the time of the West's conquering intrusion.

But if methods have been built on false premises and it is not desirable to accelerate the movement in the mistaken direction, what would be a new appropriate definition of development?

As yet no really comprehensive and convincing set of criteria has been put together to explain the total process. To state that it must bring about qualitative improvement in economic progress together with the full development of human and natural resources, and with greater equality, freedom, and rationality, is far too general. Development cannot mean the copying of set models, as there is no archetype and each country has to discover its own way, an effort that may very well be hindered by attempts to conform to any alien example. Perhaps a redefinition of the notion of efficiency itself is required, not as a superior method of higher production but rather as a means of increasing human satisfaction. But how is the process to begin? How is the new consciousness to be provoked which will bring sudden realization that sociocultural energies have been frittered away, that their effectiveness has been reduced because they were not cumulative, or that their potentialities have not been geared to any defined purpose? In other words, how do those who were formerly alloted a role acquire the self-assurance to allot a role to themselves? How does the march from passivity to self-reliance and from drifting to coordination of purposeful effort get under way? Or can the challenge of new ideas and new social forces alone set off the change in norms and meanings?

Whatever the answers, development can be properly defined only in terms of total human needs as perceived by the very societies which desire or undergo mutation. Whether it is dehumanization giving way to rehumanization, apathy turning into self-reliance, or helplessness yielding to self-confidence, the essence of development will be hope restored.

But this is too imprecise to guide action. To arrive at such a definition of universally acceptable development aims, one has inevitably to turn back to basic needs, to absolute necessities not only valued but considered indispensable by all.

At first sight, it does not seem difficult to draw up such a list. Adequate nutrition, shelter providing minimum protection and comfort, and employment enabling people to be productive and to feel useful would qualify by universal consent. Health and education might be added to a list still uncontroversial. To state that the provision of these should be the starting point of any realistic development plan need not seem overidealistic. Nevertheless, any serious attempt to gear an underdeveloped country's economic priorities to such ends would, in most cases, involve revolutionary changes almost impossible to bring about by peaceful means.

The provision of adequate food for all, for example, would require profound transformation in systems of landholding, in the content of education, in industrial priorities—to provide the implements, the irrigation facilities, the fertilizers and pesticides needed—as well as in credit and market policies, either in order to provide necessary incentives or to spread purchasing power. To offer proper shelter to all would involve planned building programs with suitable financial support. It would have to mobilize the savings of prospective beneficiaries and bring into being the required supply industries which, in their turn, could spread purchasing power over the areas affected by the new activities. Finally, to provide useful employment to the maximum number of people of working age would presuppose the reviewing of all industrial plans with emphasis on labor-intensive methods, on the decentralization of production so as to provide cheap implements and consumer goods where they are needed, on a corresponding adaptation of import policies and consumer habits, as well as agricultural changes to permit more intensive cultivation with double or even triple cropping wherever feasible; or in other words, the retention on the land in a useful role of all those who would otherwise flock to swell the army of unemployed in the cities.

Even such a summary enumeration helps to identify the central problem: the fact that any reorientation of development objectives intended to make them correspond to basic human needs inevitably involves a fundamental rethinking of prevailing economic concepts and policies. Up to now we have been considering only the first elements in any possible regrouping of more humane development aims. Food, shelter, and employment in themselves, however, are not sufficient to provide such a new content.

A growing awareness that the mere increase of the gross national product is inadequate to measure development has already produced a variety of imaginative attempts to find more comprehensive indicators. One of them, for example, has tried to find a composite standard-of-living indicator more relevant to over-all development than the usual recourse to the GNP alone. Its weighted components embrace physical needs (like nutrition, housing, and health) and cultural ones (like education, leisure, and security), as well as so-called superior needs, quantified as "surplus." While it represents incontestable progress in comparison with the usual per capita income measurements, this can be only a first step. Though it contains value judgments—that is, an interesting attempt to quantify what is more or less desired by a given population at a given moment—it still relies on only a limited number of components which may be more or less significant in any individual context.[2]

One of the difficulties in any attempt, of course, is determining whether the indispensable value judgments yield to inherited social and cultural patterns, or are rather influenced by what the person who makes the judgment considers the desirable direction their modification ought to take. Another difficulty resides simply in the paucity of quantified information about all the other factors which would be indispensable for constructing sufficiently broad composite indicators.

Indeed, even in dealing with basic needs only, consideration ought to be given to a variety of other aspirations. These might range from additional, fundamental requirements—greater economic equality, respect for the dignity of the individual, or the social utility of various categories of employment—to less tangible components, embracing factors such as social opportunities or preconditions of national and racial self-respect. For the time being, many of these might best be formulated simply as questions.

What would data show about the ownership of land, natural resources, and other national assets according to social origin, nationality, or ethnic categories? What are the differences between rural and urban incomes? What is the nature and extent of nonfunctional revenues? How much is spent on luxury housing and how much on ordinary dwellings? What is the foreign-exchange content of the goods consumed by various social categories? What does a detailed area-by-area breakdown of child-mortality rates and causes indicate? What is the social, racial, or educational composition of legislative bodies, of the senior ranks of public administration, or of the other decision-making bodies? What is the numerical importance, professional role, and income of middlemen? How do the incomes of teachers, rural medical personnel, or provincial administrators compare with urban salaries? What is the volume and what are the terms of credit facilities in rural areas, and what proportion is provided by individual money-lenders? What is the content of available education in relation to the requirements of major social groups?

Or again, what is the savings performance of various social groups according to area and profession? How important are the military facilities provided to foreign powers? What are the quantified estimates of the country's growing or diminishing vulnerability to foreign economic or political pressures?

At the present time, few such or similar questions could be answered with any precision, for lack of reliable figures. Yet their absence should not be taken as proof that it would be much more difficult to calculate serious indicators of social deprivation, exploitation, concealed unemployment, luxury consumption, inequality, or nonfunctional incomes than the indices that usually figure in statistical tabulations relating to activities less essential for the fulfillment of the human potential. Their unavailability reflects simply the priorities of statistical offices.

Answers to questions of this type would show more reliably whether development had or had not occurred than would mere averages relating to the expansion of the national product. If progress has been made towards greater equality in income distribution, if people are better nourished, if fewer children have died of preventable disease, if the number of unemployed has diminished, then there has been development. If none of these things have happened, even if in the meantime there has been growth in the national product, it would be unwarranted to speak of development. Moreover, indicators of this kind might also greatly assist the public in aid-giving countries in judging whether assistance given in its name had helped to further development or had rather been devoted to commercial, political, or strategic aims unconnected with the satisfaction of real needs.

The danger is obvious that, in the name of imported ideas, any such approach to development will be branded as unrealistically moralizing or even utopian. Simple pragmatism, however, will soon reveal the shortsightedness and lack of imagination of such patronizing strictures.

Considering both the dangers inherent in the current pathological acceleration of urbanization in the low-income countries, and a careful application of the immense potentialities of the green revolution, it is perfectly realistic to conceive of a development policy freed from the usual city-centered options. Indeed, the next ten or fifteen years will be decisive. They will determine whether or not the underdeveloped countries can escape the fatal gravitational pull of fast-growing population and agrarian stagnation. They will show whether or not the new agricultural techniques can be applied on a large enough scale to provide the economically backward countries with the agricultural detonator which was at the origin of both the West's and Japan's progress towards modern industrial society.

To help it happen, economists and planners in the preindustrial societies will have to part with their only too frequent conviction that anything worth producing must fit into the consumption patterns of foreign markets or of local minorities who have acquired foreign tastes, and begin to order their priorities in the light of what is most urgently needed to satisfy local requirements. This, of course, need not clash with the ambitions of industrialization. But instead of building factories in order to supply the needs of a limited middle-class market surrounded by a stagnant countryside, a beginning should rather be made by reviving the agricultural hinterland and industrializing on the much healthier basis of its rising prosperity and ability to provide a far broader market for the products of the new factories.

After a thorough survey of rural realities, the desirable location of potential growth-points in the countryside could be defined. On that basis, a network of market centers might be created, each benefitting from government-assisted services and investments designed to help the diffusion of new agricultural techniques. These would become decentralized seats of support institutions stimulated by government aid, ranging from cooperatives and cheap credit organizations to agricultural and vocational schools or to storage facilities, all of which, in their turn, would attract trade and light industries. By providing proper marketing facilities and processing plants, the new centers would also help to free the farmers from dependence upon parasitic intermediaries and moneylenders. The agricultural growth-points thus conceived would develop into communication centers and lively markets for consumer goods produced locally or regionally by labor-intensive methods, as well as for agricultural implements and machines, fertilizers, and pesticides manufactured in factories located on the basis of regional needs. Moreover, the new centers, with their economic opportunities rooted in the revitalized farming of the surrounding countryside, could develop hand in hand with a government-sponsored, nation-wide housing program. Relying on state-sponsored mortgages, this could well become (and experience shows that it can become) an effective way of mobilizing people's savings and, through its multiplier effect, of creating a whole chain of new employment opportunities.

Such a development strategy, built on the twin pillars of agricultural modernization and the creation of new urban networks, might provide the motive power for fundamental change capable of turning planners' abstractions into satisfaction of fundamental needs; it might begin to modify static mentalities and to replace drifting with a sense of purpose.[3]

The rethinking of development policies with the satisfaction of essential needs as their central preoccupation is both necessary and urgent. This is so not merely because it is morally imperative. It has also become unpostponable in strictly economic terms. The limited consumer needs of the urban middle classes severely circumscribe the number of industrial jobs which can be created by simply supplying substitutes for imported consumer goods. From Mexico to India expensive plants are under-utilized for lack of purchasing power on the part of potential consumers. On the other hand, from Denmark to Japan it has been amply demonstrated that modern farmers may have middle-class incomes. But beyond purely economic considerations, the spread of violence all over the Southern Hemisphere warns us that if the problem is not confronted, whatever prosperity has been created for the benefit of minorities is likely to be lost in the explosion of the discontent and the accumulated passions which statistics of economic growth have failed to reveal.

Attempts along these and similar lines to give development policies a new orientation would imply the triumph of simple logic over political considerations. It would mean the end of feudal types of land tenure and of subsistence patterns of food production, as well as of the dominance of urban interests in planning priorities. Such shifts in emphasis, however, would be to the detriment of the short-term interests of most existing ruling classes. Consequently, they would do their best to oppose them or to prevent their success. And in the prevailing world political context they would probably be able to rely on the economic and political pressures of foreign protectors. The economic tasks, already monumental, would thus become even more daunting through political complications. Some exceptional situations apart, it can hardly be expected that ruling groups who are in power, or who are kept in power by foreign help in order to maintain rather than change existing structures and institutions, could be won over to a new approach to development that runs counter to their immediate interests. Yet it is conceivable that at least in some cases, carried by the weight of local and international opinion, foreign attitudes might change and enlightened and imaginative people might be given their chance to break with the discredited old ways.

It would be misleading to think in terms of global prescriptions. Occasions for change and progress arise without logic and often as a sequel to unexpected developments. In any case, the basic need before us is not the transformation of our planet on the model of one or the other of the economic powers of the North Temperate Zone. For the foreseeable future, at any rate, there are more urgent local tasks in healing inherited inequities, with an appropriate mixture of methods in each case. The earlier this begins, the sooner a preoccupation with economic growth alone will again be feasible. But long before reaching that point, most underdeveloped countries will find themselves facing fateful choices.

They will have to assess, each in the light of its particular circumstances, the limits set to the realization of their legitimate aspirations by the constraints of the international mechanism of power, trade, and finance. Some, driven by despair and by uncontrollable passions, may disregard the retaliatory might of the system and drift into chronic revolt against its rules. But a few, invoking the fundamental freedom bestowed by political independence, and confident of their resources of inner strength and of their capacity for discipline and sacrifice, might feel impelled to go even further: to insulate themselves from the system and, perhaps, even to leave it.

XI The Temptation of Voluntary Quarantine

INTEGRATED INTO the world market as they are, and looking outward from South to North in search of indicators of their economic future, the underdeveloped countries may discern little that is really encouraging in the panorama of the coming years.

The volume of their exports will continue to grow. But they are not likely to be able to stop the shrinking of their share of total world trade. More and more often, food surpluses, wherever they continue to be available, will be needed to feed implacably expanding local populations. The low-income countries will not become better armed to protect themselves against the twin damages inflicted by the price fluctuations of their exports and by the deterioration of the terms of trade for most of them. Some of their most lucrative exports may be exposed to sharper competition from synthetics and substitutes. As for the powerful lobbies in the rich countries which have obtained the subsidization of agricultural products that the underdeveloped countries could supply at lower prices, they will not weaken their pressures. Notwithstanding symbolic gestures towards lowering tariff barriers against some manufactured exports of a few low-income countries, the drift towards preferential regional trading arrangements is likely to continue. Protectionist sentiments may spread, and the goods to be protected seem to be precisely those in which the poor might be able to compete with the rich. Moreover, the decline of aid on concessional terms will become even more rapid.

The shrinking of aid will lead to greater reliance on foreign private investments. These, in their turn, will powerfully stimulate the role of market forces within the recipient countries themselves. The immediate consequence will be sharper international competition and still greater scope for the operations of the multinational corporations. This again, in the words of Harry G. Johnson, "is likely to exacerbate problems that have already appeared in the relations between the nation-state as a powerful political entity with a bordered geographical domain, and the multinational corporations as a powerful economic entity with an unbordered world market domain. Those problems appear in one form or another as a conflict between the sovereignty of the national state and the economic liberty of the large firm. . . .[It] involves a clash between the nation-state's politically-derived ideas of what development consists in and how corporations should behave."[1]

The combined result will be the accentuation of the process whereby the growing volume of foreign investments leads to inescapable balance-of-payments difficulties. Though the new investments create additional wealth and new jobs, they also drain away more and more capital. To prevent the shrinkage of the capital base of the economy, then, a steady inflow of new foreign investments will be needed. And if they are not forthcoming on the required scale, the result will be the perpetuation of economic and political dependence.

This is what has been happening over most of the

underdeveloped world during the past decade or so. For some time it could count on a fairly large volume of foreign investments, and not infrequently, official aid came to the rescue to help service them. Economic growth, as a result, was reasonably fast in several cases. Yet gradually, debts and the servicing of investments and loans began to eat away foreign-exchange reserves. When, as a last resort, one country after another either suspended its payments or was obliged to ask for a rescheduling of them, foreign capital shied away and came back again only in response to exceptional inducements. If, on the other hand, a heroic attempt was made to continue with servicing and repayments, the capital base shrank and a deflationary crisis set in. The vicious circle could not have been more perfect.

Now, when once again private capital is being encouraged to move in in larger volume to make up for declining official aid, the hopeless race to step up exports —both to sustain acceptable rates of growth and to fulfill obligations of servicing payable in foreign exchange— will be on again. But the export sector in the underdeveloped world employs barely more than 5 to 7 percent of the labor force. And to be competitive, modern techniques must be introduced which are of little help in slowing down the growth of unemployment. Moreover, the outward-looking development implied by the prevailing North–South–North orientation of foreign trade and capital flows powerfully diverts attention from relations with neighbors. It tends to freeze the low-income countries in their bilateral, vertical integration, to the detriment of highly desirable horizontal cooperation with potential regional partners.

This is, as it were, the inner circle of reality. But beyond it, as they look out from their economic cage, the underdeveloped countries must be conscious of additional, outer circles, each one further insulating them from the elusive dream of real development, of firmer control over their own destinies, and of a dependence less humiliating in its finality.

There is, for example, what is usually referred to as the self-regulating role of market forces.

"This decline of official development aid,"—to quote Harry G. Johnson again—"will mean an increased dependence on the private market mechanisms of economic development, as contrasted with governmental planning and control of the development process."[2] Thus, "a profit-motivated development process will be different in character from [the one] planned by politicians and bureaucrats. In particular, such a development process is likely to conflict sharply with the mounting concern about social justice in the distribution of income in the course of development. . . . In concrete terms, reliance on direct foreign investment . . . is likely to mean highly uneven development."[3]

That is clear enough. Yet in "this relationship of overwhelming, one-sided power, the uncorrected market works as inequitably as it does, say, between landlord and *harijan* [untouchable] in an Indian village"—according to Lester B. Pearson's own comments on his report. "All the natural forces of a competitive and unequal economy favour the rich. Debt becomes not an ordinary commercial transaction but a desperate dependence of the pauper upon the rich man who can wait and cheat and sell him out. If we take away the fact of total inequality from our world's economic transactions we distort the harsh economic reality which underlies all our relationships whether of aid or trade or liquidity or debt."[4]

The North Atlantic world learned that much from the Great Depression. Indeed, it took the appropriate corrective measures to regulate the so-called self-regulating forces of the market—in order to protect its own citizens. Yet long after it has ceased to believe in and act on that assumption, it still pretends to believe in the virtues of the market mechanism in its dealings with the former colonial world. What this amounts to is disregarding all evidence that mere contact between rich and poor countries accentuates and perpetuates inequality, and that the economic forces generated by such an unequal relationship tend to keep the weaker partner in its subordinate role.

Decolonization and two decades of the aid experiment have not altered the fact that the small North Atlantic minority of mankind enjoys over two-thirds of the world's total income. Nor have they helped to disprove the spreading conviction that underdevelopment is still produced by the very process which simultaneously generates economic development. Yet, notwithstanding the alarm signals of growing unrest born of desperation, the disproportion in both incomes and opportunities is still increasing. But now, with all the majestic backing of theory, the low-income countries are made to understand that the price to be paid for avoiding stagnation is still less social justice.

Moving on to the next circle means, for the underdeveloped countries, the encounter with another painful reminder: comparative standards of living.

After the withdrawal of the viceroy, the governor-generals, the parachutists, and the imperial flag, it was fashionable in the course of after-dinner speeches to refer to our moral obligation "to close the gap" between the prosperity of the industrial world and the poverty of the decolonized one. Realism imposed by events soon forced a modification of rhetoric, and the promise became merely "to narrow the gap." Today, sobered by experience, we know that in the foreseeable future even this is impossible. No intellectually honest speaker could promise more than to try to slow down the speed with which the gap continues to grow.

The reasons are discouragingly simple.

A 2 percent yearly per capita growth in income doubles living standards per person in about 36 years; a 4 percent one, in less than 20 years. So the gap might begin to narrow after several decades, provided the income of the country with which the comparison is being made remains unchanged. This, until further notice, is unlikely to be the case. A more concrete example would be to compare, say, India and the United States. Even if India were to grow at a per capita yearly rate of 4 percent while the United States grew by only 2 percent—that is, India twice as fast as the United States—even then the per capita income disparity would continue to increase. The 4 percent growth would increase the average Indian's income from $100 to $104; the 2 percent growth, that of the average American from $4,000 to $4,080. Notwithstanding slower growth, the yearly increase in the American citizen's income would be still twenty times higher than in the Indian's. Indeed, in this case, the gap would continue to widen for some two generations before it began to narrow very slowly.

But even this is somewhat overoptimistic. It is not likely that the rich countries' growth rate will remain lastingly lower than that achieved by the poorer ones. Growth of population in the low-income countries may well accelerate as a result of sanitary improvements before it settles at a lower level. And even at the present rate, the population of most poor countries will double within a quarter-century; in some cases—for example, Mexico, Brazil, Indonesia, or the Caribbean islands—in less than twenty years.

The problem of this inevitably widening gap, despite its psychological significance, is given little attention in official aid and development policies, presumably because it is intractable to practical solutions. As a matter of fact, even if it were merely a simple mechanical problem of distributing the wealth of rich nations to the world's poor areas, there would be no solution. It has been calculated that it would take $1,400 billion a year to raise average income everywhere to $1,000 a year—that is, more than the total annual income of all the developed countries combined.[5]

Yet beyond leveling and philanthropy, there is another tormenting circle, the vicious one symbolizing the world-wide division of labor.

Even in the totally improbable case that all the economic demands of the underdeveloped countries' intellectuals were suddenly accepted, if grants swelled to unprecedented levels, if all tariff barriers were dismantled, if all the discriminatory policies, from nontariff barriers to insurance and shipping rates, disappeared, and if all the labor-intensive industries of the rich countries were transferred to the low-income nations, even then the fundamental cleavage would not disappear. It would simply be replaced by a new form of international specialization, with the technologically stagnant industries left to be taken over by the formerly agricultural countries. The division would merely have moved onto a higher technological level. But the gap in prosperity would only have been accentuated, and in favor of those who were already ahead in their science and organization.

The combined psychological effect of all this on the poor countries is bound to be devastating. But the reaction, of course, is not uniform.

The indifference of market forces to social justice need not worry the minority who share the profits. Those who travel and experience the opulence of the industrial world can comfort themselves with their relative affluence at home. Not even the masses feel particularly aggrieved by the wealth of faraway strangers, for their attention is forcefully diverted by the indignities they endure in the course of their daily activities. The villager and the subsistence farmer are less interested in living like a Rockefeller than in ridding themselves of the exactions of the tax-collector, the middleman, the soldier, or the moneylender. Yet even the rich resent sharing their profits with foreigners, being dependent on foreign interests, or being compelled to obey foreign pressures. As for the students, the intellectuals, and the educated who are frustrated in their hopes, they comprehend the interdependence of factors behind the problems they live with, and know to what extent the kind of regime they live under mirrors the will of the outside world. And though the large majority, scattered in countless villages, senses the whole sickness only through its own daily grievances, it is still aware that those who so visibly profit from others' misfortune could hardly feel so arrogantly safe in their privileges if they could not count on powerful foreign support.

What all are united in is their sense of humiliation. With more or less clarity but with passion proportionate to deprivation, they all vaguely identify the ultimate source of their grievance in the all-pervading, impersonal power which directly or indirectly circumscribes their place from village to planet: the force of the irresistible rich world. What brings them together in their disparate discontent is the lack of respect from others and their feeling that they are merely tools for the satisfaction of others' purposes. And the humiliation underlying it all is becoming the common denominator of a world-wide, racially motivated, insurrectionary protest.

This is something new. It is spreading, and it is fueled by greater awareness and by deepening passion. For if people can get used even to physical pain, they can never reconcile themselves to humiliation. The popular base of the revolt exists, and an overabundance of facts helps to build upon it an imposing rationale of unpredictable force.

It is empirical in its reasoning. And like all analyses which are also meant to be programs for action, it is untainted by self-criticism, is harsh in its self-justification, and is overoptimistic in its generalizations.

The great economic powers, it maintains, relying on their enormous technological, financial, and military coercive power, impose their goals on the poor countries with utter disregard for their personality or their preferences and drag them into forced and deforming conformity. To serve their ends, they have brought into being and continue to sustain local groups who support and profit from the foreigners' designs. Having replaced their soldiers and gunboats by impersonal market forces, the rich countries have fitted the poor ones even more tightly into their commercial strait-jacket. But market forces channel resources only into profitable activities and neglect the essential and useful ones which might prepare the ground for satisfactory progress. The longer the sovereignty of the market lasts, then, the more the ruling minorities will support the outsiders in order that their own preferences and options may prevail. In the meantime, the economic surpluses generated remain under their control, and the way they make use of them frustrates development and the satisfaction of essential needs.

The convergence of forces strengthens the same basic thrust. The central pillar on which the edifice is built is the outward-looking nature of the economic organization imposed. Its purposes are focused on metropolitan markets rather than on home needs. Yet by the very nature of the system, export possibilities can never catch up with import requirements. The gap has continually to be filled in by foreign capital: by investments, loans, or aid. The inevitable result is still tighter incorporation into the dominant economic structures. But the organization and technology that accompany foreign capital extinguish jobs faster than new ones can be created. Thus the vulnerability to economic pressures and to the vagaries of primary-product markets is further accentuated and the captive economies, rather than really being aided, transfer growing resources and thereby aid more and more the industrial world.

As for the collaborating privileged groups, they are neither desirous nor capable of freeing themselves from the barely concealed blackmail attached to aid. On the other hand, dependence on foreign methods, on foreign equipment, or on technical assistance becomes a habit-forming drug and continually deepens the cleavage between parasitic, westernized cities and the neglected and frustrated rural areas. The lack of self-confidence born of such dependence cannot be remedied. The permanent prodding to adopt Western-style attitudes, techniques, and incentives kills any attempts to boost self-reliance. And the seeking out of creative potentialities in inherited patterns of thought, attitudes, and institutions is constantly short-circuited by the decisive might of foreign economic forces.

Somewhere at this point the indictment gives way to prescription. To break out of the vicious circle, in order to recover lost identity and self-respect, the very orientation of economic development has to be changed. Instead of looking outward, it must become inward-oriented and more preoccupied with the solution of local problems than with the confrontation of those created by contact with the industrial world. The degrading aid relationship must be liquidated. Integration into the world market, dependence on foreign capital, the whole South-North fixation of economic thinking, must come to an end. Instead, each country must find its own path to development, and there must be experimentation with indigenous methods and reliance on local means. Structural changes must prepare the ground for popular participation in constructive tasks, for greater savings efforts, and for more rational investment priorities. To replace the metropolitan nexus, there must be an endeavor to create regional heavy-industry bases producing greater solidarity and interdependence between neighbors. Moreover, the new sense of participation and enthusiasm should help to consolidate national consciousness, to reconstitute damaged national self-respect, to stimulate self-reliance—in short, to obliterate humiliation. And to do it all, if necessary, there must be no hesitation in accepting the price of isolation or even the need for sealing oneself off from the almost inevitably interfering and hostile rich world.

It would be unwise to dismiss reasoning of this kind as irrelevant or unrealistic. Examples are not lacking to show that some underdeveloped countries have known their periods of most rapid development precisely when historical circumstances had severed their ties with the advanced industrial powers. In the case of Latin America, for example, the only underdeveloped region then free of direct foreign control, three such interludes brought acceleration in structural changes and often rapid industrialization as well. These occasions were the two world wars and the years of the Great Depression. The rapid expansionary phases of industrial development of Argentina, Brazil, Mexico, and even of Chile occurred during these periods, when the loosening of established investment and trade ties seems indeed to have favored autonomous industrialization and faster economic growth. It was during periods of temporary isolation, when deprived of capital, of imports, and of foreign experts, that the domestic potential for entrepreneurship, for skill, and for capital formation could be deployed and that those countries were most successful in their attempts to reverse the process of underdevelopment. Moreover, so it would seem, they soon lost this new élan once the temporary barriers between the developed and the underdeveloped countries disappeared.[6]

Similar situations, bringing freedom from foreign interference, providing protection to infant industries, and offering incentives to experiment, to take risks, and to alter established policies were created by the voluntary isolation first of Japan and later of Russia and China. Though purely economic purposes may not have been their dominant motivations, nonetheless the economic results have certainly been impressive.

Both during the Tokugawa Shogunate—a military regime with a feudal structure lasting from 1603 to 1867—and after the Meiji Restoration in 1868, Japan, in almost complete self-imposed isolation, remained free of the structural limitations implied by the integrating and satellizing impact of superior economic powers. Isolation, in a sense, provided the protection that high transport costs had offered at the time of the West's own industrial revolutions.

Japan's early exports were tea, rice, copper, coal, marine products, and handicrafts such as paper, pottery, and lacquer. Gradually, however, silk emerged as the main item and became the principal source of foreign exchange over the half-century up to the Second World War.* Relying on this good foreign-exchange earner, improving its quality and its production methods with great care, Japan was able to broaden its industrial base, advancing it from textiles to technologically more sophisticated levels. This, however, is almost the end of the story. At the beginning, there was the single-minded, disciplined concentration on the mobilization of previ-

*Had silkworm disease in Europe in the nineteenth century not reduced production, or had nylon appeared a few decades earlier, Japan's rise, and with it contemporary economic history, would have been very different.

ously untapped material and human resources, and this with almost exclusive reliance on the country's own efforts. To that end, feudal regulations and restrictions were modified with constant concern for the constructive integration of the dispossessed and for the provision of appropriate incentives to serve the new economic goals.

When the restoration brought to power a remarkably competent and progressive ruling class, there was no inertia to fight. Increased incomes and productivity came mainly from the steady broadening of the volume of internal trade, and it was the domestic market that provided the decisive stimulus to growth. The authorities played a central role in industrialization and both stimulated and channeled the exceptionally high rate of savings into investments in the most productive directions. The foreign experts hired at great cost were selected from numerous countries, their numbers never exceeded 2,500 at a time, and they were replaced as soon as possible by Japanese who had been sent to be trained abroad in the meantime. Characteristically, there is no evidence that the returned Japanese specialists were given salaries comparable with those their foreign predecessors had received. The selection of students to be sent abroad, the choice of what they should study, decisions as to the kind of foreign experts to be hired, as well as the building of institutions around the knowledge thus acquired, were methodical and coordinated policies. Before the end of the nineteenth century literacy was almost universal, and against about 26,000 primary schools in 1962, over 20,000 existed already in 1874 for a considerably smaller population. And if universal modern education was Western in its scientific aspects, it remained purely and emphatically Japanese in its cultural and moral content.

Notwithstanding its meager natural resources, during its period of guided transformation Japan borrowed abroad only insignificant sums and permitted very little investment by foreigners. Basically, the principal source of growth was in continuous, deliberate, and planned structural change and in the constant adaptation of social and economic institutions, as well as values and incentives, to the central endeavor to move from less to more rewarding economic activities. And throughout the metamorphosis, indigenous sociocultural patterns were carefully preserved as constant frames of inspiration and strength, and indeed, remained guarantors both of its solidity and its authenticity.

The isolation of the Soviet experiment, though on an infinitely richer base of natural wealth, was comparably independent of foreign loans or investments. The state's economic role and the enormous savings and scientifically oriented educational effort were other common features. The experiment was no less successful than Japan's with respect to rapid industrial transformation. Yet the skill of the Japanese in structural adaptation and their devotion born of inherited social solidarity were missing, and indeed the retarding weight of agricultural failure may perhaps be accounted for by the doctrinaire obstinacy with which they sought to impose structures manifestly unsuited to tap the rural masses' productive potentialities. If in Japan modernization was greatly helped by readiness to fit into purposeful coordination of economic, social, and educational policies, the Soviet Union could not rely on the hierarchical and institutional loyalties which had been so decisive in Japan's case.

Also in self-imposed isolation, China is currently attempting to apply the lessons of the experiments of both Japan and Russia. Once again external trade is but a marginal factor and the momentum comes mainly from the domestic market. Neither foreign loans nor investments are being relied upon. In fact, the departure in 1960 of the Soviet technical assistants seems to have stimulated determination to rely only on indigenous effort, and the economic expansion of the years since the Cultural Revolution appears to prove its success. Starting out from an industrial and technological base much narrower than the Soviet Union's in 1928, and relying only on students returned from abroad or on a very few foreign experts hired at high cost, at least in some fields China seems to have made remarkable technological progress. Moreover, unlike heavily aided India, it has no foreign debts and its development is sheltered from the vicissitudes of the world economic conjuncture. A policy of decentralization aims at the involvement of growing segments of the rural world in industrial processes. And, as in Japan and unlike in Russia, particular efforts are being deployed to reinterpret imported ideas—Western or Soviet—in terms of Chinese traditions and impulses and, relying on their galvanizing influence, to mobilize indigenous skills and initiatives in the service of the over-all, planned transformation.

Although it could scarcely be denied that modernization, industrialization, and rapid development have been shown to be possible in isolation from the world system, still a certain number of objections might be formulated.

In the first place, the kind and degree of initiative-forcing isolation that Japan chose, and half a century ago Russia repeated, has become much more difficult in view of the deeper and more widespread penetration of foreign economic interests in command of decisive economic levers all over the underdeveloped world. In the Japan of the 1870s, there were practically none. In pre-1918 Russia, foreign economic interests were present much less in the form of direct private investments than in that of loans. In China up to 1948, however, direct private investments had been more important. But even if today the total volume of foreign private investments is impressive in global figures, in the majority of low-income countries they control only a few specific sectors of over-all economic activity. These, however, may be vital. Also, alliance with local oligarchies bolsters their power and represents a formidable obstacle to structural change. Nevertheless, in most of these countries there exists a vocal or potential opposition, perhaps even public opinion is becoming more articulate, and a change of regime and orientation is not excluded. Should such change occur, short of direct intervention and war, there is very little that foreign powers could do to reverse the trend leading to nationalization or other forms of greater local participation in formerly foreign-dominated economic activities. Nor is it probable that in the prevailing international context recourse to open intervention, and even less to war, would be easily decided.

The second objection might be that large-scale mass communications and irreversible scientific and other influences of all sorts render isolation from the world system unlikely. Considering what is happening in China, this is hardly convincing. Like Japan earlier, China is not hermetically sealed off. It hires some foreign experts, and it certainly keeps itself informed about technical and scientific developments in the rest of the world. Yet, though not an island, China can keep itself free of all unwanted influences. And although "China-watching" has become a profession for large numbers of highly trained individuals—a sizable proportion of whom practice on the very doorstep of the country, in Hong Kong—whenever China chooses to be secretive, the outside world knows barely more about what is going on inside the country than it did about Japan throughout the last century.

Finally, the objection might be made that the underdeveloped countries of today do not command resources, material or human, comparable with those of Japan, Russia, or China to enable them to repeat the same lonely performance. This, of course, is a debatable generalization. Abundance of material resources, as Japan demonstrated, is not indispensable. A development strategy which reduces to a minimum the need for foreign exchange may still produce economic progress aiming either at near autarky or at a situation where the country could become internationally competitive in carefully selected items of processed primary products or manufactured goods. If isolation is considered the only way for a country to retain its authenticity or to revitalize its sociocultural heritage in the service of modernization, this is, in fact, the major justification for opting for it. Moreover, only unforeseeable challenges can reveal unexpected qualities. If isolation is self-imposed, presumably it is in order to reassert a sociocultural identity menaced by alien formative influences. It is a choice responding to a felt need, and to what extent it will satisfy that need, no one can predict.

In any case, the question may legitimately be asked whether the aim is primarily economic or sociocultural. Rural majorities will hardly experience major material change as a result of a break with the world system. Yet, long before material benefits, the ensuing social and structural changes may render their life more meaningful and more satisfactory in terms of self-assertion, new purpose, or regained dignity. Though the city of Rangoon may have become even more run-down than usual, it is by no means impossible that in their self-imposed isolation and even without much economic growth, the Burmese now derive more satisfaction from the display of their inner psychological resources, from ordering their lives free of foreign influences, or from their ability to be able to learn from their own mistakes, than a mere increase in the quantity of available consumer goods could offer.

The desire to be released from imported stereotypes and imposed ways of living, to return to a more comfortable and more secure national or cultural identity, or to adapt to them what seems indispensable in what the outside world has to offer, will not disappear. It may even become stronger as the standardizing pressures mount. Indeed, it may very well become the fascinating central theme of the concluding quarter of this century, as one human group after another attempts to domesticate the oncoming waves of alien influences, to select, digest, and transform them, and thus to hammer out on its own anvil its own authentic personality. Some may succeed. Many more may not feel the need, will lack the will or the stamina even to try, or will give up under the strain of the effort and succumb to mere material rewards. But there may also be unexpected and entirely original experiments brought about by historical circumstances, by passions, or by the sheer arithmetic of material constraints. Who could foresee the outcome of Islam's fateful struggle with the imperatives of modern technology? In what kind of social framework might the Indians of South America recover their self-respect and re-enter the mainstream of history? And if one day thirty or forty million modern farmers feed India, who would dare to forecast the kind of sociological framework within which the hundreds of millions who have become almost redundant will be retained inside society?

The only thing certain is that once the pendulum of sociocultural identity has swung out too far through prolonged exposure to alien forces and values, it will inevitably tend to move back nearer to its original and natural position. After three centuries of Western supremacy, that pendulum is now on its way back and self-imposed isolation, wherever possible, may be but a station along the road of corrective de-westernization.

Seen in such a perspective, the wish of the vulnerable to put a protective distance between themselves and the overwhelming power of the industrial world should not be rejected in contempt or in anger. It should rather be given the understanding due to people who really wish to mobilize and expand their resources by relying on their own efforts and who, to do so, have decided to work out their own solutions. It would better befit those who have not yet demonstrated their ability to be really effective in their help to show compassionate consideration for people who consciously proceed to exchange their hitherto aimless sufferings for suffering with a defined purpose. It is an endeavor that merits sympathy and encouragement and, whenever possible and in appropriate indirect forms, even assistance.

For if the temptation is irresistible, it may well be in the interest of the developed countries to see to it that the dangerously disoriented, tormented, and indigent segments of humanity which have chosen to pass through the terrible tunnel emerge from it the soonest possible, with renewed self-respect and ready for a more equal partnership in a plural world.

XII Institutions, Intentions, and Practice

THE INSTITUTIONS within which economic relations evolve between the rich and the poor countries are either bilateral, multilateral, or global.

When the essential interests of a rich country are involved, it will rely mainly on the bilateral channel. When several powers share such interests, or when the means required are beyond the resources of any one among them, there is recourse to joint action within pragmatic, consortium-type associations. When a still greater depersonalization of economic relations is desired, funds will be channeled through world-wide or regional multinational institutions. And when it comes to negotiations concerning over-all attitudes and obligations, or the fundamental rules of the game, the forum will be global: either within the United Nations and its specialized agencies, or within other intergovernmental organizations created for the purpose.

The bilateral relationship is usually the direct descendant of the colonial link, and can thus be most easily branded with the neocolonialist epithet. Notwithstanding its advantages in terms of continuity or reciprocal familiarity, it is also most susceptible to exploitation on behalf of ruling groups in need of powerful protectors. The consortium is, as it were, a cooperative of neocolonialist design. It spreads the burden, provides pressure with the respectability of international censure, and, for the assisted, might produce a larger volume of financial assistance. The multinational institutions aim at being considered neutral, but their operations depend on loans and grants and, to that extent, could scarcely deviate too far from what the dominant members of the system consider essential for the furtherance of their aims. Finally, the global negotiating forums have their origin in the idealism of the immediate postwar years, and in the Economic and Social Council of the United Nations in particular. They were created with the intention of adapting the rules of international economic relations to the imperatives of greater equity. But with the real causes of world poverty receiving diminishing attention, the debates of these organs are increasingly centered around principles and less and less around how these could be harmonized with concrete commitments. Thus, they tend to become propaganda platforms where the numerical majority (usually assured of the verbal backing of Communist countries) can take its rhetorical revenge upon the materially invincible. For precisely the same reasons, whenever the rich countries find it in their interest to seem responsive to pressure and to concede marginal advantages to the other side, they formalize them within the intergovernmental organizations, in quest of publicity and, in the long run, also of votes.

This new institutional framework provides opportunities to replace the monologue of colonial times by dialogue between bargaining partners. The genuineness of the dialogue broadens as one advances from the bilateral to the global frame. The forces facing each other are grossly unequal, but the global dialogue offers opportunities to appeal to public opinion and thus, perhaps, to temper interests by whatever degree of sense of justice may be mobilized.

Yet behind the debate are the more or less irresistible intentions of the stronger side. Their central purpose is identical: to prolong both the world-wide division of labor and the postwar liberal world economic order, with its theories, rules, and market forces, all inevitably favoring the already stronger. The alternatives the models offer are within well-defined limits: to accommodate different kinds of reasoning and motivations in the industrialized countries, and to put varying emphasis on short-term or long-term interests, but without ever surrendering any of the basic components of the existing supremacy.

To simplify, then, the major economic powers might permit three possible models.

The dominant model implies the continuation, perfection, and intensification of the present main trend. Official aid and private investment should continue to provide assistance in the construction or extension of infrastructure to prepare the ground for a still broader and more efficient exploitation of natural resources and, in the second place, to help accelerate industrialization, mainly in the form of import substitution through the building of local consumer-goods industries. The help provided by international organizations, technical assistance, or emergency aid in food or other forms in time of need are part of the package. The danger persists that international competition could lead to the shrinking and perhaps even to the elimination of certain lines of local production built on indigenous capital and entrepreneurship. On the other hand, it is not excluded that the industrial powers could gradually accept the idea that certain labor-intensive industries should be yielded to the underdeveloped countries as their legitimate share of progress. In fact, the multinational corporations too might find it advantageous to transfer some of their productive units to cheap-labor areas.

This model, a mere acceleration of the traditional attempt at westernization and of urban-centered planning, does not dispose of the familiar social and political drawbacks. With rural hinterlands stagnant and increasingly crowded, purchasing power remains concentrated in the more prosperous layers of the urban sector. The slums and even more the villages do not advance much towards entry into the consumer society. To cater for only the remaining one-third, however, still provides interesting markets. But they would remain indefinitely below the promise of the country's potential in terms of its total population.

The second model is only a more liberal variant of the first. It resembles what the Alliance for Progress rhetoric promised: an enlightened, reformist partnership aiming at greater social justice, and at redistributive reforms achieved through reliance on the shock-absorber of foreign capital. Mutually more satisfactory arrangements might govern the exploitation of natural resources. Industrialization could benefit from alliance with local capital and entrepreneurial talent and form the new élan provided by spreading purchasing power. It might even include the creation of heavy industries capable of providing capital goods in growing quantities. Though not tried yet within the present context, this model is unlikely to produce satisfactory results. For in the short run, land reform and income redistribution through taxation remain incompatible with what is referred to as a "favorable climate" for private foreign investments. Moreover, what is achieved in agriculture these days depends very largely on the social and political purposes of those responsible for development. Indeed, the greater the pressure for reforms, the greater is likely to be the reluctance to tamper with the status quo lest it get out of hand. To make such a model workable would require, on the one hand, a ruling group exceptionally honest in its social and political purposes and unusually experienced and shrewd in its bargaining techniques, and on the other, negotiation partners on the side of the industrial powers who, to appreciate what might be gained, would also have to be aware how temporary are the benefits won by postponement.

Although for different reasons, the third model is even more theoretical. A few smaller industrial powers excepted, its feasibility is not yet really admitted. It would consist in acceptance of the fact that a low-income country could fully wield its sovereignty and in the virtual end of privileged treatment wrought by political or economic pressure. It would admit the weaker partner's right to nationalize existing foreign enterprises, to circumscribe carefully the scope of possible newcomers, to operate structural reforms in disregard of established foreign or its allied local interests, and to do it all while remaining a profitable economic partner, or while maintaining only those bridges to the system which it regards as consistent with its ideas of self-reliance and self-respect. Up to now no underdeveloped country has fully achieved such a role. Mere political neutrality has been tolerated, as in the case of Pakistan or India. But attempts to go beyond it and aim at both structural reform and economic neutrality—such as have been made in varying forms by Tanzania, Ceylon, Peru, and Chile—have already provoked economic reactions sometimes barely distinguishable from sanctions. Nor is it yet certain how long, if at all, such and similar experiments will remain sheltered from the full retaliatory powers commanded by the dominant system.

Of the three models, then, one is operational. Whether the second will be experimented with again, or whether the third will really be admitted as an alternative, the next few years will tell. In the meantime, with the exception of those which have already made their choice, or those refusing all three alternatives, the underdeveloped countries will have to envisage their role within the framework of one or the other of these models.

By doing so, they will step out of the anonymous crowd constituting the imaginary "third world" and find their place within distinct categories. It will not necessarily be final. Direct interference and power-political rivalries will not respect their sovereignty, nor will economic, racial, or other tensions stop at their borders. Moreover, the more illusion and the less realistic reasoning went into their decision, the more easily will they be deflected from their chosen course. Their economic situation will evolve, the mood of their people and circumstances in general will continue to change, and they may move from one category to another later on. The broad division, however, should serve at least to put unrealistically general aid and development policies on a more selective basis.

In practice, then, the underdeveloped countries belong to one of three main categories. First, those which can pin their hopes on the overspill effect of the dynamism of one of the great growth areas along whose borders they find themselves. Second, those which, for specific reasons, can draw best advantage from the acceptance of a client-state status. And third, the countries which, in one form or another, prefer and can afford a more aloof stance, with more or less pronounced isolation from the forces of the dominant world market.

In shorthand, as it were, they may be (dependent) partners, (docile) clients, or (disciplined) rebels. Within each category, of course, there are various shades and grades. But even so, a certain degree of generalization within each appears to be permissible on the basis of observable common denominators.

Taking first the countries whose economic prospects are largely influenced by the effect of the dynamism and growth of neighboring dominant entities, the typical case in the Western Hemisphere is Mexico. The Central American republics and some of the Caribbean islands also belong to this group. All these areas have the United States as their dominant trading partner. They receive an exceptionally heavy volume of American private investments, and a sizable proportion of their foreign-currency earnings comes from expenditure by—mainly American—tourists. The role of the English language among the ruling classes, the orientation of educational institutions, and the impact of technology in the form of equipment and personnel are additional factors. Moreover, being within easy reach of the United States' military presence, for the multinational corporations these are areas relatively free of risk and manipulable should social unrest threaten established structures.

In relation to Europe, the countries most affected by its economic growth are those on the southern shore of the Mediterranean basin: Morocco, Algeria, Tunisia, Lebanon, and Cyprus, and perhaps also Egypt and Libya. Here too, language and educational links, in this case mainly French, provide a bridge to the ruling elites. Heavy investments and large volumes of trade and tourism are supplemented by migrant labor and the bonds of reciprocal familiarity arising from prolonged intercommunications, the less pleasant memories of which usually fade with time. In this case, too, the multinational corporations can rely on Europe's stabilizing presence while the likelihood of serious change in sociopolitical orientation is limited by lack of any nearby growth center capable of offering comparable advantages.

In connection with Japan, the countries which find

themselves in a similar situation are South Korea, Taiwan (so long as its present status remains unchanged), Indonesia (more and more each day), later on (depending on the evolution of Sino-Japanese relations) perhaps Malaysia, Thailand, and the Philippines. Here language, educational links, and traditional bonds are not positive factors, but their absence is amply compensated by others. Japan is rapidly becoming the dominant trading partner, the source of technology and equipment and, with its fast-rising standard of living, also of tourism. Japanese investments in all these countries are mounting rapidly. Moreover, the effect of Japan's dynamism is likely to be particularly strong for a number of specific reasons. Far more than the United States or Europe, Japan depends on imported raw materials. As it is unlikely to admit large numbers of foreign workers, and given its growing shortage of skilled labor, more and more of Japan's labor-intensive industries will be transferred to these outer regions. Finally, the conscious planning of Japan's industrial development onto technologically higher levels coincides with its rapidly increasing potential to export capital on a large scale. The combined effect of all these factors foreshadows the emergence of an impressive sphere of influence within which Japan's mounting economic power will be felt all along the western Pacific basin.

Which of the underdeveloped countries will be in the second category and find option for the client-state status most rewarding depends on a still wider variety of factors.

In this case, historical circumstances, national character, or even climate may be important determinants. Geographical situation, excluding or permitting the playing off of rival contenders, may be even more decisive. States in the interior of continents, with a narrow economic base or with a single source of natural riches and without the means to exploit and market them, and devoid of skills or essential infrastructure to sponsor other important economic activities, have scarcely any other choice until the faraway day when regional collaboration may alter their economic perspectives.

In South America, Bolivia alone is in that situation, so long as its potential resources in the warm lowlands remain under-utilized and no regional collaboration offers an alternative. Paraguay and, in a different context, Ecuador and Venezuela may reach similar conclusions. In Asia there is practically no parallel situation, and this for two main reasons. First, single-resource or resource-poor countries are rare, or their opening on the sea, as in the case of Malaysia, assures them access to politically rival markets. In the second place, the others find themselves along the divide of the contemporary world's greatest power rivalries and so, even with modest skill, they can—like Afghanistan, Nepal, or Mongolia—draw greater profit from their situation than client-state status could offer. Inevitably, then, the largest number of countries in the second category belongs to Africa. So long as the economic and trading influence of the Soviet Union and China on the African continent remain marginal, the majority of the states between the colonial South and the Arab North will have no other choice. Of the 38 African states south of the Sahara, those large enough and with a sufficient diversity of resources to offer adequate markets for future industrialization—as, for example, Nigeria, Congo (Kinshasa), the Ivory Coast, Ghana, or Kenya—number barely half a dozen. States with small populations but with large and easily exploitable resources of mineral or other industrial raw materials—like Zambia, Mauritania, Guinea, or Gabon—are not more numerous. The rest, with unrepresentative ruling groups grafted onto populations living off subsistence agriculture, depending on foreign subsidies and in some cases even on foreign military presence, can scarcely expect to play a more independent role than that of mere subordinate outposts of the West's, and particularly Europe's, economy.

These two categories, then, have to live with the dominant economic model offered by the major economic powers. Most of them do not command the bargaining assets to force advance towards the second model with its reformist intentions. Thus the stark reality for all these states is the dual economy the dominant model implies.

This does not exclude hopes that the benefits of mere economic growth may slowly trickle down to the villages. Quite often, however, this is not even intended, and the governing minorities prefer to rely on more or less brutal repression to contain the resulting discontent. And where it is intended, it just does not happen.

Even in Mexico, notwithstanding the structural changes wrought by its revolution, its fast economic growth, and its relative agricultural success, half the country's population—the rural half—earns only 15 percent of all incomes. The federal district, in which the capital lies, with 14 percent of the total population, produces 40 percent of the national wealth. Industry, catering mainly for the purses and tastes of the urban population, works at only 60 percent capacity and over a third of the labor force is unemployed.[1]

Since the Korean War the 31 million South Koreans have been flooded by $7 billion in American funds alone, but despite additional foreign investments and economic-growth figures surpassing even Japan's yearly average of around 11 percent, the agricultural sector is withering away. If it contributed nearly half of all exports as late as 1962, it now receives a bare 6 percent of all investments, and in 1969 food-grain imports cost $300 million.[2]

The message is similar from countries in the first two

categories from one end of the world to the other, from the Philippines and Indonesia to Congo (Kinshasa), from oil-rich Iran to Venezuela, or from Gabon to Thailand. In spite of plentiful private investments, aid, and impressive growth rates, the gap between rich and poor, between urban opulence and rural degradation, continues to grow. And as the inevitable consequence, in all these cases there is universal and mounting preoccupation with keeping the excluded one-half to two-thirds of the population under control.

But to contemplate the long-term promise of the dominant model, it may be best to look at the three countries where its working has been least interfered with, where it has been longest at work, and where it could exert its influence under optimum conditions. They are Puerto Rico, the Philippines, and Liberia.

Puerto Rico's special relationship with the United States places the island inside the American tariff wall and under its military shield. No other country will ever have freer access to the United States market, and no other country could possibly provide a safer haven for American investments or for the activities of the multinational corporations. As a result, Puerto Rico has received per capita more private foreign investments and has had higher tourist income than any other state in the world, and it has known proportionately rapid industrialization. A tiny wagon attached to so powerful a locomotive, its growth rates have been fast, as expected. Urban prosperity mirrors American ways of living. But the total labor force has barely increased during the past fifteen years, there is widespread unemployment, and nearly as many Puerto Ricans have emigrated to the United States in search of an income as have remained in their own country.

In the case of the Philippines, local capital has played a larger role. But lavish aid and preferential United

States treatment of sugar exports have been decisive ingredients generating high growth rates. Once again, there has been a great deal of industrialization. But the servicing of debts is canceling out new inflow of capital and balance-of-payments crises are growing chronic. The spread of prosperity to rural areas has been no more than modest. Unemployment is widespread and two-thirds of the 38 million inhabitants of the country live in degrading poverty. The cultural depersonalization of the privileged groups has probably been nowhere more complete. And for several years now, guerrillas have been profiting from the deepening discontent.

Thanks to the Americo-Liberians (descendants of returned, liberated slaves) and to the dominant role of American companies in the country, Liberia has had a long and special relationship with the United States. Most of its aid, its private investments, and its equipment come from America. Moreover, since 1950 Liberia has become one of the world's major producers of iron ore. A typical concession-dominated economy, it benefits also from exports of rubber and from income provided by a large merchant fleet operated in its name for reasons connected with advantages in taxation. Indeed, during the decade up to 1961 the Liberian economy grew at a rate outstripped only by that of Japan. But there is still forced recruitment of labor for mines and plantations, conditions in rural areas are more backward even than in neighboring countries, and iron-ore mining by modern methods provided employment to few Liberians. The growth the country has known "did not lead to development, that is, to structural economic change absorbing larger numbers of Liberians in new productive activities and with more advanced training and skills. On the contrary, the returns from Liberia's economic growth, insofar as they accrued to Liberians, went almost exclusively to the small ruling minority of Americo-Liberians, thus reinforcing their political power and the economic and social divisions between them and the country's tribal majority."[3]

Considering this panorama, it is not surprising that impatient and rebellious voices are heard from the Southern Hemisphere, calling for greater detachment from the dominant industrial world. The purpose of these possible candidates for the third category may simply be limited and controlled isolation. It may go beyond that and aim at relations comparable to those now existing between East and West. But in some exceptional cases the determination to cease to be a helpless toy in the hands of the world market may lead to an even more radical break, to the self-imposed quarantine.

Decisions of such a nature would have to rest on the solid foundations of a long-term vision of one's destiny. Isolation might be difficult without geographical assets offering a degree of immunity from direct foreign intervention. It would certainly require broad popular support, born of a community of purpose, to help shoulder the inevitable hardships or to consider them less significant than the nonmaterial satisfactions self-reliance might offer. And the attempt might well be impossible without an ideological basis capable of galvanizing convictions and enthusiasm and of sustaining sacrifices.

Trying to guess where this might happen, one inevitably turns towards the large, potentially self-contained entities like Brazil or India. But developments of this nature have never been predictable. It is impossible to foresee the particular constellation of circumstances—such as a sense of humiliation, xenophobia, or the quality of leadership—which might ripen decisions. They might be motivated by fears of imminent threat to national identity or security, or by the combination of such fears with exasperation caused by inadmissible dependence. Past experience with a too-powerful Indian minority, and being sandwiched between two of the most populous countries, may have prompted Burma's current seclusion. The desire to reassert cultural identity and threatened traditions, to attain a new equilibrium after excessive exposure to the radiations of an alien civilization, may one day lead to comparable developments in India or in some of the larger Moslem countries. On the African continent, it may come about in Nigeria, or perhaps within some future regional entity under strong and self-reliant leadership. It may possibly happen, and perhaps is most likely to happen, in countries which have already achieved economic progress rendering the tutelage of the dominant economic powers too heavy to bear, or justifying the belief that, free of the constraints of foreign economic influences, development could be accelerated and channeled into socially more desirable directions. This may happen, or perhaps has already started to happen, in Latin America. Over the past quarter-century a few Latin American republics have accomplished a considerable degree of industrialization. Some are already producing an increasing proportion of the equipment goods they need. And in particular situations the racial resentments of the Andean Indians might complement merely economic aims.

Prognostication, however, is too risky. Unpredictable and imponderable factors will sway events. Some of the candidates may be influenced by their more or less justified aspirations to become world powers. A few may be caught in irresistible racial tensions generating uncontrollable passions. Others, again, may be made disagreeably aware that they are one of the few bridgeheads in the Southern Hemisphere which one or another of the superpowers will not allow to determine its own course because of its key importance in terms of strategy or essential raw materials. The only thing certain is that more and more underdeveloped countries are becoming increasingly disillusioned in their relations with the advanced industrial powers. Many of them are growing reluctant to be either partners, clients, or mere rebels. Indeed, countries with non-Western civilizations and with distinct cultures may feel the need for a pause for introspection, for a secluded interlude to find their compromise with what they have to retain from outside. Moreover, in some of them a great deal of intellectual groundwork has already been done to prepare minds for a change of course.

Like all attempts at categorization, all this may be either not comprehensive enough or too rigid to contain possible variants. The rivalry of existing and emerging great powers will keep on transforming the context. The models may evolve, and countries belonging to the first category may qualify simultaneously for the second. Partners may also be clients, and both may one day turn into rebels. Yet notwithstanding its evident shortcomings, even such a rough classification might help to render more realistic any attempt to reconsider aid and development policies.

XIII | *Palliatives and Alternatives*

THE LIBERAL WING of the development establishment has by now a standard kit of components which, fitted together, are presented as a desirable world strategy for aid and development.

It considers financial assistance to underdeveloped countries an international obligation, the beginning of a global income tax. Thus, for the time being, 1 percent of the rich countries' GNP should be offered in aid, untied, and with the largest possible proportion of it in grants or soft loans. Moreover, an increasing volume of private foreign investments should help the process, both as provider of capital and as conveyor of modern organization and technological know-how.

Trade in raw materials and primary commodities should be organized within a rational framework with price stabilization as its base. The industrialized countries should cover a stipulated proportion of the increment of their needs by imports rather than by synthetics or substitute materials. In addition, a kind of international insurance scheme should compensate the poor countries for unforeseeable shortfalls in the earnings from their exports of primary commodities. Also, they should be assisted in the diversification of their production in order to be less dependent on the fortunes of a handful of commodities. Furthermore, methods should be devised to remedy the deterioration of the underdeveloped countries' terms of trade.

Hand in hand with such changes would go unilateral measures to eliminate trade barriers. Tropical products should not be taxed. Restrictions on others ought to be removed and harmful policies of subsidization brought to an end. Simultaneously, tariff structures should cease to penalize progress towards industrialization, and as a logical sequel, all other obstacles, from quotas to administrative restrictions, should be dismantled in order to enable underdeveloped countries to set up their own factories in the knowledge that prosperous and open export markets will sustain the growth of their new industries.

All such measures, it is argued, would serve the interests of rich-country consumers. The shirts, the shoes, or the alarm clocks they bought would become cheaper. Moreover, all this ought to culminate in a long-term policy shifting labor-intensive industries to the low-income countries. The hardships this would cause should be alleviated by appropriate adjustment policies and by the retraining of redundant workers for technologically more advanced industries where they would earn higher wages. And they would sell more of their sophisticated products to the underdeveloped countries, whose purchasing power would have improved.

Finally, the combined economic and political influence of the industrialized countries ought to be utilized to encourage and strengthen regimes in poor countries which would be able and willing to create congenial surroundings for the utilization and equitable distribution of the benefits thus provided.

In a nutshell, such is the content of the kit.

In one form or another, the components of this liberal prescription have been the subject of intergovernmental discussions ever since the end of the Second World War.[1] The need for modification of the system came to be universally admitted. What remained to be determined was to what extent and with what speed.

It is one of the merits of the United Nations and its specialized agencies that they have provided a platform on which the rich and the poor could engage in dialogue in search of an answer. The danger that it would be utilized to gain time and to divert pressure into rhetorical contests seemed compensated by the fact that the debate itself was bound to have some impact on world public opinion. Thus, the poor majority has been trying to persuade the rich minority to consent to the largest possible modifications and with the greatest possible speed. Its endeavors, however, have invariably encountered the immovable obstacle of national sovereignty. Mere majority votes have been helpless against it. Citing their own public opinion, representatives of the rich countries could evade both logic and moral imperatives. Nor was the situation rendered easier by the fact that the painful structural adjustments implied by the requested concessions could not be matched by any undertakings on the part of the rulers of the underdeveloped countries to operate corresponding reforms to permit the really effective utilization of the benefits eventually obtained.

The liberal wing of the development establishment is, of course, right in proclaiming that the time has come to replace "aid" by a genuine international development policy, that is, by a global strategy planned and executed in "equalitarian interdependence." Though their prescription fatally ignores both contemporary realities of power and history's lessons about human behavior, it still forms a logical and coherent whole. If it could be applied in its totality and with the required speed, it might help to improve the situation of most underdeveloped countries. The aid and trade measures proposed could considerably increase their capital resources, which, suitably utilized, might speed their economic advance. Whether these would be properly utilized, no one could be certain. Whether the economic growth would benefit majorities and so lead to real development is a matter of opinion. What is more certain is that, within foreseeable circumstances, far less of the prescription will be translated into practice, and far more slowly, than would be required to produce any significant impact.

Though conceived by some as the beginning of a systematic process of the redistribution of the world's resources, aid-giving has been a reluctant and contradiction-ridden operation right from the start. In real value its volume is already declining. Its terms are in rapid deterioration. Even if the economic growth rate of the rich countries were to accelerate steadily, in view of the prevailing scarcity of capital and high interest rates it is more than doubtful that the quality of aid would improve in the foreseeable future. Moreover, even if aid targets may seem a means of stimulating international solidarity, they might just as well be turned into harmful soporifics. Without detailed analysis of the purposes for which assistance is given or of the ways it is employed, measurement of its mere monetary volume is bound to remain almost meaningless. The small fraction of a donor country's GNP devoted to rural improvement may be of far greater importance than a much larger proportion destined to finance the purchase of supersonic aircraft.

After long years of negotiations, there are today five international commodity agreements in operation: for coffee, sugar, wheat, tin, and olive oil. The European Economic Community and the United States have refused to sign the sugar agreement. The one regulating the price of coffee—the second most important primary commodity in value after oil—is in permanent difficulties. The arrangements concerning wheat are of benefit primarily to the high-income countries. No agreement has yet been concluded on a series of other products of capital importance to underdeveloped countries. Protracted negotiations have usually been short-circuited by the inability of the producing countries to synchronize their attitudes, or more often, by speculative interests reluctant to part with benefits accruing from operating in an unregulated market. Limiting recourse to synthetics and substitute materials has revealed itself a futile enterprise, and after several years of debate, the international insurance scheme has practically been shelved.

How to improve the low-income countries' terms of trade is as yet a mere academic subject. Those who question the very need for remedial action assert that in the long run gains and losses cancel each other out. Alternatively, they invoke the example of petroleum or of a few metals such as copper, concerning which, at given moments, the producing countries' bargaining position is relatively favorable. And within the prevailing economic framework it is hard to see how the problem could really be confronted.

Thanks to the growing role of synthetics and substitute materials and to the "miniaturization" of modern technology, primary products, including foodstuffs, face increasingly inelastic demand. For some time the Communist countries will provide expanding markets for tropical foodstuffs such as cocoa, coffee, or citrus fruits, which they have not consumed in important quantities in the past. But that market, too, will grow saturated in due time. Nor is it easy to regulate supply when individual small farmers account for a large proportion of total output. On the other hand, the stepping up of production in times of high demand fatally leads to overproduction and to falling prices once scarcity is over. In fact, fixed prices in themselves are not enough in the face of aggressive selling methods. Whatever price levels are agreed upon, they soon tend to become redundant without simultaneous agreement upon both national production levels and the sharing of world markets. In the meantime, increased productivity in the factories of the rich countries is absorbed by mounting wages. The example spreads by osmosis: to industries whose productivity may be stagnant or even in decline and, in due time, to the public sector and to service industries as well. The resulting inflationary trend is reflected in higher prices for the goods the underdeveloped countries need to buy. Under these circumstances, short of price reductions proportionate to increased productivity, it is difficult to see how the poor countries' terms of trade could effectively be safeguarded.

Similar contradictions between interventionist policies at home and so-called free trade with the poor world characterize also the trade measures which would be indispensable components of the liberal prescription.

Farm-support policies and the subsidized exports they lead to are eloquent illustrations. Sugar is a flagrant case in point. But it is not the sole example. And the picture is not much more encouraging when it comes to import restrictions. Escalating tariff structures continue to penalize the advance towards the processing of local raw materials. And whenever the low-wage countries have a real advantage in international competition, as is the case with textiles and footwear, quantitative restrictions complete the already formidable panoply of obstacles.

Hedged around by qualifications and escape clauses, the unilateral tariff preferences for selected exports, granted in 1970, are barely more than a symbolic gesture to appease pressure and criticism. They may encourage some private investors to move to low-wage countries in order to export to metropolitan areas. But the practical effects will be slow to appear, and it is estimated that they are unlikely to generate additional income in excess of one-half to one billion dollars a year. And the concessions are revocable whenever they may hurt.

What alternatives are left?

Among the complex variety of factors leading to development, the mobilization of internal resources remains by far the most important. But even in the most favorable and most successful situations, certain goods and services have to be imported and paid for in foreign exchange. During the past few years roughly four-fifths of the underdeveloped countries' foreign exchange has been earned by exports. Only one-fifth of it has been provided by aid, loans, or foreign investments. Thus real aid alone accounted for only a small part of even that one-fifth. More concretely, the additional purchasing power provided to the developing countries by real aid amounts to barely more than a twentieth of their combined export earnings of nearly $50 billion.

Nevertheless the trade-versus-aid debate is not pointless. It is true that trade implies self-help and offers advantages proportionate to effort. It also calls for competitive standards of efficiency, technical progress, and capacity for adaptation. Aid, on the other hand, can be instrumental either in complementing the benefits derived from trade or, on the contrary, in discouraging such efforts owing to its availability irrespective of performance. Governments of underdeveloped countries have had occasion to learn that to run a big balance-of-payments deficit—that is, to live beyond the means provided by their own efforts—tends to generate more aid. Yet even so, within the framework of a rational and moral policy of international cooperation, aid might be justified as an accelerator. Implicit in the assumption, however, is that aid should be made available in rational and moral ways. In practice this has rarely been the case. Instead of lightening the sacrifice involved in a high rate of local savings, it has more often served different and less reputable ends.

It is not impossible that more countries will follow Sweden's example in its official endeavor to allot its aid mainly to reformist governments attentive to social justice. But Sweden, of course, is something of a newcomer in the field of aid, without a colonial past and with relatively few established interests overseas. It is equally possible that, through bilateral or multilateral channels, the major donor countries will try to agree upon criteria whereby to measure performance in the positive utilization of their aid and to penalize the recalcitrants. But it would be surprising indeed if such a policy became standard practice before rational and moral considerations overrode short-term political and economic interests. Thus, possible as such and similar changes may be, they are unlikely to occur fast enough or in a sufficiently comprehensive fashion to eliminate in time the self-defeating major shortcomings of prevailing aid methods.

It is not, then, the principle of aid one is obliged to question, but rather the probability of any timely and serious change in its present forms. And if it is unlikely that the motivations determining its employment will seriously change, the problem is in what other forms foreign assistance may be provided so as to preclude the possibility of its misuse by the recipients or of its serving mainly the interests of the donors.

Direct charitable or voluntary relief activities come nearest to fitting such a definition. The succor they offer to the needy is irreplaceable in the instant relief they provide. Frequently they are the only means available to save lives. Nor should their quantitative importance be belittled. In their multiple and scattered forms they channel each year assistance worth $600 to $800 million. And neither governmental intermediaries nor excessive bureaucracies take their toll of them. Moreover, unlike public or multilateral aid, charitable or voluntary relief action means direct involvement and provides the individual donors with means to communicate their interest and concern. However, this type of action may often treat symptoms only. This is particularly the case with food aid, which, when on a large scale, might even help to depress local prices and thus offset remedial action in the form of higher local production. Yet charitable and direct relief activities satisfy real needs as they arise. And often a small and unspectacular improvement in local conditions may liberate individual initiatives which may contribute more to change or to development as a whole than some of the more imposing projects conceived by distant, impersonal authorities.

Another desirable way to provide assistance is in the form of long-term, low-interest loans, and this on the assumption that no investment is psychologically or materially worthwhile if it cannot yield benefits convertible into at least modest interest on the capital employed.

A variety of proposals have been put forward to devise mechanisms permitting both the expansion of the volume of loans and the lowering of interest rates without heavy sacrifice to donors. The best known among them suggested that aid-giving countries should allow an international organization—perhaps the International Development Association, the World Bank's soft-loan arm—to borrow from capital markets at commercial rates of interest and to lend the funds so raised at concessional terms. The lending countries would guarantee the capital borrowed and would make up the difference between interest paid and received. In simpler terms, $100 borrowed at 6 percent interest and loaned at 1 percent would cost the donors $5 only, plus the risk involved in their guarantee.[2] By this method, important additional funds might be mobilized for development purposes. But it would deprive donor countries of the advantage they usually derive from their carefully identified generosity. And that, no doubt, goes a long way to explain why the idea has never advanced beyond the stage of experts' reports and exploratory discussions.

But charity and concessional loans apart, one may seek further alternatives to prevailing forms of aid. Countries really desirous of offering effective assistance ought to find it more logical, for example, to devote their grants to the gradual liquidation or at least to the alleviation of the debt burden of the states they wish to aid. New aid involves new obligations, and the conditions invariably attached to it restrict the recipient country's freedom in its use of the new funds obtained. In contrast, the same amount devoted to the liquidation of debts would liberate a corresponding volume of export income for unrestricted use in the best interests of the recipient.

Another alternative to direct aid might be the provision of compensating knowledge and services. Scientific and technological research directed towards serving the interests of the populations of underdeveloped countries is by far the most effective aid rich countries can donate to poor ones. Its quantifiable value might well be far greater than the real worth of the aid now provided, and by its very nature it could not be turned to the advantage of privileged minorities only. As an illustrative prototype, one may invoke the example of the green revolution.

The research effort which resulted in the development of the new high-yielding varieties of wheat, rice, and maize is variously estimated to have cost no more than two to four million dollars.[3] Yet the use of the new seeds has already led in some countries to a substantial reduction of imports, representing foreign-currency savings of tens of millions of dollars. Moreover, under suitable social and economic conditions, their generalized use might not only eliminate the need for cereal imports but also result in exportable surpluses, all together providing foreign currency amounting probably to far more than the total volume of foreign aid over several years.

This is but a single, though a spectacular, example of a well-selected scientific contribution capable of offering far greater and far more universally beneficial advantages than any probable amount of financial aid might provide. As a variant of a proposal by Professors Hirschman and Bird, it is perfectly conceivable that scientists, technicians, and specialists of all kinds, in the company of respected public figures, might create a series of private development Funds, each devoted to a carefully selected problem of universal relevance to the underdeveloped countries.[4] Free of the power-political shackles and of the bureaucratic ballast of giant international organizations, such Funds could begin to plan and to coordinate study, research, and other practical activities aimed at the solution of the problem they had selected to deal with. Surely, neither talent nor idealism would be found lacking for modestly paid or even voluntary collaboration.

One such Fund might amplify the plant-research work which led to the high-yielding wheat, rice, and maize varieties. Another one, or several of them, might turn to the perfection of simple technologies capable of providing goods and equipment based on local materials for local use and related to the level of technical sophistication of their prospective users. Agricultural implements, low-cost ways of lifting and moving water, simple and cheap building techniques, portable sources of energy, or small-scale productive units capable of turning out "modern" goods but utilizing dispersed small deposits of mineral resources inadequate for large-scale industry, are but a few examples among all the needs and possibilities.[5] Low-cost robust means or rural transport or small fertilizer plants utilizing local raw materials might be subjects for other Funds.[6] Visual methods for agricultural education in illiterate communities, the design and equipment of simple, mobile birth-control dispensaries, or visual aids in the formation of personnel for cooperatives would be equally useful and important.

One of the Funds might concentrate its energies on the organizational problems involved in the chronic under-utilization of industrial plants already installed in underdeveloped countries. How to squeeze maximum productivity from already imported equipment before new factories are bought could well be one of the most rewarding subjects for study and improvement. Indeed, given their neutral and disinterested nature, it is conceivable that one or more of such Funds could acquire the functions of a consultative service with a pool of specialists at its disposal, capable of advising underdeveloped countries either in their negotiations with prospective foreign investors, or, perhaps, in the drawing up and appraisal of their economic plans.

There would be no shortage of urgent and promising subjects. And in place of pompous declarations and charters devoted to unattainable goals, members of the Fund, men of prestige and solid reputation, could appear on television to explain to their listeners how their contributions and the work done with their help had enabled masses of indigent people to accede to a more dignified life. Indeed, the idea of independent research and science Funds might be coupled with a contributory aid scheme whereby the individual citizen could select the specific field of activity he wished to support, thus promoting the direct involvement of taxpayers.

Should governments in the industrial countries be

disposed to offer tax credits for individual foreign-aid contributions, the revenue thus gathered might enable the Funds to channel their own financial assistance either through multinational organizations or in direct support of projects resulting from their own research efforts.[7] Successfully experimented with in one donor country, the example of private contributory development Funds might spread to others. Gradually they might grow into alternative mechanisms for transferring knowledge or funds capable in the long run of superseding present bilateral aid programs. And thanks to the element of individual choice and financial participation involved, they might also help rekindle public interest in the aid and development process.*

These are but a few of the possible alternatives to direct aid, but there are other methods to replace it. These would, in fact, enhance the import capacity of the poor countries much more effectively and would be free of the influences associated with foreign gifts and assistance. They would simply consist in replacing aid by refraining from causing harm.

The net result of abstention from inflicting damage on the economies of underdeveloped countries might be measurable. If a current practice deprives a low-income country of $100 worth of export revenue, then the termination of that harmful practice might be considered the equivalent of an identical volume of aid. This way, international aid objectives set for grants and concessional loans might be fulfilled, not necessarily by gifts and soft loans only, but also by the elimination of practices which have been causing measurable harm.

Indeed, economic damage might be quantifiable in

*The very fact that voluntary and charitable organizations could mobilize almost $850 million for development purposes in 1970 seems to confirm the feasibility of voluntary private contributory schemes as possible alternatives to official governmental aid.

several fields. The somewhat controversial examples which come to mind first are capital flight and armaments. It is conceivable that the rich countries might devise methods rendering it less easy for flight capital from the underdeveloped regions of the world to take refuge behind secret bank accounts. It is equally desirable, though perhaps even more difficult, to reach international agreements to restrict the sale of at least "major weapons" to low-income countries, and to deter the transfer of other arms which fatally involve neighbors in ruinous armaments competitions. It would be much less difficult to throw light on and to restrict discriminatory practices in the field of invisible services and in freight-rate policies in particular. And it would be easier both to quantify and to put an end to the economic damage inflicted on the poor countries by the more or less open encouragement of the brain drain. A variety of methods could be devised, ranging from modification of immigration regulations to possible compensation in proportion to the advantages the rich countries derive from the services of the highly trained personnel they admit. It will be remembered that some rough estimates put the yearly damage in the region of one billion dollars.*

But approaching the more concrete examples, one moves from aid to trade.

It is true that only a small part of the rich countries' imports from the poor regions of the world are subject to significant tariffs. If one excludes the part admitted duty-free, under low duty, or with preferential arrangements, as well as crude petroleum, only about one-fifth remains. In other words, only about $10 billion worth of poor-country exports are encountering really important obstacles to their entry into the rich markets. But within this segment are all the articles which have a significant

*See p. 126.

export potential. They are either kept out by these obstacles, or their volume is seriously reduced, or else they are not produced at all for export because of the existing trade barriers.

How much more of such articles the underdeveloped countries might sell on the industrialized countries' markets cannot be estimated. A variety of imponderables are involved. Just as an indicative figure, the total duties collected on all imports from the underdeveloped countries entering the United States are in the region of half a billion dollars each year. The total in Europe and Japan together might be roughly comparable. Quite apart from the new opportunities it would open up, the elimination of these tariffs might each year offset about one billion dollars' worth of aid.

In the meantime, and notwithstanding the limited and selective unilateral preferences just granted, existing tariff structures enable the rich countries to supply their industries with cheap imported raw materials but protect them against all really effective competition. Tariffs rise for each stage of processing, assembly, or manufacture. Textile fabrics confront much higher duties than yarns. Oilseeds (in the Common Market, for example) enter duty-free, at 10 percent in semiprocessed form, and at 15 percent as refined oil. But the effect of the escalation, already a serious impediment in low-income countries to the local transformation of their raw materials, is compounded by the intentional confusion of nominal and effective protection.

A nominal tariff is the rate of duty expressed as a percentage of the total value of the imported article. But the effective rate is much higher because the raw material that went into the processed article is taxed at the same, higher rate as the value added in the process of transformation. Suppose that leather enters with 10 percent duty and shoes with 20. In that case, the effective protection against the imported shoe is much higher than the nominal 20 percent, as its leather component too (which alone would have entered with half that duty) will be taxed at the higher level.

If \$250 of yarn is needed to produce \$500 worth of fabric and the first enters at a duty of 10 percent and the second at 20 percent, the duty on the imported yarn is \$25. But the \$100 duty paid on the imported fabric represents an effective rate of 30 percent rather than the nominal 20 percent. In the case of refined oils, the effective rate of protection works out at no less than 150 percent.

Thus the rich countries see to it that the employment opportunities, the value added, and the foreign-exchange savings are reserved for themselves. And if, in spite of the discriminatory tariff structure, a few of the underdeveloped countries still manage to export important quantities of their processed or manufactured products, their efficiency is likely to be recompensed by additional, quantitative obstacles, usually in the form of quotas.

Simultaneously, the neomercantilist trend in the farm policies of the industrially advanced countries is creating additional grave problems for the underdeveloped world. Agricultural protection, massive subsidies, and price supports as well as the subsidized exports they lead to, do not affect Temperate Zone foodstuffs alone but also products of vital interest to the preindustrial countries, such as sugar, vegetable oils, and oilseeds. Countries previously dependent on imports grow self-supporting. Others have even become exporters, as is the case with German wheat and Japanese rice. Their low-priced, subsidized exports or their food aid does enormous damage to the export possibilities of low-income countries who may have nothing else to sell abroad, or of those who hoped to become sellers of wheat, rice, or maize should their hopes attached to the green revolution ever be fulfilled. The subsidies causing these problems cost billions of dollars each year. The economies of the countries indulging in this luxury may be strong enough to remedy the resulting disequilibrium. But the underdeveloped countries are unlikely to be able to cope with it without serious implications for their economic progress and probably also for their political stability.[8]

Escalating tariffs and extravagant agricultural price support policies serve to protect the interests of home producers. But the arguments invoked in their support cannot possibly justify the taxing of imported tropical products which cannot be grown in the Temperate Zone industrial countries, and thus could not compete with local growers. Nevertheless the Western industrial countries, and the European Economic Community in particular, impose fiscal duties on imported beverage crops and bananas. By doing so, they limit demand and cause the exporting countries considerable and measurable damage. Cocoa, coffee, and tea apart, sugar, oilseeds, oranges, bananas, and tangerines too are affected. Though the abolition of such taxes may not raise sales considerably, the exporting countries' earnings could be increased by at least as much as the amount of taxes removed. In 1961, in the Common Market and EFTA countries as a whole, they amounted to $785 million.[9] It is hardly believable that countries of such affluence, and presumably anxious to aid the underdeveloped countries, could not forgo such punitive taxation. By doing so and restituting that sum, at one stroke they could undo damage amounting to nearly one-third of the real cost of the combined aid effort of the world's richest countries.*

Finally, there is the steady squeezing of the poor countries' capacity to finance their imports due to the continuous deterioration of their over-all terms of trade. The downward drift in world prices of most primary

*That is, countries that are members of the Development Assistance Committee (see p. 49 above).

products since 1955 has produced a fall of 7 percent in their terms of trade. Over the same period, the upward trend of the prices of manufactured articles has led to a 10 percent improvement of the industrialized countries' own terms of trade. Thus for sixteen years now an ever-growing quantity of primary products has had to be offered in exchange for the same volume of manufactures and equipment goods. According to one estimate, since 1955 the underdeveloped countries have lost on the average $2.5 billion a year owing to the deterioration of their terms of trade—a sum probably superior to the real cost of all the aid they have been receiving.[10]

Serious departure from any of these established practices would raise fundamental questions involving formidable forces and interests. Will inflation, for example, remain a permanent feature of the advanced industrial economies, and will the present protectionist trend intensify or recede? Are the industrial countries really decided and do they command the material, social, and political means to go beyond mere marginal adjustments and effect the structural changes and the massive retraining and transfer of their workers from labor-intensive to high-technology sectors? Or can the exports of merely those processed or manufactured articles which do not seriously compete with rich-country products ever procure the volume of foreign exchange the underdeveloped countries need to satisfy their minimum requirements in accelerating their economic progress? Finally, as is likely to happen with textiles, will not the modernization and automation of the rich countries' own industries in the long run either cancel out the low-cost producing countries' competitive advantage, or alternatively, compel them to maintain socially unacceptable wage levels in their endeavor to remain competitive?

Attempts to answer these and similar questions would soon point up existing contradictions between the occasionally enlightened economic and political intentions of governments in the industrialized countries and the resistance of their farmers and of their inefficient, marginal economic sectors, so effectively represented by pressure groups and trade unions. For the paradox helps to reveal the real nature of the contemporary international variant of the class struggle. The fundamental conflicts of interest are not necessarily located between the poor countries and the modern, dynamic or multinational capitalist concerns, for the great multinational organizations may have a somewhat positive role to play in poor countries after the elimination of major structural distortions. But a fundamental, perhaps unresolvable conflict exists between the low-income producers of the underdeveloped countries and the farmers, the craftsmen, and the historically condemned labor-intensive industries of the rich world.

It is their rear-guard fight to maintain uneconomic production in the face of the competition of the cheap-labor countries that now constitutes one of the most important obstacles to any rational aid and development policy. Yet, as they are both electors and taxpayers, their interests are likely to prevail. Quotas and customs dues will not speedily be abolished. Effective opposition, if not violent revolt, will remain the alternative to the only international trade policy likely to make a serious impact on North-South economic relations. Such a policy would consist, first of all, in a generalized system of preferences which would admit in agreed quantities, through long-term agreements and at fixed prices, the products of the underdeveloped countries, and would retain barriers only against those exports of the other industrialized countries (particularly agricultural ones) which the poor countries could supply more cheaply.

Short of such a complete transformation of the pattern of international trade, unlikely if not impossible within the liberal economic context, at best only unconnected components of the liberal prescription will be put into practice. Aid will remain inadequate and is unlikely to be freed of its political strings. Regulation of commodity markets will occur mainly when it offers greater advantages to the industrialized than to the underdeveloped countries. Unilateral preferences will provide only narrow and precarious openings. In the other fields, it would be futile to expect any really important progress. Or what can be expected will be so modest that it could scarcely bring about fundamental modification in the prevailing situation.

Before brushing aside such conclusions as unduly pessimistic, it is advisable to part with some illusions about the magnitude of the changes required.

A really serious and systematic policy of economic emancipation would imply an immense effort by rich countries. It would require a massive transfer of really productive resources amounting to several times the present still-unfulfilled target of 1 percent of their gross national product. It would also demand a radical transformation of their own economic structures to permit the coordination of the poor and rich countries' industrial policies, the creation of entirely new rules and mechanisms of international trade, and an unshakable determination and courage to confront the internal political consequences the indispensable adjustments would entail. And it would also imply the subordination of all political and strategic interests, as well as ideological predilections, to the overriding need to support governments devoted to social and economic change in order to permit optimum mobilization of internal resources.

It would be morally and intellectually untenable to exclude the possibility of all this happening. But it would be morally and intellectually dishonest to sustain illusions regarding its probability.

Yet with the social and economic climate of the underdeveloped countries in rapid change and with their populations in fast expansion, thinking about the future has to respect boundaries in time. The fragmentary halfhearted measures which, at best, may be forthcoming are unlikely to bring us much nearer to the goal, and in time. Indeed, the sum total of concessions and modifications which might most optimistically be expected is not likely to go beyond just what is necessary to prolong the consent of client states or to discourage voluntary associates from turning to rebellion against the system.

Thus the aid and development problem, already, calls for two distinct approaches. First, to see to what extent the likely marginal modifications might improve the situation of clients and partners. Second, to consider what forms of cooperation may be desirable or would be possible with the others who have, or will have, come to the conclusion that in order to satisfy their basic aspirations they had better loosen or sever their ties with the system dominated by the advanced industrial powers and put an end to their dependence on them.

In the first category, with skill and luck, an exceptional few may accede to a halfway status between the aristocrats of opulence and the states condemned to the role of proletarians of the world order. Some of the most acute problems of certain Mediterranean and African states may thus be solved at the expense of other poor countries. The same may happen to Mexico and a few Central and South American republics not too far from the United States, or to a handful of East Asian states within Japan's emerging sphere of economic influence. They may be able to attenuate, though not to undo, the structural deformities they have inherited. They will have to bargain hard for compensating advantages to render their heritage more supportable. But they will not be able to get rid of their vulnerability and of their dependence.

With the others, constituting the second category, the system as a whole will have to experiment with new methods with long-term aims. The initial shock of frustration may gradually give way to constructive attitudes. And in due time, it may even be recognized that what was regarded as unwelcome change may have been a prelude to developments which alone are capable of offering at least long-term solutions to what seemed to be insoluble problems.

With isolationist and protectionist sentiments fast corroding the universalist ideals of the postwar period, in the coming years part of the underdeveloped world may split into separate economic regions, each made up of associates and economic dependencies of either the European Community, the United States, Japan, or in a different context, of the Soviet Union and China. This may lead to the vertical linking together of rich metropolitan areas and some underdeveloped peripheral partners who, behind protective barriers, might attempt to build interdependent economic entities.

Within these entities, the benefits of collaboration would be shared in proportions determined by the realities of power. The requirements of private investors, and of the multinational corporations in particular, might enable the low-income countries belonging to such entities to obtain some of the palliatives the liberal prescription recommends in favor of all. There may even be more public aid, and at more favorable terms, to help pay for the servicing of private investments. Deepening collaborations would short-circuit all serious attempts at economic integration between the underdeveloped countries themselves in favor of an ever more pronounced North–South orientation of the peripheral economies. National incomes may increase at the price of a steadily growing portion of domestic resources being owned by foreigners. But economic and political privilege will remain the monopoly of the minorities devoted to the prolongation of dependence.

How rigid the political and economic frontiers between such vertical entities would be, or what degree of coordination between them could emerge, it is impossible to guess. But whether the aid and development problem will be confronted within a universal framework or within such economic spheres of influence, the two categories will still call for two different approaches. For if some countries are gradually attracted into them, there will be others that wish to break away. And they may attempt this in order to join those who had refused to be included or had been left out because they were too cumbersome or economically irrelevant.

These latter countries are already beginning to constitute the second category, which is only in its formative phase. Countries belonging to it have been experimenting with political neutrality, with the lessening of their dependence on foreign aid and investments, with nationalization and expropriation of their foreign-owned resources, or with social and cultural institutions more in conformity with their new aspirations. The corrective de-westernization implicit in most of these experiments has invariably provoked more or less violent external opposition. Successful resistance to such opposition has usually owed more to big-power rivalry than to local strength. And in most cases the isolation it has led to was much less self-imposed than it was the outcome of foreign sanctions.

The implacable arithmetics of growing numbers and diminishing shares, leading to a rising trend of political upheaval in one poor country after another, is likely to swell the number of candidates for this second category. With the arrival of the postcolonial generations on the public scene, with the inability of either communist or capitalist imported models to offer solutions, and perhaps with the lessons provided by the fate of the countries within the emerging vertical entities, the experiments are bound to spread and grow more radical. The hardships of self-reliance will remain intimidating. But more and more often autonomy will appear as the only and irresistible alternative left to attempt liberation from intolerable conditions.

It is possible that for some time to come the great powers will persist in their attempts to thwart these experiments, mainly for fear that ultimately these may tip countries into their rivals' camps. But they will be able to persist in their obstruction only so long as they can offer material advantages capable of lessening the temptation, or so long as the situation remains controllable. The thrust for change, however, will grow more and more desperate. It will reach a point where the feared dangers of the experiment will no longer be proportionate to the cost of its abortion. The United States has gone through that experience in Vietnam. Half a dozen similar attempts all over the globe might eventually convince even the superpowers not merely to let countries beyond their immediate sphere of influence go their own way, but also to cease their sanctions and interventions for fear both of the material burden and of the dangers of involvement and ultimate confrontation.

The role the great powers in such a situation would allot themselves would not go beyond mutually neutralizing abstinence. In exchange for the lessening of the dangers of direct involvement, they would forgo past privileges on condition that the others did not try to gain new ones. Depending on the evolution of relations between themselves—relations which in their turn could be greatly influenced by their attitudes in the face of the growing turbulence of the underdeveloped countries—it is then conceivable that large regions in the Southern Hemisphere might be enabled to attempt their own transformation free of interference, pressures, or imposed models.

Unprecedented as such developments would be, they would not fail to provoke the antagonism of all those not yet reconciled to the rhythm of contemporary change. Opposition would manifest itself on three main grounds: moral, political-strategic, and economic.

Invoking moral duty and forgetting all the gruesome massacres, starving crowds, and columns of refugees they have silently watched on their television screens, some people will suddenly grow loud in their condemnation of what is happening. Their humanitarian concern for those enduring the physical exertion and harsh discipline of delayed self-emancipation will barely conceal their inability to conceive of any deviation from the familiar submission and servility of the past. Others, idealists in rich countries, will speak of desertion of duty and of the abandonment of economic ghettos. They may not know how much they have underestimated what the real cost of their prescriptions would have been. They may disregard the fact that what they proposed, even at that cost, never had any chance of offering real solutions. They may even be unaware that what they consider a retreat from solidarity may seem to other idealists, in poor countries, to be liberation and advance towards hopeful new possibilities. And they may also fail to see that in place of their past efforts in the service of aid that failed to help, they may render more effective assistance by helping to prevent harm being done.

As for the political and strategic objections, they are usually based on two main assumptions: first, that only economic integration into the dominant system can offset the danger of a given country passing under hostile political influence; and second, that support for collaborating elites is the most effective way of ensuring continuity of dominance. Such assumptions govern the fates of countries from Guatemala to Czechoslovakia. But they are realistic only within agreed spheres of influence and insofar as recourse to force can be envisaged. From Iraq to Cuba and from Ceylon to Chile, results have been different. And at least in Cuba's case, neither geographical proximity nor the overspill effect sufficed to counterbalance the popular verdict.

The validity of these assumptions, however, hinges on the meaning given to their vocabulary. Suppose, for the sake of illustration, that India decided to insulate itself from unwanted influences and embarked on self-reliant policies, ending its dependence on outside forces. Suppose also that the great powers reached a tacit agreement to let India go ahead unhindered and considered it a sociopolitical no-man's-land. Developments of this nature would be the result of strong nationalist sentiments, perhaps even mixed with xenophobic passions. Under such circumstances arms purchases, import and export policies, and other external relations would be diversified in order to achieve the least possible dependence on any one great power. The first among them which attempted to upset the balance would automatically provide all the others which had respected the tacit agreement not to intervene with immense psychological and political assets. Counteraction which became necessary or which was requested would then be far more welcome than any interference before the experiment had got under way.

There is no great power today with such irresistible territorial ambitions that, after the winding up of the largest colonial enterprises in history, it would embark on conquest in distant areas. Nevertheless, the appearance of an irrational conqueror cannot be entirely ruled out. But even in that unlikely situation, the counteraction of the other powers would occur under far more auspicious circumstances than if it had been undertaken as preventive action against hypothetical dangers. Still, support for subversion or guerrilla action might be risked by one of the great powers wishing to circumvent agreement. If so, local determination to resist might acquire a dangerously popular base. Even so, the ultimate possibility would have to be faced that, with or without foreign support, a given underdeveloped country might completely change its sociopolitical personality. Almost certainly the result would be an authoritarian regime, probably exercising a high degree of control over the economy, and possibly even communist in its ideological orientation. But would the emergence of the seventh or tenth variant of communism in, let us say, India necessarily offer greater political or strategic advantages to any outside power than, for example, China is offering to the Soviet Union? And does not recent history prove that nationalism generally assimilates and outlasts passions aroused by any ideology?

But irrespective of such considerations, the political and strategic opposition to the sociopolitical neutralization of underdeveloped countries desirous of taking their destinies in their own hands is basically due to disbelief in the feasibility of reliable great-power cooperation. Evidently, this is the crux of the problem. Yet nearly all the major international crises of the postwar period have had their origin in underdeveloped countries, and fearful of being sucked into armed confrontation, the great powers have invariably managed to limit their involvement. Granted a modicum of rationality and interest in self-preservation, the procedure is unlikely to change. But hidden behind the skepticism may also be the veiled hope that the emergence of self-reliant countries in formerly easily manipulable regions can be prevented.

Centuries of history, from the Anglo-French wars to the intervention in the Soviet Union and the sanctions against China, prove the ultimate futility of such attempts. Their failure has punctuated the dispersion of modern power from the British Isles throughout the North Temperate Zone. Moreover, outside the vertical entities to be constituted, the underdeveloped countries which sought voluntary quarantine would not all do so at the same time.

It would be a gradual process, with the emergence of successive sociopolitical no-man's-lands. Each would provide the great powers with opportunities to experiment and to perfect their methods and appropriate mechanisms of noninterference. It is only over a long period of time that the individual cases might begin to shape a generalized system, one susceptible of modifying the very nature of North-South relations.

The political and strategic objections, however, are not dissociable from the economic ones. For even in the near-ideal situation of a lasting stalemate within the North Temperate Zone, economic rivalry in the Southern Hemisphere would not end.

The underdeveloped countries combined account for less than one-fifth of world exports. The major oil-exporters' share of this is nearly a third. Some of the most important of them are geographically near either to Europe or to the United States. Like the others, under whatever regime they choose to live, they will have to sell their oil, and the question is merely at what price. Camels do not drink petroleum. The Soviet Union has exportable surpluses. Even if China's needs surpassed its domestic production, it might not have the means for some time to import really large quantities. And in the meantime new deposits are being discovered, and some of them in the Northern Hemisphere.

The remaining two-thirds of the underdeveloped countries' exports are made up mainly of raw materials and of primary commodities. Here again, whatever their political orientation, they will have to export, and the more so if they wish to accelerate their economic progress. There may be some diversion from export crops to food production for home needs. Japan, the Soviet Union, and China may increase their purchases of some essential commodities, such as copper or rubber, which are still important to Western economies. There may also be larger sales of tropical products to non-Western markets. All this may lead to some price increases but not to real shortages, and in any case, synthetics and substitute materials could take care of the problem.

As for sales by the West and Japan to the underdeveloped countries, they amount to roughly $50 billion. Machinery, transport equipment, and chemicals make up over half, consumer goods about a quarter, and food, beverages, and tobacco nearly one-eighth. All these exports, however, amount to barely 2 percent of the non-Communist industrial countries' gross national product. Even their total cessation would be no serious blow, though specific industries specializing in supplying the poor countries' needs might suffer. Of course, nothing of the kind is likely to happen. In fact, even radical political transformation in a few poor countries leading to a faster tempo of industrialization would change merely the composition of exports. In place of imports to satisfy luxury needs, the foreign exchange earned could pay for more machinery, chemicals, and equipment goods. The Soviet Union and eventually China might be able to supply a growing share. But for a very long time the West and Japan would remain by far their major sources.

Foreign investments in general and the activities of the multinational corporations in particular might be more directly affected.

According to one estimate, the direct-investment stake of the Western industrial powers in the underdeveloped countries (by the end of 1966) amounted to about $30 billion.[11] This represented nearly a third of their total investments overseas. Since 1966 it may have grown to about $40 billion, remaining still about a third of the total. United States investments form nearly half. About a third originate in France and Great Britain. The rest come mainly from Germany, Japan, Italy, Holland, and, to a lesser extent, Canada, Sweden, and Switzerland. The direction of the main flows has been from the United States to Latin America, from France to the franc area overseas, and from Great Britain to the low-income Commonwealth countries.

Virtually half the cumulative total is in petroleum (nearly 40 percent), mineral exploitation, and smelting. Only a little over a quarter went into manufacturing. The building of industries attracted private investors only to the underdeveloped countries with relatively high levels of income. These were primarily in Latin America, where Argentina, Brazil, and Mexico had the lion's share. In East and South Asia only a few countries qualified, and industrialization in most of the rest of Asia, in Africa, and in the Middle East could scarcely rely on foreign private investments.

Radical political and economic changes in underdeveloped host countries would no doubt seriously affect such investments. In this context, then, Latin America, the Middle East, and some East African metal-producing countries are the sensitive areas. Confiscating nationalization, however, has hitherto been a relatively rare occurrence.

Yet with General Motors the tenth largest nation in the non-Communist world as measured by revenues or gross national product, with about two hundred corporations controlling two-thirds of all manufacturing assets in the United States, with about one-third of all world exports believed to be sales within multinational corporations, and with even important industrial powers declaring themselves helpless to control the activities of these transnational giants, it would be surprising indeed if an underdeveloped country that was really determined to regain control over its economic and political destiny did not find itself in conflict with foreign private enterprises operating inside its borders.

Within the vertical economic entities now emerging, the irritants and the claims may for some time be counterbalanced by other advantages inherent in association. But with the underdeveloped countries embarking on the transformation of their economies with a view to lessening their dependence, the conflict is bound to deepen. This is particularly likely in relatively advanced low-income countries where the beneficial role of foreign investments is already being questioned. These are the countries where foreign private enterprise is stifling available entrepreneurial talent, where it is strangling already existing but still vulnerable local enterprises, and where its superior productive, financial, and marketing resources represent a monopolistic lock on major sectors of the economy. In all such situations the problem will be, and is already, to evolve orderly equivalents to the more revolutionary methods of transfer to local ownership. Perhaps regulated buy-out and sell-out options may gradually be devised, and discussion about the feasibility of international "divestment companies" is already acquiring at least academic respectability.[12]

In their activities the multinational corporations respond to business imperatives. Their motivations for going into underdeveloped areas are diverse. Extractive industry goes because that is where resources lie or because that is where they can be extracted most cheaply. Other corporations go to the underdeveloped countries for quick profits. Many more, however, are interested in establishing a foothold to be there before their rivals. The demographic mirage, too, plays its role. Convinced that the prosperity of the privileged minorities, the present customers for their products, is bound to spread, they are lured by the prospect of tens if not hundreds of millions of future customers. Their obsessive preoccupation with security and stability, however, turns them into powerful underwriters of the political and social status quo. And the resulting vicious circle denies them the much-desired price, the spread of purchasing power and the ever-growing market.

Meanwhile tensions will grow more acute, and when the contradictions finally collide and explode, the time for rethinking will have arrived. The multinational corporations will not be able to prolong their present role in the countries which succeed in breaking away from the system. There will be losses and bitter feelings. Yet later on, the multinational corporation may return into a changed setting, in a different role, and so, in a broader perspective, reactions need not be disproportionate. In a typical recent year (1968), the Western industrial powers' *total* private investments in *all* the underdeveloped countries amounted to only $2.8 billion. In comparison, the private investments of United States industry in France *alone* (in 1965) reached $2.5 billion.[13] And as a matter of fact, the cumulative total of the combined private investments of all Western industrial powers in all the underdeveloped countries is not much higher than the yearly cost of America's war in Vietnam.

The damage that nationalization or expropriation might inflict in a few radically changing underdeveloped countries would be insignificant in comparison with what preventive action, with its political and military implications, would cost. Nor should policies of such a nature be thought of as the irrevocable end of possible and mutually profitable cooperation.

Notwithstanding hunger and mass unemployment from India to the Nordeste of Brazil, the pathological spread of giant slums around skyscrapers from Caracas to Manila, or the fact that one country after another is being bailed out of bankruptcy caused by unbearable debt burdens, no doubt waves of chamber-of-commerce lyricism will mount to proclaim that free enterprise could have done it quicker and better. Structural changes and growing public control of underdeveloped economies will continue to be derided, overlooking the fact that a far larger proportion of the gross national product is controlled and disposed of by the state in "free enterprise" America than, for example, in "socialist" India. Or that the market economies of some Western European industrial powers have far larger public sectors than have, or are likely to have, even those underdeveloped countries which will turn to a socialist organization of their economies.[14]

Fortunately, however, the multinational corporations may be capable of responding to the inevitable. More or less successfully, private investors all over the world are trying to adapt to substantial institutional changes. Faced with astute or well-advised negotiating partners, they will have to experiment with a variety of methods to replace outdated relationships. These may involve the reinvestment of profits, built-in export obligations, or joint ventures. They may lead to coproduction arrangements through which capital, equipment, technology, and skills may be transferred, with repayment in kind and on a long-term basis. The financial and institutional problems of orderly collaboration, of transfer to local management and eventually to ownership after a specified period, are not insoluble. There will be a need, too, for research to make Western technology applicable to local conditions and to develop labor-intensive production methods. Much will have to be done also to make the multinational corporation an agent of meaningful regional economic integration in underdeveloped regions. And with the new approaches might also come suitable training arrangements and, it is to be hoped, even changing assumptions about social and political stability being a precondition for development.

In this connection it may be worth recalling that in its insular solitude, almost completely sealed off from the rest of the world, even Japan relied on some foreign experts, loans, and equipment. Later, during the Soviet Union's rigidly isolationist period of early industrialization, much of the transfer of technology occurred in collaboration with Western industrial powers. The main vehicles utilized were either the employment of Western specialists or what were known as "concessions," that is, reliance on Western entrepreneurship and capital. Either foreign firms were granted the right to develop and exploit a given project without acquiring property rights, or mixed corporations were created with 50 or 51 percent Soviet participation. Western consulting engineers, entrepreneurs, or technical directors were not rare in the Soviet economy at the time. Gradually, however, emphasis shifted to the importation of complete plants and equipment, to technical-assistance contracts, or to purchase of patents, plans, and designs. Indeed, according to an estimate, in one form or another over 90 percent of the early Soviet industrial structure obtained technical assistance from abroad.[15] At present, with varying emphasis on the different elements, China, too, has recourse to similar methods. And it would be difficult to deny that after their isolation from the dominant system, Japan, the Soviet Union, and China have emerged as more important economic partners than they were before their radical structural transformation.

The story need not be very different with the underdeveloped countries, which may come to the conclusion that imported ideas cannot galvanize their energies, that change must come from within their societies in accordance with their own experiences and needs.

During the coming years the energies of the industrial powers of the North Temperate Zone will be fully absorbed both in the organization of their nuclear coexistence and in the complex problems arising from their own technological revolutions. They will hardly be able to spare the volume of material aid or the political interest involved in any serious confrontation of the problems of even those underdeveloped countries which continue to rely on them. They ought to welcome the constructive disengagement of those to whom they can offer no real solutions. Indeed, they might follow with sympathy the efforts of countries condemned to major upheavals as they turn to the satisfaction of their needs mainly by their own means and attempt to spread the benefits more evenly than in the past, as they attempt to involve hitherto passive masses in their endeavor to lift themselves from indigence to at least a modest level of decent material existence and from humiliating dependence to the rebuilding of a self-assurance which is the precondition of their return to international partnership in a more equitable plural world.

How, where, and when such developments will gather momentum is impossible to foretell. But they are becoming inevitable. They will offer no infallible keys to success, nor will they lead to quick solutions. How harsh the forced marches undertaken will have to be may depend on how far they are left unobstructed or how long they remain unaided. For large segments of humanity this may be the only way left to defuse forces of despair seeking outlets in destructive violence. It may even prove to be the only process able to provide the hope and the self-respect which alone may divert dangerously mounting racial passions into constructive channels. And feeling the shock-waves caused by enormous exertions, the rich world may even be moved to a new dimension of tolerance: to the compassion of disinterested solidarity capable of being helpful without trying to deflect people from their chosen paths.

At best, it would be a long and difficult enterprise. It would involve much suffering. But at least it would be endured with a clear purpose. And existing international organizations, the United Nations in particular, might have an important role to play. Rules, norms, and methods would have to be devised, made acceptable, and acted upon. In the place of unattainable global aims, they would be in the service of more modest but perhaps more realistic ideals.

And the attempt will have to be made. For failing this, there will be nothing left to do but try to humanize the process of economic re-colonization that will have become unavoidable.

Concluding Remarks

THE VIOLENT global disequilibrium that lasted for over two centuries has given place to a virtual world directorate of five power centers across the North Temperate Zone. Power has been dispersed from its Western stronghold. Direct colonial rule is practically gone. But the members of the directorate, though uneasily neutralizing each other, remain rivals. Perhaps they compete most dangerously when, under the pretext of exporting their utopias, they try to recruit clients or to gain other advantages in the underdeveloped Southern Hemisphere. The old disequilibrium between the West and the rest of the world, then, has been replaced by an equally untenable new one between the industrial powers of the North and the preindustrial masses seething below their opulence, in the South.

When decolonization revealed the gravity of the disequilibrium, people asked how to put an end to it. Today, twenty-five years later, the question has changed. By now it is not so much how to solve the problem as how to live with it.

It may be too early to assess the relative importance of the various developments which have brought about this change. Nevertheless, two among them stand out with stark clarity. They even seem to ensure that the

North-South problem will become the dangerous leitmotif of the remaining quarter of this century. One of them comprises the complex ramifications of what is generally referred to as the demographic explosion. The other is connected with the beginnings of really cosmopolitan production, and in particular, with the role of the multinational corporations in this new phase.

The merely quantitative aspects of the population problem have received abundant publicity. Following centuries of near stagnation, from about 1650 onward world population doubled in two centuries, reaching 1 billion by about 1850. It had doubled again by 1930, after eighty years. The next doubling, from 2 to 4 billion, will have been accomplished in only forty-five years. And beyond 1975, the rise from 4 to 8 billion will probably require less than thirty-five years. Children now in primary school may very well reach retirement age in a world with over 12 billion people. Indeed, in the totally improbable case of present growth rates continuing unchecked, by 2200 the grandchildren of our grandchildren may be condemned to live in a world where 500 billion people will give the surface of all continents a population density equal to that of the biggest cities today.

What is practically certain is the doubling of the world's population by the end of this century. And behind that figure are related problems which cluster around three main themes: food, environment, and equality.

The extent of malnutrition today is subject to debate. Statistics are often unreliable. Essential requirements may have been overestimated. With only 11 percent of total land area under cultivation, there are still huge potentially fertile regions in reserve. It may even be true that the world nutritional situation has not been getting worse during the past two decades. That situation means, however, that the great majority of contemporary mankind is made up of peasants producing merely enough to keep their families alive and with only a rainfall or two separating them from famine. Sometimes because of ignorance, but much more often because of shortages, hundreds of millions live on a diet insufficient to sustain normal health. Caloric, protein, and vitamin deficiencies are widespread. With or without natural or man-made disasters, countless millions go permanently hungry. And tens of millions of children suffer from a lack of essential foodstuffs which, medical science has revealed, impairs their mental development for the rest of their lives.

Some observers believe that the situation is overdramatized. The surplus areas of the world can export a yearly 40 to 70 million tons of grain whenever necessary. High-yielding seeds, fertilizers, and modern agricultural techniques could bring self-sufficiency to even the most deficient areas. Moreover, proteins obtained from petrochemicals, photosynthesis, and new techniques of recycling and production of synthetic foods connected with space exploration open up limitless possibilities. The world, we are told, might feed several times its present population.

This may be so, under certain circumstances, of course. To begin with, hunger and poverty are inextricably linked. So long as potential consumers live in abject poverty, there will be no incentive to make the effort and to take the risks to produce beyond immediate needs. Markets are lacking both at home and abroad. The social and political preconditions of the new production techniques are not being fulfilled. The scientific knowledge and means, as much as the available surpluses, are in the hands of the industrial powers. The solution, insofar as there is one within certain demographic limits, remains in the domain of the rich countries' charity, commerce, or politics. At this point, however, quantity gets mixed up with quality.

In the underdeveloped world as a whole, a little less than 400 pounds of grain a year is available for each person. At that level nearly all has to be consumed merely to meet essential energy requirements, and little if anything is left to convert into animal protein. In contrast, the average North American or West European requires nearly a ton of grain each year to maintain his dietary levels. Of that he consumes less than a tenth directly. Most of the rest is consumed indirectly in the form of all those foodstuffs—meat, milk, and eggs—which guarantee his good health, his mental development, and quite often, his overweight. This proportion of one to five is not likely to change quickly or even in the foreseeable future, and on a global scale, it will prolong the dilemma already defined by Plato and Aristotle: between preoccupation with the quality of man voiced in *The Republic*, and the fear expressed in *Politics* that excessive population "is a never-failing source of poverty, which is in turn the parent of revolution and crime."

But beyond the arithmetics of food, uncontrolled population growth also has other implications of comparable gravity.

The yearly gross product of the 1 billion people in the industrially advanced countries is about $2 trillion, increasing by no less than $100 million each year. In contrast, the combined gross product of the 2.5 billion population of the underdeveloped regions is only about $700 billion. Its distribution is grossly unequal and, in absolute terms, grows much more slowly than the income of the rich countries. Two-thirds of the population producing the $700 billion is tied up in primitive agriculture, while the same proportion in the rich countries is only around 10 percent.

Simultaneously, accounting for only 6 percent of the earth's population living on 7 percent of its land area, the United States controls close to 40 percent of the world's productive resources, consumes one-third of its energy production and one-third of its steel. With living standards in Western Europe and Japan approaching those in the United States and with a larger population total, much that remains of natural resources and of energy passes under their control. Yet if the current total world production of energy were distributed on the basis of American standards, it would barely cover the needs of 650 million people. At American levels again, the total world supply of fertilizers would be adequate for a population of only 900 million. And the production capacity of the total industrial complex in the world today could cover, by American standards, the needs of 1 billion people, or barely more than a quarter of mankind.

Industrialization and technological progress theoretically could no doubt take care of the problem. But in order to raise the level of consumption of all mankind to *present* American standards, the removal of natural resources from the irreplaceable deposits in the earth would have to be increased several times over its present level. If the possession of automobiles, for example, became as widespread as it is in France today (twice less per capita than in the United States), it would mean 4 million cars in the Congo (Kinshasa), 130 million in India, and nearly 200 million in China. Add refrigerators, washing machines, television sets, schools, universities, hospitals, and private swimming pools, and project the steel and timber, the petroleum and other energetic resources, or the educational requirements they imply, and the argument that we could run short of metals and lack energy, clean streams, and fresh air before we ran out of food will become plausible. The population problem due to riches is becoming no less a problem than that due to poverty. And in the meantime the population of the industrially advanced countries grows by about 1 percent while that of the rest of the world grows by nearly 3 percent. Moreover, in the rich countries a yearly increase in consumption of 3 to 5 percent—that is, a doubling every fifteen to twenty years—is now taken for granted, while an improvement of 2 to 4 percent is aimed at in the rest of the world.

To come anywhere near the satisfaction of such needs while progress is also being made in narrowing the material gap between poor and rich regions of the world appears quantitatively unrealizable. And in any case, it would involve environmental problems of unforeseeable dimensions.

It is estimated that every day the United States produces 800 million pounds of rubbish, a fair proportion of which goes to befoul the landscape—48 billion rustproof cans and 26 billion nonbiodegradable bottles are discarded each year. Nine million cars, trucks, and buses are abandoned annually, a large proportion of them being left to disintegrate in the countryside. Of the billions of pounds of paper used every year, only one third is reclaimed. And the yearly 8 billion pounds of plastics used are made of nonbiodegradable materials. That is in the United States alone. Western Europe and Japan, not to speak of the other industrial powers, are catching up fast both as waste-makers and as inventors of new needs. And in this respect a fast-rising poor population inflicts less harm than a slowly rising rich one on the ecology of the earth, on its rivers, its woods, its animal life, and its biosphere.

True, the environmental problem is receiving growing attention. Yet it is practically impossible to reach quantitative estimates of the level at which the catastrophic plundering of the biosphere, the destruction of natural environment, the pollution of air, water, and soil, or the decay of cities and human beings—in other words, the upsetting of the world's ecological equilibrium—would begin to provoke irreversible changes in both social habits and the quality of the individual. It may be at the 8, 10, or 12 billion mark; no one knows for certain. But clearly, at some point the rate at which natural resources are used up must be drastically cut. Should technological solutions to these problems ever appear, they will develop but slowly and will inevitably serve primarily the interests of their inventors, the industrially advanced countries. Meanwhile, given the finite nature of the world's resources and the limited powers of the human organism to adapt to ecological mutation, the maniacal acceleration of consumption will carry in itself the destructive tensions of inequality, rivalry, and conflict.

Such considerations, all traceable to uncontrolled population growth, throw up a series of questions. These are either unanswerable or they cast long shadows of grave probabilities directly relevant to the future of North-South relations.

The first series of questions has food as its starting point. Will national and international policies be adjusted so as to give appropriate priority to the material and social preconditions of higher output on the land in the underdeveloped countries? Alternatively, will most of the subsistence farmers be bypassed by large-scale, industrialized farming? If so, with an estimated 225 million newcomers on the labor market in the next ten years in the low-income countries, will all those who have become redundant in the countryside continue to swell the army of unemployed in the mushrooming cities of the poor world? In that case, will the industrially advanced powers keep on covering the food deficit of the overcrowded rural and urban areas? And if they have to assume that role permanently, what will be the material and political cost, and what will be the long-term effect on the world balance of forces? Finally, should this be the likely trend, what political or ideological arguments will be invoked to justify the division of mankind into an affluent and well-fed minority and a needy and ill-nourished majority condemned to a physically and mentally inferior status?

The other sequence of questions centers around resources other than food. As natural resources grow scarce, what kind of criteria will be invoked to determine who may or may not continue to raise their levels of consumption? More generally, and force apart, what principle will preside over the distribution of material possibilities in the world? When the dangers of ecological disequilibrium have become menacing, will the rich minority apply self-discipline, or will the poorer majority's hopes of higher consumption rather be barred? And once it becomes clear that population growth and industrialization are approaching the limits of the earth's capacity to support them, who will be the arbiter, and in the name of what political or moral principles, to determine by whom either industrialization or procreation will have to be stepped down?

While the world is seeking answers, the demand for equality is likely to spread. Intergovernmental organizations still project the future—and build their strategy on irreconcilable quantitative prescriptions—on the assumption that the gap can be narrowed. They raise such hopes without spelling out how population growth could actually be slowed down, without even hinting at the possibility that in the already affluent societies further growth of consumption may have to be brought to a halt, yet firmly maintaining that the desirable leveling of material opportunities should be in an upward direction. And should it become clear at a given point that leveling is feasible only downward, they offer no devices to be relied upon to contain the inevitable confrontation.

At present, then, there is no solution in sight to the equation involving these frightening combinations of material, political, cultural, and moral elements. A mere hint of a possible answer, however, may be discernible in developments in the field of multinational production. It is not reassuring. Yet, paradoxically, it is connected with what ought to be the next stage in material well-being: with progress towards the transnational rationalization of the division of labor and the emergence of truly cosmopolitan production techniques.

Given the existing imbalance between North and South and the limiting power of the national state as a frame of reference, the international corporations are today in the vanguard of forces shaping a future less controlled by the constraints of national sovereignties. Their interests and means, and therefore their perspectives, are supranational—that is, proportionate to contemporary possibilities. Since the Second World War they have been organizing production and consumption above and across national boundaries. What is still in doubt is whether their immense power and dynamism will further egalitarian interdependence on a transnational scale or whether it will rather ally the interests of Northern and Southern elites in a new global hierarchy of power.

For the time being, few underdeveloped countries seem ready to reshape their priorities in order to satisfy the most urgent mass needs. They continue to favor the building up or expansion of the so-called modern sector, professing to believe that in the long run at least, this will raise the standard of living of the bottom two-thirds as well. Even so, given the grossly uneven distribution of incomes, this modern sector alone provides a sizable market for the satisfaction of the needs of the minority whose consumption habits are modeled on those prevailing in the rich countries. Average-income statistics tend to disguise their real importance. Although India's nearly 550 million people are very poor in the majority, the number of westernized modern consumers may constitute a market comparable in importance to, let us say, that of Spain. Or among almost 95 million Brazilians, those who can afford to buy luxury cars, air-conditioners, tranquilizers, and tape recorders may perhaps be as numerous as those in Austria. These are the markets, real or potential, that the large international firms are after. By arranging to precede their rivals, undoubtedly they bring capital, technology, and organizational ability that the host countries badly need. The supplying of local components and the provision of supporting services may go some way towards spreading purchasing power. Within certain limits, then, the market may even grow. The real question, however, is whether such policies will enhance the chances of more equal distribution or will rather fortify and perpetuate the present uneven trend, spreading and deepening underdevelopment as a price of economic growth.

Naturally, a variety of imponderables are involved. The underdeveloped countries might attempt to create their own regional, multinational production units as a countervailing force. They might try to unite on joint negotiating platforms in order to force concessions or to impose conditions. Or, by infiltrating their personnel into key posts and by acquiring the necessary technical and organizational competence, they might endeavor to tame the manners of the alien giants and to domesticate their aims. In all this, international organizations might one day be able to help them. But possible as such developments may be, in practice they are far from likely. Those in power in the underdeveloped countries, who might pressure the international corporations to adapt their policies and research to the satisfaction of mass needs, usually have no interest in doing so. Their outlook and their personal preferences are nearer to the foreigners' conceptions than to indigenous aspirations.

It is much more likely that the combined weight of Western and Japanese corporations will succeed in shaping a world-wide hierarchical division of labor. High-level decision-making, concentrated in the industrialized countries, will direct regional echelons in the Southern Hemisphere. Structural decisions, consumption patterns, and even the nature of the end products will continue to come predetermined down the organizational pyramid. Almost automatically, they will help perpetuate dependence and with it the prevailing pattern of inequality. Though this may be a simplified image, it is recognizable in what is unfolding.

The more powerful the new transnational productive apparatus becomes, however, the greater will be the tensions its weight will generate. The dominant international economic and trading system will continue to guarantee its markets. What advantages structural change might offer will remain a distant and uncertain promise. Thus stability will continue to be the supreme aim, and no effort will be spared to maintain it. Yet to do so, some essential prerequisites will have to be met. The food and housing problem must not get out of hand. To pay for indispensable imports and to permit the repatriation of profits, either more public aid or new export opportunities will have to be provided. Even education may have to expand, at least to the extent necessary to man the posts created by industrial and urban growth. Above all, the two-thirds of the population excluded from the emerging structure will have to be kept under control.

This indeed may pose the most difficult problem. A rigid managerial hierarchy composed of a small multinational elite and of its indigenous collaborators facing the great mass of the disqualified is not a reassuring prospect. The decisions they make are bound to affect the daily existence and the future of masses of people. Yet hundreds of millions in the world's underdeveloped regions are already either unemployed, underemployed, or living by dispensable occupations. For the coming two or three decades at least, their numbers will swell. The urban unemployed will multiply and grow more desperate. All these multitudes will have to be cut off from agitators, local or foreign, and prevented from gaining social consciousness. Or if they have reached that stage already, they will have to be politically defused. Birth control is too slow. Mere anti-insurgency technology may not be enough. In view of contemporary progress in sophisticated scientific savagery, one day drugs may come to be considered a more effective means of keeping the masses submissive and docile.

Excessively gloomy forecasts? Maybe. But what is happening already should not be overlooked. Indeed, during the decade that began with the liquidation of colonialism on earth and ended with its beginnings on the moon, no development has been more disquieting than the staggering acceleration of the process whereby mankind got used to organized cruelty on an unprecedented scale. Auschwitz and Hiroshima happened, but they were not televised. Horrors of similar magnitude are now regularly projected in our homes while we quietly take our meals. The almost continuous slaughter of millions of people all over the Southern Hemisphere or ingeniously organized torture hardly produces significant reactions any longer. The neutralization of moral indignation has become a professional skill. Random indifferent technological bestiality and the unprincipled destruction of anything human have numbed sensibilities to a point where degrees of tyranny or degradation are no longer appreciated. With racialist and xenophobic pseudotheories providing anesthetics, the ground seems well prepared for the acceptance of the sufferings of the "underdeveloped" with a moral discrimination which implies that even meriting compassion or indignation indicates inferior status. Uncannily, the whole process begins to resemble the subconscious forging of moral and mental shields in expectation of even greater horrors vaguely felt to be inevitable.

The blind consistency of the trend is unmistakable. But it is not yet irreversible. Fortunately, a variety of scattered symptoms are discernible which mitigate despair.

In both the rich and the poor countries self-confident new social forces are seeking outlets. All over the underdeveloped world, an acute sense of failure and mismanagement is turning into revolt against the diversion of energies from urgent constructive tasks to artificial problems and futile political maneuverings. Countless rural teachers, social workers, priests, and men-at-arms work with devotion and often at the risk of their lives to help awaken the political consciousness and the dignity of people who were forced to part with it long ago. Educated men in exile or in prisons wait for the day when they may be useful again. In the meantime, in the rich countries, people in revolt against mechanical commercialism and against money as the sole measure of man begin to challenge the quality of life in their societies, grow aware of the price their comfort exacts in other parts of the world, and seek liberating change for both sides. Even among leaders of the industrial world, doubts are beginning to arise as to whether profits and higher consumption alone are aims worthy of the means they command and whether there are no ways to harmonize efficiency and productivity with more positive social and international purposes.

Above all, there is the world-wide, confused, but immensely promising refusal of the young to fit into a world that treats them as commodities. In North and South and in East and West, the new generations are in revolt against styles of living shaped by tradition or by monumental impersonal organizations. They want to fill in the emptiness that is left when old doctrines have been found wanting. The young of the industrially advanced world may be distressingly vague when it comes to defining, not what they are against, but what they favor. Their critique usually ignores the sterile sequels of revolutions. Yet what they dislike is not likable, and the love, solidarity, and human warmth they seek are not there. And their strictures are likely to become the familiar views of the future. In place of the hard materialist and acquisitive world of today, they want one that is humane, that appreciates idealism and beauty, that provides fraternity with meaning. And in their unshaven, barefoot, and rugged extravagance, perhaps unconsciously they may be finding their way towards that *selective affluence* which, after all, might be the indispensable prelude to the voluntary leveling which could lead to the solution of what seemed insoluble.

Although within vastly different settings, these new strivings and energies in both rich and poor worlds have parallel aims in the elimination of deprivation and humiliation. They train for the same struggle. They both dream of turning the machine to human ends. Each desires hope more than comfort. And if by any chance they make real progress in the coming years, combined they might change again the question asked about North-South relations: instead of being merely how to live with the problem, it may become once again how to solve it.

And should they achieve that much, then it might be possible to provide answers with more experience, with fewer illusions and less hypocrisy, and with much greater realism than ever before.

APPENDIX 1

How the Communists Do It

If an overabundance of data makes it difficult to estimate the real worth of Western aid to low-income countries, the opposite is true for Communist donors. Reliable statistics are rare, the distinction between commitments and actual disbursements is vague, and there is semantic ambiguity particularly when it comes to separating aid from trade.

Soviet thinking on underdevelopment has also suffered from oversimplification which, in the long run, could not stand up to confrontation with reality. The Soviet Union's aid program began about fifteen years ago, with only a small, heavily doctrinal literature to rely on and with very limited direct experience of tropical and subtropical regions. The economic backwardness of the newly independent countries was readily ascribed to colonialism. The revelance of tradition and of psychological or cultural factors was admitted only gradually. Thus thinking on development started out from somewhat simple premises, which dictated three essential prerequisites: *(a)* rapid domestic capital accumulation (to sustain heavy, planned investments), *(b)* limitation of trade with capitalist powers (because it is exploitative and prolongs dependence), and *(c)* emphasis on the building of a heavy industrial base (machine-building and the manufacture of means of production, because it is the only firm foundation of economic independence). These prescriptions were complemented by the additional advice to underdeveloped countries to nationalize foreign property, stimulate the expansion of the public sector, and collectivize their agriculture—all within the framework of centralized planning.

Such views, however, recommending the adoption of basically the 1917 model of a communist economy gradually acquired more subtlety and realism. Practical experience and unavoidable difficulties forced rethinking of both ideology and methods. As an intermediary stage, the "national democratic" state became acceptable. In these states, "the national bourgeoisie" was to introduce "noncapitalist changes" and thus provide a shortcut to socialism without revolution. Simultaneously, the idea of a "socialist division of labor" made its appearance, timidly opening the door to notions of comparative advantage and of specialization on the most competitive products. With the erosion of unconditional faith in the primacy of the heavy industrial base, and once the need for economic interdependence had been admitted, what remained to be demonstrated was the basic identity of interests of the former colonial countries and the Communist states. But the discrimination by the capitalist world market against colonial types of vulnerable economies, and its power to impose deteriorating terms of trade, meant that Communist countries could really help create new economic activities capable of modifying the interited colonial structure. Trade being more important than aid, the provision of an alternative outlet for the underdeveloped countries' trade was in itself often the most effective form of international cooperation. Thus trade on "mutually advantageous terms" would serve the interests of both sides. And it is at this point that aid and trade become undistinguishably intertwined and foreign trade often seems to be equated with aid.

Thus it is practically impossible to dissociate the Communist countries' aid effort from their over-all trade relations with the underdeveloped countries. Since 1955 there has indeed been a very rapid expansion of trade between them: its volume almost doubled between 1955 and 1960, and nearly doubled again during the next five years. From a few hundred million dollars in 1955, the exports of the Soviet Union and of the Eastern European Communist countries to the underdeveloped states have grown to nearly $5 billion, while their imports from the underdeveloped countries have risen to about $3.5 billion. This, of course, amounts to barely more than 6 percent of the underdeveloped countries' total exports, and to only about 12 percent of the combined imports of the Soviet Union and Eastern Europe. Nevertheless, for the past fifteen years it has represented by far the most dynamic growth sector in the low-income countries' external trade and, indeed, in world trade in general.

The impressive percentual growth of these exchanges is explained mainly by the very low level from which they started out. Before the war the Soviet Union's direct trade with colonial areas was very limited. But decolonization completely changed prevailing trade patterns. The newly independent countries were understandably anxious to diversify their foreign trade independent of ideological considerations. Thus direct trade between the Communist countries and the newly independent states grew very rapidly. Moreover, rising incomes in the Communist countries provided expanding markets for certain articles, particularly tropical food products like coffee, cocoa, or oranges, which had previously been considered inadmissible luxuries. Last but not least, the underdeveloped countries' need for machinery and equipment goods rose rapidly, and it is in this field in particular that the Communist countries have secured for themselves a steadily growing share.

But whatever the reasons, the rapid growth of trade has been associated also with expansion of development credits to the underdeveloped countries. The bulk of Soviet aid probably still goes to other Communist countries—such as Cuba, Mongolia, North Vietnam, and North Korea—which, in terms of average income, still belong to the underdeveloped category. For various reasons, however, such aid is not included in official aid figures. As for the importance of the Communist countries' aid to non-Communist underdeveloped states, it is still subject to interpretation.

Indeed, neither the Soviet Union nor the other Communist countries have ever published over-all official statistics about their aid effort. Estimates issued by Soviet academic institutions, on the other hand, present lower figures than the ones reached by either the United Nations or the analysts of the United States Department of State. According to these American estimates, economic aid from the Communist countries to the underdeveloped ones between 1954 and 1968 amounted to nearly $10 billion. This included $949 million from China. The share of the Soviet Union alone accounted for $6,296 million. To this $10 billion of aid could be added—still on the basis of the American estimates—military supplies of about $5.5 billion between 1955 and 1967. This gives a total of some $15.5 billion over thirteen years; a sizable sum, though only a small fraction of what the DAC countries have provided, however their aid figures are interpreted.

If assistance given by the Communist countries to the underdeveloped among them is added, these aid figures are almost doubled. According to estimates by the OECD Secretariat, between 1947 and 1968 the Soviet Union and the Eastern European Communist countries provided assistance to Mongolia, North Vietnam, North

Korea, and Cuba amounting to approximately $6.2 billion—to which about $2 billion of Soviet aid to China ought to be added.

On the basis of all these figures, the flow of development assistance from the Communist to the underdeveloped countries is estimated at roughly 0.3 percent of the joint gross national product of the Soviet Union, the Eastern European Communist countries, and China (including the nearly $1.5 billion of aid that it provided to Cuba, North Vietnam, and North Korea). The Communist countries' aid to non-Communist underdeveloped countries alone, however, would amount to only 0.1 percent of the GNP since its beginning in 1954.

As a matter of fact, the Communist countries—unlike the members of the OECD—have so far refused to accept even the moral obligation to devote 1 percent of their GNP to development assistance, the official Soviet argument being that underdevelopment is a consequence of colonialism; it does not consider itself responsible for this and therefore refuses to accept quantitative obligations.

But returning to the Soviet Union's aid to non-Communist underdeveloped countries, inaccuracy of statistics apart, the curious discrepancy between Soviet and foreign estimates may have a variety of causes. To begin with, Communist aid is heavily "project-oriented" and the shortage of local skills and specialists often causes considerable delays in the execution of aid projects. Secondly, the United States estimates are probably based on figures supplied by the receiving countries, and these may have their own good reasons to inflate rather than to minimize them. Thirdly, invisible services (such as shipping and insurance) are probably not included in the Soviet estimates. Finally, it is quite possible that the Communist countries are reluctant to reveal the relative modesty of their aid effort, or alternatively, that they may fear that even a yearly $300 to $400 million worth of largess on their part may seem inadmissible to their own public, often short of even essential commodities. But whatever the reasons, there has been intentional confusion between aid commitments, usually fully publicized, and actual disbursements, rarely if ever announced.

It is interesting to note that during the last ten years the Communist countries of Eastern Europe have been shouldering a fast-growing share of the over-all aid effort of the Communist camp. If between 1954 and 1963 Soviet commitments were three times higher than those of Eastern Europe, between 1964 and 1968 the latter accounted for over half the total. Indeed, in 1968, for the first time, the commitments by the Eastern Europeans combined surpassed those made by the Soviet Union, with Czechoslovakia and Poland as the principal donors.

About two-thirds of all Soviet aid has been concentrated on industrial projects and infrastructure and nearly a tenth on transport and communications; geological prospecting, consumer goods and food industries, and cultural, scientific, and health facilities have accounted for most of the rest. As for conditions, grants account for only a very small share (schools, hospitals, and training facilities mainly). Most of Soviet and Eastern European aid is made up of development credits, the major part of it by the state, about a tenth by commercial export organizations, and the remaining tenth to pay for technical assistance. The standard formula is 2.5 to 3 percent interest, and amortization over a period of eight to twelve years with repayment usually beginning the year after the final delivery of equipment. Commercial credits carry a somewhat higher interest rate (3 to 5 percent), are repayable in three to ten years, and a down payment of up to 20 percent has not been unusual in more recent commitments. All Communist aid is fully tied to procurement and other services in the donor country, though some triangular arrangements within the Communist camp have been known. Repayments are made either in goods or in local money, but prolonged clearing imbalances may occasionally be settled in convertible currencies. Technical assistance too is supplied on credit, though salaries are far lower than those of Western specialists. The Communist countries participate only modestly in multilateral aid, contributing less than 3 percent to the United Nations Development Program's funds, and to some of the United Nations' specialized agencies. However, the Communist countries do operate their own "multilateral" schemes, insofar as several of them may offer credits and help in the execution of the same project.

Though Soviet economic assistance is extended to over forty countries and military aid to about twenty, the bulk of it is concentrated on a handful of selected recipients. In 1954–1967, India, the United Arab Republic and (pre-Suharto) Indonesia alone absorbed nearly half of Soviet aid and nearly two-thirds of military assistance. India and the United Arab Republic between them have taken 43 percent of Soviet economic assistance and 40 percent of its military aid. They are also the Soviet Union's chief trading partners in the underdeveloped world. According to the United States Department of State estimates (1954–1966), the ten chief trading partners of the Soviet Union in the underdeveloped world absorbed 82 percent of its economic aid and 95 percent of its military assistance. In order of importance, the chief recipients of its economic aid were India, the United Arab Republic, Afghanistan, Indonesia, Iran, Syria, Algeria, Turkey, Iraq, and Pakistan. By and large, the aid patterns of the People's Democracies have followed the Soviet selection.

The aid projects range from relatively modest enterprises to enormous industrial schemes like the Bhilai and Bokaro steel complexes in India or the Aswan Dam in Egypt. Credits from the Communist countries have no doubt made a sizable contribution to industrialization in some selected countries. In Afghanistan, for example, 60 percent of all foreign aid for implementing the 1956–1961 five-year plan was supplied by the Soviet Union and Czechoslovakia, as well as nearly half the foreign aid for the next plan. Under India's third five-year plan (1962–1966) 17 percent of public-sector investments came from the Communist countries, as did about a fifth of all investments under Mali's 1961–1965 plan.

Technical assistance, usually on a credit basis, has been proportionate in importance. Like Western aid donors, the Communist countries too have seen their aid projects delayed or under-utilized because of shortages of technical skills and administrative and managerial personnel. As part of their project agreements, they provide training in the Soviet Union and in Eastern Europe to foremen and technicians who will be working in the new plants. As for the number of experts and specialists they have sent out, these are believed to have numbered over 20,000 during each of the past few years, with the Soviet Union accounting for about half the total. Though as a rule the personnel thus provided is attached to specific schemes, in Africa fairly large numbers of specialists are engaged in nonproject activities as doctors, teachers, advisers, or planners, with those from Eastern Europe in the majority.

Since 1956 an estimated 30,000 to 35,000 students from underdeveloped countries have received academic education in the Soviet Union and Eastern Europe, probably the majority of them on scholarships. (Since 1964, however, there has been a noticeable decline in numbers, variously ascribed to stricter academic standards, to language difficulties, and to problems of integration.) The subjects most frequently chosen were medicine and engineering. A fair proportion of these students went either to the Lumumba University in Moscow—especially established for scholarship holders from underdeveloped countries—or to the equally specialized November 17th University in Czechoslovakia.

A field where aid from the Communist countries offers specific advantages not usually available with Western assistance is the transfer of up-to-date technology. The Communist state being the sole owner of patents, it is far better placed to transfer patent rights than are firms operating in a free-enterprise system. There is no need to keep secret manufacturing processes introduced into underdeveloped countries, to require royalty payments, or to claim virtual monopoly on the local market. Though this is a particularly effective means of weakening the position of Western-controlled firms, as a rule the Communist countries do not share with the underdeveloped countries production processes still unknown in the West or Japan. Nevertheless, the Communist countries can rightly point out that their equipment incorporates the latest techniques in manufacturing processes. And in support of their case they invoke, for example, the production of antibiotics in India.

Such rapid developments in trade and aid relationships, however, could not fail to produce their attendant problems. The trade deficit of the underdeveloped countries with the Communist world is steadily growing, and especially that with the Soviet Union. From 18 million rubles in 1961 it increased to 307 million in 1966 and to over 500 million in 1967—a total of nearly 2 billion rubles (about $2.2 billion) for the 1961–1967 period—or a deficit of about $2.5 billion if all the Communist countries are considered. Correspondingly, the debt burden too is acquiring serious proportions. According to American estimates, it has been steadily growing from a yearly $40 million to $171 million between 1962 and 1968. In a parliamentary answer (on July 8, 1971) the Indian finance minister revealed that in 1970–1971 his country paid back to the Soviet Union 210 million rupees (about $28 million) more than the 490 million rupees it received as aid. The position in respect of Czechoslovakia and Poland was said to be similar, though not of the same magnitude.

The aid program of China is, of course, on a more modest scale, and most of it goes to North Vietnam and North Korea. Nevertheless, the years of the Cultural Revolution apart, it has been a continuous process ever since 1954, when China itself was still relying on Soviet assistance. Up to 1970, Chinese aid to non-Communist underdeveloped countries amounted to over $1 billion, spread over twenty-four countries. Pakistan, the largest recipient, was accorded about $300 million. Tanzania was next, with about $160 million, followed by Algeria, (Nkrumah's) Ghana, and the Sudan.

In contrast to Soviet and East European aid methods, less than half of Chinese aid was project-tied and aid to agriculture has been playing a far bigger role. Chinese assistance concentrated on immediately productive, small-scale and medium-scale import-substitution industries in the form of textile mills, plywood, match, cigarette, and cement factories, sugar refineries, radio transmitters, and plants for the production of agricultural implements. In some countries—as in South Yemen—Chinese interest-free loans helped to finance extensive road-building, involving also the supplying of Chinese laborers. Unlike the case of other Communist countries, however, the gaining of commercial advantages does not seem to have been a major consideration in China's aid policy. In fact, notwithstanding China's modest means, its aid terms have been unusually generous: in most cases, interest-free loans with a ten-year repayment period beginning only ten years after delivery of equipment. Moreover, about a fifth of all Chinese aid has been in the form of grants, occasionally even in convertible currencies. By far the most spectacular Chinese aid item is the building of the 1,056-mile "Tan-Zam railroad" to link Dar es Salaam to Lusaka, the construction of which started in 1970. It is being financed by an interest-free $400 million loan repayable jointly by Tanzania and Zambia, from 1983 and over thirty years. In addition, the cost of the 5,000 or so Chinese laborers and technicians will be paid out of profits on sales of Chinese consumer goods in state-controlled stores. The railroad will open a sea route from Tanzania to landlocked Zambia's copper mines and will render possible the development of mineral resources in Tanzania's southern highlands. It is a project that was greatly desired by the recipient countries for economic, political, and even racial reasons. And like the Aswan Dam, its financing had been rejected by the West. This is a new departure in Peking's aid policy, both in its scale and in its obvious political motivations. With the renewal of China's interest in its external relations and with the deepening of Sino-Soviet rivalry for the sympathies of underdeveloped countries, it may herald a new, more active phase in Peking's aid policies.

In conclusion, to return to the Soviet Union, by far the most important provider of assistance among the Communist countries, its usual secretiveness invites widely differing appraisals of its aid methods and performance. Some critical Western analysts maintain that its aid policy is but a barely concealed instrument of trade expansion. As the Soviet Union itself is a large-scale producer and exporter of raw materials, it is also a fervent supporter of liberalism in international trade. It buys its primary products and raw materials from the underdeveloped countries, profiting from market fluctuations, and re-exports an unknown proportion of them. It can impose its own terms of trade, and it protects its home market, not by tariffs, but by import taxes which raise the selling price of the imported goods to that of the corresponding goods produced within the Soviet Union. The inevitable long-term result is the underdeveloped countries' mounting debt burden and growing trade deficit, which, according to some interpretations, is the outcome of deliberate policy, for whenever settlement can be obtained in convertible currency, the Soviet Union utilizes it to satisfy its own needs on Western markets.

In a less critical vein, it may be pointed out that since Khrushchev set out to make the Soviet Union a major aid-giver, it has delivered over $3 billion worth of goods, industrial equipment, and technical assistance which have incontestably contributed to the industrialization and the economic progress of some underdeveloped countries; that its long-term credits were on soft terms; and that the major part of them have been repayed in export commodities. In the case of Egypt's cotton, the result has been mainly export diversion, as the cotton sent to the Communist countries might have been sold against hard currency. But in the case of India, for example, available evidence suggests that the bulk of the country's rapidly expanding exports to the Soviet Union (and the other Communist countries) has constituted a net addition to India's export earnings. As for terms of trade, in India's case at any rate they seem to have been no less favorable than in its exchanges with its traditional trading partners.

If the underdeveloped countries' hopes to repay Soviet credits not merely by traditional exports but increasingly by manufactured ones—and by products of the enterprises built with Soviet assistance in particular—could not be fully satisfied, that may not be entirely the Soviet Union's fault. There is some evidence of recent Soviet preoccupation with factors inhibiting imports of manufactured goods from the aided countries and with delays in the execution of aid projects. Quality standards and lack of diversification, which do not necessarily explain the delays in the projected growth of industrial imports, receive more attention. Moreover, since about 1966 there are signs of a wider reconsideration of Soviet aid methods as a whole. It would seem that the Soviet Union too has encountered the difficulties so well known to Western providers of aid. One of the answers was greater emphasis on comprehensive "turnkey" plants, whereby the Soviet Union assumes over-all responsibility for both the supplying and the building of entire industrial complexes. Also, it seems that extensive cost and feasibility surveys are being carried out before any broadening of aid programs. They come together with efforts to end the under-utilization of already installed productive equipment and with greater insistence on quality production.

For the first time, specialized Soviet publications are beginning to discuss both the debt and the balance-of-payments problems free of simplifying clichés. There are even suggestions for multilateral settlements between the Communist countries and individual regional groupings. But the discernible softening of doctrinal rigidity implies also a new recognition of the enormity of the development problem. What this recent, more pragmatic approach may bring, it is too early to say. Yet it is not impossible that it may be the beginning of a long process which, in due time, might convince the Soviet leaders that the development problem is far too complex and too dangerous to be considered merely an aspect of the rivalry of the great powers.

APPENDIX 2

Aid Flows—Statistical Table

SINCE THE TEXT of this book was completed, provisional figures for 1970 of the total net flow of financial resources from the sixteen DAC states to the underdeveloped countries have become available. They modify only marginally the over-all picture presented and based on 1969 figures. Grants by private voluntary agencies are included for the first time ($840 million for 1970). Without them, the flow of resources was $1 billion higher than in 1969. Increase in direct investments and in export credits accounts for most of it. Official development assistance rose by $190 million (to $6.8 billion in 1970), but declined as a percentage of the donors' GNP from 0.36 to 0.34 percent. The share of grants continued its decline. Moreover, at least 3 percent of the over-all total ought to be deducted when comparison is made with 1969, if allowance is to be made for inflation.

Net Disbursements[1]	1960	1961	1962	1963	1964	1965	1966	1967	1968	1969	1970
					MILLIONS OF U.S. DOLLARS						
I. Official Development Assistance	4,703	5,198	5,471	5,812	5,955	5,872	6,070	6,618	6,325	6,625	6,813
1. Bilateral grants and grantlike flows	3,716	4,031	4,050	3,972	3,807	3,705	3,737	3,608	3,340	3,262	3,298
2. Bilateral loans at concessional terms	452	646	910	1,473	1,761	1,802	1,992	2,292	2,303	2,316	2,400
3. Contributions to multilateral institutions	535	521	511	368	387	364	341	718	682	1,046	1,115
II. Other Official Flows	262	945	513	203	–73	302	384	396	725	582	1,135
1. Bilateral	195	715	498	206	–66	297	331	377	735	597	864
2. Multilateral	67	230	15	–3	–7	5	53	19	–10	–15	271
III. Private Flows	3,150	3,106	2,453	2,557	3,200	4,182	3,828	4,226	6,008	6,473	7,604[2]
1. Direct investment	1,767	1,829	1,495	1,603	1,783	2,496	2,187	2,118	2,919	2,703	3,412
2. Bilateral portfolio	633	614	147	327	416	687	502	796	880	1,386	837
3. Multilateral portfolio[3]	204	90	239	–33	141	248	15	306	610	419	343
4. Export credits[4]	546	573	572	660	860	751	1,124	1,007	1,598	1,964	2,172
IV. Grants by Private Voluntary Agencies	..	..	..	..	..	..	..	..	..	..	840
Total Net Flow	8,115	9,249	8,437	8,572	9,082	10,355	10,283	11,240	13,057	13,680	15,552[2]

[1] Gross disbursements minus amortization receipts on earlier lending.

[2] Including grants by private voluntary agencies. On the same basis as for other years, total private flows (item III) would read 6,764 and the figure for total net flow would read 14,712.

[3] These funds of private origin are mingled with those under I.3, and II.2 and other funds from non-DAC sources, in programs governed by criteria similar to those applied in bilateral official development assistance programs.

[4] Measured by some countries as change in outstanding amounts guaranteed, by others as change in outstanding amounts due on disbursed credits. Interest is included in the sums recorded as outstanding, so that the net flow tends to be overstated if gross new guarantees are rising, and vice versa.

SOURCE: OECD Press Release (A/71/22) June 28, 1971.

NOTES

PART ONE

Chapter I. The Inimitable Original

1. See Paul Bairoch, *Révolution industrielle et sous-développement*, 2nd ed. (Paris: SEDES, 1964), pp. 71–75. Several of the facts and conclusions in this and the next chapter are based on the findings of this remarkable work.
2. W. W. Rostow, *The Stages of Economic Growth* (Cambridge: Cambridge University Press, 1960), p. 34.
3. Clarence E. Ayres, *The Theory of Economic Progress* (Chapel Hill: University of North Carolina Press, 1944), pp. 129, 137.

Chapter II. Distorting Encounter

1. Bairoch, *Révolution industrielle*, p. 178.
2. On the poverty of tropical and subtropical soils, see Pierre Gourou, *L'Asie* (Paris: Presses Universitaires, 1953); by the same author, *Les Pays tropicaux* (Paris: Presses Universitaires, 1948); and René Dumont, *Economie agricole dans le monde* (Paris: Dalloz, 1954).
3. J. D. Durand, "The Population Statistics of China, A.D.2–1953," *Population Studies*, vol. 13, no. 3 (March 1960); and Bairoch, *Révolution industrielle*, p. 141.
4. Simon Kuznets, *Modern Economic Growth* (New Haven, Conn.: Yale University Press, 1966).
5. Bairoch, *Révolution industrielle*, p. 183.
6. Ida C. Greaves, "Plantations in the World Economy," in Pan-American Union, *Plantation Systems of the New World* (Washington, D.C., 1959), p. 15.
7. Bairoch, *Révolution industrielle.*
8. United Nations, *Measures for the Economic Development of Under-*

Developed Countries: Report by a Group of Experts appointed by the Secretary-General of the United Nations (E/1986 ST/E-CA/10), 1951, p. 77.

9. Organization for Economic Cooperation and Development, quoted in *Le Monde*, August 11, 1970.

10. The average annual growth rate of the per capita share of gross national product between 1961 and 1968 was 5.9 percent for Puerto Rico, 19.4 for Libya, 4.7 for Israel, 8.1 for Hong Kong, and 7.2 for Saudi Arabia. It was 3.4 percent for Mexico, 4.3 for Malaysia, 4.6 for Thailand, 5.6 for South Korea, 6.5 for Taiwan, and 4.8 percent for the Ivory Coast (*World Bank Atlas*, 1970). (The GNP is calculated on the basis of 1968 and its growth for the period of 1961–1968.) With even greater reservations, Mauritania (11.3 percent), Iran (5.0), Panama (4.6), as well as Trinidad and Tobago (4.4), may be included in the list.

Chapter III. From Ideal to Practice

1. United Nations, *Measures for Economic Development.*

2. In 1969, for example, a sharply reduced request for foreign aid was cut by Congress by more than half. In 1970, without being requested by the administration, congressional committees added over $50 million to the military appropriations for Korea and Taiwan—in the latter case, in order to supply fighter planes.

3 *The Colombo Plan for Co-operative Economic Development in South and South-East Asia: Report by the Commonwealth Consultative Committee*, Her Majesty's Stationery Office, November 1950.

4. *The Economist*[London], June 7, 1969.

Chapter IV. The Cost of Being Generous and of Being Aided

1. To obtain the approximative but over-all total of the net flow of financial resources from rich to poor countries, a yearly $300 million to $350 million ought to be added as the socialist countries' contribution (see Appendix 1). To complete the picture, approximately another $700 million should be included for aid from private, non-profit-making organizations (such as religious missions and various charitable and welfare organizations). This DAC estimate is made up of $400 million to $500 million per annum from the United States, some $200 million from European DAC member states, and $50 million from Australia, Canada,

and Japan *(Development Assistance, 1970 Review*, OECD, December 1970).

2. At the invitation of Robert S. McNamara, president of the World Bank, Lester B. Pearson, former Canadian prime minister, in the company of seven international personalities, agreed to draw up a balance sheet of twenty years of experience in development assistance and to complete it with recommendations for its future course. The result, the "Pearson Report," was published in 1969 under the title *Partners in Development: Report of the Commission on International Development* (New York: Praeger Publishers). See p. 140.
3. The best-known estimates are contained in G. Ohlin, *Foreign Aid Policies Reconsidered* (Paris: OECD Development Center, 1966); J. A. Pincus, *Costs and Benefits of Aid: An Empirical Analysis*, Proceedings of the United Nations Conference on Trade and Development, Second Session, New Delhi, vol. 4; *Flow of Financial Resources to Developing Countries, 1961-65* (Paris: OECD 1967); and I. M. D. Little and J. Clifford, *International Aid* (London: G. Allen & Unwin, 1965).
4. See Jagdish N. Bhagwati, *The Tying of Aid*, Chaps. 3 and 4 (Proceedings of UNCTAD, vol. 4); as well as estimates for Pakistan, Iran, Tunisia, and Chile, *ibid.*, vol. 4.
5. Pearson, *Partners in Development*, p. 172.
6. Spurred on by the recommendations of the Pearson Commission, the progressive untying of aid is now widely discussed. In his foreign-aid message to the United States Congress in 1970, President Nixon admitted that "because recipients are not free to choose among competing nations, the value of the aid they receive is reduced significantly." He added: "These strings to our aid lower its purchasing power, and weaken our own objectives of promoting development. Aid with strings can create needless political friction." These remarks were made, however, in support of his order to eliminate those tying restrictions on procurement which hinder the United States' guarantee program supporting American private investments in developing countries. Welcome as the trend towards untying is, a number of important donor countries are reluctant to modify their attitudes, and it would be over-optimistic to expect rapid or fundamental change within the next few years.
7. For example, PL480 food aid represented 55.9 percent of total aid supplied to India up to March 31, 1965, and in the fiscal year 1966 represented almost two-thirds. See P. J. El-

dridge, *The Politics of Foreign Aid in India* (New York: Schocken Books, 1970), p. 113.

8. See John Pincus, "The Cost of Foreign Aid," *Review of Economics and Statistics*, November 1963.

9. In 1967 there were 11,027 students and 8,215 trainees from underdeveloped countries in the United States. Their numbers in Germany were 4,663 and 7,200; in France, 6,309 and 5,938. As for teaching personnel, in 1967 the United States had only 431 in the field, as against 1,960 Germans and 29,683 from France. When it comes to "advisers," Germany's share was 792 and that of France 5,256, as against 9,009 Americans. The situation was quite different in the case of "volunteers": 18,654 came from the United States, 1,650 from Germany, and 437 from France.

10. In the 1969 United States Foreign Assistance program, for example, the Peace Corps accounts for $101 million of aid. In 1967, from the DAC countries, the expenses of 25,083 volunteers were included in official aid figures (11,890 were teaching personnel and 13,193 were in other technical-assistance activities).

11. Between 1961 and 1968 the grant element declined from 87 to 63 percent.

12. Great Britain's Ministry of Overseas Development calculated in 1965 that the United Kingdom's aid program in that year constituted a charge on the country's balance of payments equaling somewhere near a third of the aid total. In other words, about £66 of every £100 of aid was spent in the United Kingdom. This figure, however, has been contested as an understatement. The situation is probably not very different for the other major donor countries. In some cases, even smaller proportions leave the donor country. As an interesting sidelight, it may be mentioned that contributions to multinational aid agencies, for instance, may produce export orders far in excess of what was given. Sir Eric Errington, speaking in the aid debate in the House of Commons on December 2, 1968, mentioned that Great Britain, by way of procurements, obtained more than it had contributed, for example to the International Development Association: "for every £1 we have presented, we have received 30s. back" (Hansard Parliamentary Debates, Commons, vol. 774, no.24, p. 1052).

13. Public debt here relates to debts contracted by the governments of ninety-one low-income countries, or to debts guaranteed by them. Transfer of profits and dividends on private investments or private credits are not included (Pearson, *Partners in Development*; and World Bank, *External, Medium*

and Long-Term Public Debt Outstanding, Transactions and Payments, 1956–1976*).*

14. *Liberalization of Terms and Conditions of Assistance, Debt Service Projections: 24 Developing Countries,* UNCTAD 1968.

15. Suppliers' credits, that is, private export credits, are particularly onerous. Those who offer them are usually in a monopoly position, since there are rarely competitive tenders. They usually carry high interest rates and often compensate "reasonable" terms by inflated sales prices. Their volume has been sharply rising: from $1 billion to $4 billion between 1963 and 1968. Though suppliers' credits can be valuable, they enable unscrupulous contractors to exploit the absence of other suppliers and may tempt imprudent governments—and highly placed but corrupt officials in particular—into rash expenditure. (For figures see *The Use of Commercial Credits by Developing Countries for Financing Imports of Capital Goods,* International Monetary Fund Staff Papers, March 1970, vol 17, no. 1.) In 1968, no less than 41 percent of the underdeveloped countries' total debt-service payments were on account of guaranteed export credits (with relatively hard terms, although they represented only 20 percent of total outstanding debt (UNCTAD, TD/B/C.3/77, App. II, p. 6).

16. These figures relate to the period 1965–1967. By now the debt service as a percentage of gross lending has grown further. Grants and private investments, however, are not included. In the table of figures quoted, South Asia is grouped together with the Middle East and there the percentage is 40. In the Middle East, however, export credits have been less prevalent and this distorts the total. The figure for India and Pakistan alone would be much higher (Pearson, *Partners in Development,* p. 74).

17. *Problems and Policies of Financing, 1968, Proceedings of UNCTAD,* vol.4.

18. Charles R. Frank, Jr.; *Debt and Terms of Aid,* Monographs of the Overseas Development Council, No. 1 (Washington, 1970), chap. 4 (co-authored with William R. Cline). Ghana and the United Arab Republic, though among the most indebted countries, were not included in the list for lack of adequate data.

19. Frank, *Debt and Terms of Aid,* chap. 4.

20. In chronological order they were Argentina, Turkey, Brazil, Liberia, Chile, Yugoslavia, Indonesia, United Arab Republic, Ghana, Peru, and India. For the methods applied in each case, see pp. 26–28 in Frank, *Debt and Terms of Aid.*

21. Pearson, *Partners in Development,* p. 50.

Chapter V. Who Aids Whom and Why?

1. *Development Assistance, 1970 Review*, OECD, Paris, pp. 196-97. Aid from the socialist countries is not included in these figures.
2. *The Guardian*, August 1, 1967.
3. *What Is British Aid?* Her Majesty's Stationery Office, 1970, p. 6.
4. International Cooperation Administration, *Questions and Answers on the Mutual Security Program*, Department of State Publication no. 7027 (Washington D.C.: Government Printing Office, p. 17).
5. William S. Gaud, "Foreign Aid: What It Is; How It Works; Why We Provide It," *Department of State Bulletin*, vol. 59, no. 1537 (December 9, 1968), p. 605. AID stands for Agency for International Development.
6. *The OECD Observer*, February 1970.
7. "There is . . . general acceptance of aid as a necessary defense against Communist expansion—even to the extent of obliging its adversaries to temper their opposition with disclaimers alleging support for the 'principle.' . . ." Even the most consistent and passionate opponent of foreign assistance, Representative Otto Passman, had to proclaim that he was not opposed to its anticommunist aspects. See John D. Montgomery, *The Politics of Foreign Aid*, published for the Council on Foreign Relations (New York: Frederick A. Praeger, 1962), pp. 198–99.
8. *The Guardian*, January 11, 1967.
9. Most of this applies also to the Soviet Union. Its armed interventions in Eastern Europe, particularly in Czechoslovakia, were prompted primarily by the fear that closer economic ties with the West would lessen the economic dependence so essential to maintaining the Soviet Union's dominance. Ideological considerations, however, introduce an additional element somewhat different from those characterizing the underdeveloped countries' relations with the non-Communist economic powers. See Appendix I.
10. In 1969 the underdeveloped countries' exports to the non-Communist industrial countries amounted to about $46 billion. Of this, a little less than $7 billion represented processed and manufactured articles. Practically all the rest was in raw materials and basic commodities.
11. United Nations Conference on Trade and Development, *Review of International Trade and Development, 1969/70*, Part One (TD/B/309), Geneva, August 7, 1970, p. 48 of roneotyped version.

12. United Nations Conference on Trade and Development, *The Flow of Financial Resources: The Outflow of Financial Resources from Developing Countries* (TD/B/C.3/73), Geneva, 19, pp. 13–14.
13. Based on export and import figures for 1969.
14. *Development Assistance, 1970 Review*, OECD, Paris. The $7 billion estimate, from UNCTAD, *Review of International Trade*, p. 48.
15. Called together by the Brookings Institution, the meeting, held on December 9–10, 1965, was intended to discuss confidentially the issues raised for American foreign-assistance policy by the first UNCTAD conference held in Geneva in 1964. See Harry G. Johnson, "U.S. Economic Policy Toward the Developing Countries," *Economic Development and Cultural Change*, April 1968, p. 382. Professor Johnson was the author of the background paper for the occasion.
16. The principle of temporary, nonreciprocal tariff preferences for the manufactured and semimanufactured exports of underdeveloped countries was accepted at the second UNCTAD conference, held in New Delhi in 1968. Negotiations about the mosaic of concessions continued during the following three years. When they will be ratified by all the industrialized countries is not yet known. One explanation of why the United States government unexpectedly rallied to the scheme is that it seemed to be the only answer to the proliferation of discriminatory preferences negotiated by the Common Market with a number of underdeveloped countries.

Chapter VI. The Mercenaries of the Status Quo

1. John D. Montgomery, *The Politics of Foreign Aid: American Experience in Southeast Asia*, published for the Council of Foreign Relations (New York: Frederick A. Praeger, 1962), pp. 247, 250–51.
2. Total official receipts, annual average 1967–1969, from official bilateral and multilateral aid as percentage of 1967 imports of goods and services, amounted to 39.45 percent for India; 35.03 percent for Pakistan; 38.34 percent for Tunisia; 36.82 percent for Indonesia; 29.58 percent for South Korea; 27.25 percent for Turkey; and 22.29 percent for Bolivia (*Development Assistance, 1970 Review*, pp. 202–3).
3. Lester B. Pearson; *The Crisis of Development* (London: Pall Mall Press, 1970), p. 105.

4. Gunnar Myrdal, *The Challenge of World Poverty* (New York: Pantheon Books, 1970), p. 195.
5. UNESCO, *Adaptation of Education to the Needs of the Modern World in Rural Areas*, I.E.Y. Series No. 9 (Paris, 1970), p. 2.
6. Address to the Board of Governors by Robert S. McNamara, Washington, D.C., September 29, 1969.
7. UNESCO, *Adaptation of Education*, p. 3.
8. "Even among those who run the full course there is waste as an increasing number of graduates are unable to find employment. In one Asian country alone, a half-million high school and college graduates—fully 10 per cent of the total —are out of work. Many graduates who do find employment are in jobs which do not actually require the relatively costly education they have received" (address to the Board of Governors by Robert S. McNamara, President, World Bank Group, September 29, 1969).
9. Gregory Henderson, *The Emigration of Highly-Skilled Manpower from the Developing Countries* (New York: United Nations Institute for Training and Research, 1970), p. 84.
10. E. K. Ramaswami, "Problems of Unemployed Engineers," *Hindu Weekly Review*, February 19, 1968. According to another author, in India the "dislike for occupations entailing manual operations could be due either to nutritional deficiencies or merely to social inhibitions. . . . Even an engineer craves government positions where he is for all practical purposes an office worker. . . . By the prevailing social standards, workers engaged in jobs involving the operation of the productive apparatus are regarded as socially inferior to desk-workers" (Brahmanad Prasad, "Is Unemployment Increasing in India?" *International Development Review*, January 1970).
11. *Ibid.*, p. 84.
12. *UNESCO Statistical Yearbook 1967*, pp. 259–68.
13. Guy Hunter, "The New Africa," *Foreign Affairs*, July 1970, pp. 713 and 720.
14. McNamara, address to the Board of Governors.
15. For a summary of Tanzania's experiment, see Brian MacArthur, "Education in East Africa," *Venture*, February 1971.
16. Education related to development has a voluminous literature. For a brief but excellent analysis of the problem, see Myrdal, *Challenge of World Poverty*, chap. 6, "Education."
17. See on this subject Gunnar Myrdal's *Asian Drama* (New York: Pantheon Books, 1968), or in shorter form, Myrdal, *Challenge of World Poverty*, chap. 7, "Corruption"; particularly on the economists' lack of interest in the subject and on the paucity of research relating to it.

18. Robert K. Merton, *Social Theory and Social Structure*, rev. ed. (Glencoe, Ill.: Free Press, 1967), p. 72.
19. See Karl Polanyi, *The Great Transformation* (New York: Rinehart & Co., 1944).
20. Edward Van Roy, "On the Theory of Corruption" *Economic Development and Cultural Change*, October 1970, p. 98.
21. *Ibid.*, p. 109. The author's conclusions, however, are based primarily on his examination of the situation in Thailand. See also David H. Bayley, "The Effects of Corruption in a Developing Nation," *Western Political Quarterly*, vol. 19, no. 4 (December 1966).
22. UNCTAD, *Flow of Financial Resources*, p. 21.
23. United Nations, Economic Commission for Latin America, *External Financing in Latin America* (E/CN 12/649), 1965, p. 82.
24. Laurence Whitehead, "Aid to Latin America: Problems and Prospects," *Journal of International Affairs*, vol. 24, no. 2 (1970), p. 187.
25. *The Economist*, December 5, 1970, p. 17.
26. *SIPRI Yearbook of World Armaments and Disarmament, 1968/69* (Stockholm: Almqvist and Wiksell, 1969), p. 45.
27. Geoffrey Kemp, *Arms Traffic and Third World Conflicts*, International Conciliation Series (New York: Carnegie Endowment for International Peace, 1970), p. 74.
28. *SIPRI Yearbook, 1968/69*, p. 66.
29. *Financial Times*, May 20, 1970.
30. *SIPRI Yearbook, 1969/70*, p. 24.
31. In January 1971, of the 40 independent African states, 15 had military governments. According to *Croissance des jeunes nations* (Paris, January 1971), African states devote 2.4 percent of their combined gross national product to defense costs. This, however, according to the same source, amounts to two-thirds of what is spent on education, two-and-a-half times the spending on health, and 90 percent of all external aid received.
32. For more detailed export estimates, see *SIPRI Yearbook, 1968/69* and *1969/70*. The complexity of the estimation of second-hand arms traffic need not be underlined. Recently, for example, there appeared in Pakistan, "for servicing," jet fighters built in Canada under United States license, originally sold by West Germany to Iran.
33. *SIPRI Yearbook, 1968/69*, p. 54.
34. On November 30, 1965 and on November 21, 1968. See United Nations document GAOR: 20th Session, 1st Committee, 1394th Meeting, December 2, 1965, para. 56, as well as United Nations document A/C.1/PV.1631, December 5,

1968, p. 16. As a result, scattered research apart, only two private institutions systematically disseminate information regarding arms transfers and force levels: The Institute of Strategic Studies in London, and the International Peace Research Institute in Stockholm.

35. Pearson, *Crisis of Development*, p. 96.
36. *L'Exode des cerveaux: Travaux de la conférence de Lausanne* (Lausanne: Centre de Recherches Européennes, 1968), p. 3.
37. Henderson, *Emigration of Highly-Skilled Manpower.*
38. *L'Exode des cerveaux*, p. 4.
39. *The Times* [London], August 20, 1970.
40. Mr. Malcolm Adiseshiah, quoted by *The Times*, August 20, 1970.
41. Advertisements in the *British Medical Journal* and the *Lancet*, offering posts abroad, rose from a yearly average of 134 in 1951 to over 4,000 in 1966 (*The Times*, April 11, 1967).
42. Henderson, *Emigration of Highly-Skilled Manpower*, p. 117.
43. P. G. Frank, *Brain Drain from Turkey* (Country Study for Education and World Affairs), quoted by Henderson, *Emigration of Highly-Skilled Manpower*, p. 118.
44. *Scientific Brain Drain from Developing Countries*, 23rd Report of the Committee on Government Operations, House of Representatives, March 28, 1968) pp. 16–18.
45. Henderson, *Emigration of Highly-Skilled Manpower*, p. 131.
46. Richard M. Titmuss, Professor of Social Administration at the London School of Economics, in his address to the British National Conference on Social Welfare, as reported by *The Times* of April 11, 1967.
47. "In the last one hundred years significant economic growth has been achieved only in those countries in which a high proportion of the total population is found in primary schools." Countries "with the best records of economic growth expanded primary education first, secondary education next, and university enrollment last." Yet university education in some underdeveloped countries comes long before there is a broad enough primary base. This has been the case in the majority of the Latin American republics and in both Egypt and India. See Alexander L. Peaslee, "Education's Role in Development," *Economic Development and Cultural Change*, April 1969, pp. 293 and 307. Indeed, "some educated elites may even impede developments relative to what could occur without them. . . . There can be wasteful and even dysfunctional investment in education." See Bowman and Anderson's chapter, "Concerning the Role of Education in Development," in Clifford Geertz, ed., *Old Societies and New States* (New York: Free Press, 1963).

Chapter VII. Trahison des Clercs—North-South Version

1. Simon Kuznets, *Six Lectures on Economic Growth* (New York: Free Press 1959), p. 15.
2. Pearson, *Partners in Development,* p. 12.
3. An additional factor is added in the form of a differential birth rate. It is usually lower among the upper classes and higher among the low-income groups. Thus, here, the 2.5 percent average is applied as 1.8 percent for the top minority; 2 percent for the middle stratum, and 2.6 percent for the remaining 80 percent of the population.
4. *Towards Full Employment: A Programme for Colombia,* prepared by an interagency team organized by the International Labour Office (Geneva, 1970), pp. 140–41.
5. *World Bank Atlas.*
6. Economic Commission for Latin America, "La distribución del ingreso en América Latina," mimeographed (Santiago, April 1969).
7. *The Economist,* January 2, 1971.
8. Sunethra Bandaranaike, "Politics and Wealth in Ceylon," *Venture,* March 1970.
9. Speaking to a Pakistani audience in 1958, Professor Harry G. Johnson of Chicago declared that "the remedies for the main fault which can be found with the use of the market mechanism, its undesirable social effects, are luxuries which underdeveloped countries cannot afford to indulge in if they are really serious about attaining a high rate of development. In particular, there is likely to be a conflict between rapid growth and an equitable distribution of income; and a poor country anxious to develop would probably be well advised not to worry too much about the distribution of income . . ." (originally published in the *Pakistan Economic Journal,* June 1958, and incorporated into Harry G. Johnson, *Money, Trade and Economic Growth: Survey Lectures in Economic History* [Cambridge, Mass.: Harvard University Press, 1962], p. 153).
10. See, among others, Edwin Dean, *The Supply Responses of African Farmers: Theory and Measurement in Malawi* (Amsterdam: North Holland Co.; New York: Humanities Press, 1966); Dharm Narain, *The Impact of Price Movements on Areas Under Selected Crops in India, 1900–1939* (Cambridge: Cambridge University Press, 1965); J. R. Behrman, *Supply Response in Underdeveloped Agriculture: A Case Study of Thailand 1937–1963* (New York: Humanities Press, 1969); W. P. Falcon, "Farmer Response to Price in a Subsistence Economy: The Case of West Pakistan," *American Economic Review,* May 1964; as well as Keith Griffin, *Underdevelopment in*

Spanish America: An Interpretation (London: G. Allen & Unwin, 1969), pp. 22–23 and 182–83.

11. Quoted from Keith Griffin's article in the *Bulletin of the Institute of Development Studies* [University of Sussex], May 1969, p. 17.
12. *Ibid.*, pp. 23 and 182–83.
13. ". . . there is mounting evidence that growth and more equal distribution of family income are under certain circumstances related and not inconsistent, especially since consumption expenditures in the lower income groups may have a favourable impact on productivity and saving may not diminish with more income inequality. It is interesting to note that Japanese economists regard high savings ratios as much a concomitant and consequence of growth as cause, and that greater income equality did not reduce personal savings rates but probably raised them in the postwar decades" (Harry T. Oshima, "Accelerated Growth: Japan's Experience," review article in *Economic Development and Cultural Change*, October 1970, p. 126).
14. Ragnar Nurske, *Problems of Capital Formation in Underdeveloped Countries* (Oxford: Basil Blackwell, 1953), pp. 58–75.
15. In 1969 in Colombia, for example, the approximate import content (as percentage of the total value) of processed food was 8 percent; of furniture, clothing, and footwear, 1 percent; of metal products, 23 percent; and of electrical appliances, 28 percent (DANE, *Cifras y coeficientes de la industria manufacturera nacional* [Bogotá, 1969], quoted from *Towards Full Employment*, p. 148).
16. *Towards Full Employment*, p. 146.
17. ". . . the Meiji Resotration brought forth a number of reforms in agriculture . . . and these must have raised incentives in agriculture, which in turn led not only to rapid diffusion of best techniques but perhaps to higher intensity of work, to higher labor force participation rates, for even the poorer peasants. The resulting higher productivity could have led, in addition, to more saving and to increases in the demand for wage-goods, which may then have led to greater output in the small wage-good and service industries, this in turn serving as an incentive to the diffusion of better techniques . . ." (Harry T. Oshima, "Accelerated Growth," p. 125).
18. Pearson, *Partners in Development*, pp. 11 and 10. In the authorized French translation, "self-sustaining growth" is less ambiguous: "*à assurer leur croissance économique par leurs propres moyens.*"
19. *Ibid.*, p. 125.
20. *Ibid.*, p. 124.

21. Rostow, *Stages of Economic Growth*, p. 10.
22. Pearson, *Partners in Development*, p. 49.
23. Myrdal, *Asian Drama*, vol. 1, p. 34.
24. Joan Robinson, *Economic Philosophy* (Harmondsworth, Middlesex: Penguin Books, 1962), p. 114.
25. Samir Amin's expression.
26. For example, Keith Griffin, "Foreign Capital, Domestic Savings and Economic Development," *Bulletin*, Oxford University Institute of Economics and Statistics, May 1970. Developed in greater detail, and applied to the Spanish American situation in particular, see Keith Griffin's *Underdevelopment in Spanish America.*
27. Griffin, *Underdevelopment in Spanish America*, p. 124. A cross-country analysis of 37 underdeveloped countries showed a negative relation between domestic savings and the net inflow of foreign capital (Rahman M. Anisur, "Foreign Capital and Domestic Savings . . . ," *Review of Economics and Statistics*, February 1968). Another study of 18 out of 20 Latin American countries showed that an increase in foreign capital would reduce rather than increase gross domestic savings if other things remained unchanged (Luis Landau, *Determinants of Savings in Latin America*, Memorandum 13, Project for Quantitative Research in Economic Development, Center for International Affairs, Harvard University). These are but random examples from the mounting literature on the subject.

PART TWO

Chapter X. The Pillar of Fundamental Needs

1. E. A. Ackerman, *Japanese Natural Resources* (Tokyo: GHQ, SCAP, NRS, 1949). Quoted from Shigeto Tsuru's contribution to *Essays on Japanese Economy* (Tokyo: Kinokuniya Shoten).
2. Twenty countries are examined and the subdivisions, individually weighted, are under *nutrition* (calories, proteins, and carbohydrate grams); under *housing* (quality, density, and privacy); under *health* (medical services, infectious disease mortality rates); under *education* (enrollment, output, and teachers); under *leisure* (free time, newspapers, radio, and TV); under *security* (personal, insurance, old age); plus "surplus" (*The Level of Living Index*, prepared by Jan Drewnoski and Wolf Scott, UNRISD Report no. 4, Geneva, September 1966).
3. See Barbara Ward's articles in *The Economist* on urbanization in

underdeveloped countries, edited in pamphlet form under the title *Poor World Cities* (London: Catholic Institute for International Relations, 1970).

Chapter XI. The Temptation of Voluntary Quarantine

1. "The Multi-National Corporation as an Agency of Economic Development: Some Exploratory Observations," paper prepared for the Columbia University Conference on International Economic Development, February 15–21, 1970, p. 6.
2. *The Crisis of Aid and the Pearson Report*, a lecture delivered at the University of Edinburgh on March 6, 1970 (Edinburgh: Edinburgh University Press, 1970), p. 23.
3. "Multi-National Corporation," p. 2.
4. From Lester B. Pearson's address at the same Columbia University Conference, as reproduced in *Ceres* (FAO Review, March–April 1970), p. 23.
5. The calculation was made by John Pincus in the Columbia University's *Journal of World Business*, autumn 1967 issue.
6. "Wars and depression have historically no doubt been most important in bringing industries to countries of the 'periphery' which up to then had firmly remained in the nonindustrial category," states A. O. Hirschman in his article "The Political Economy of Import-Substituting Industrialization in Latin America," *Quarterly Journal of Economics*, February 1968. According to A. Kafka: "In the Great Depression, there appears . . . to have been a curious association between the degree of violence of these adverse shocks and growth" (from "The Theoretical Interpretation of Latin American Economic Development," his contribution to H. S. Ellis and H. C. Wallich, eds., *Economic Development for Latin America* [New York: St. Martins Press, 1961]). A. G. Frank goes even further and adds the Spanish depression of the seventeenth century and the Napoleonic wars as additional examples for Latin American development stimulated by the loosening of established trade and investment ties between dominant and dominated powers.

Chapter XII. Institutions, Intentions, and Practice

1. *The Times*, July 9, 1970, and the periodic publications of the United Nations' Economic Commission for Latin America.
2. *The Economist*, December 5, 1970.

3. Quoted from Gwendolen M. Carter's review of Robert W. Clower et al., *Growth Without Development: An Economic Survey of Liberia* (Evanston, Ill.: Northwestern University Press, 1966) in *Economic Development and Cultural Change*, October 1968, p. 132.

Chapter XIII. Palliatives and Alternatives

1. By and large, the two United Nations trade and development conferences—in Geneva in 1964 and in New Delhi in 1968—revolved around these issues. Simultaneously, an enormous amount of literature dealt with and refined the kit's components. The prescription as a whole was set out in great detail in the Pearson Report.
2. This was first proposed by David Horowitz, governor of the Bank of Israel, at the first UNCTAD in 1964 and later metamorphosed into a plan for a *multilateral interest equalization fund* (see UNCTAD, TD/B/C.3/76, February 1970).
3. Speaking in the House of Lords debate of March 4, 1970, Lord Snow stated that the cost of research that led to the green revolution was only about $2 million.
4. Albert O. Hirschman and Richard M. Bird, *Foreign Aid—A Critique and a Proposal*, Essays in International Finance, no. 69, Princeton University, July 1968.
5. With similar intentions the Intermediate Technology Development Group Ltd. was created in London. A charitable trust formed to collect and present data on simple low-cost technologies, it brings together some seventy administrators, economists, architects, doctors, and engineers in panels to advise on practical aspects of low-cost technology in the fields of rural health, water development, agricultural equipment, and cooperatives.
6. Intermediate technology and small scale industries are a major instrument in Chinese planning, destined to take over the burden of supplying agricultural communities with new types of inputs and equipment and with simple consumer goods. By 1966, two-thirds of the gross value of agricultural machinery production came from small local plants. Small units of production contributed one-third of total nitrogenous fertilizer production in 1968 and, according to reliable sources, even synthetic ammonia was produced in small-scale local factories (UNIDO, *Industrialization and Productivity*, no. 7, 1964). Complete sets of equipment for installation in small synthetic-ammonia plants at the district and community levels have been turned out by Shanghai factories since 1962 (Carl Riskin, "Small Indus-

try and the Chinese Model of Development," *The China Quarterly* [London], April–June 1971).

7. The Hirschman-Bird variant of the proposal suggests that no one should be granted more than a 5 percent tax-free share of his total tax obligation, that in any case an individual ceiling of $10,000 should be fixed, and that corporations should not be eligible, all this in order to eliminate the possibility of undue influences on the Funds' activities. On the 5 percent tax-free basis, it was estimated that in 1965, in the United States, the maximum amount that could have been made available for development in this way would have been about $2.3 billion, as against about $2.5 billion of actual United States public economic assistance in the fiscal year 1966 *(Foreign Aid)*. Similar tax-free contributory schemes might perhaps be envisaged to help free underdeveloped countries of their debt burden in cases considered particularly deserving by individual contributors.
8. For a brief but excellent summing up of the subject, see H. B. Malmgren and D. L. Schlechty, "Rationalizing World Agricultural Trade," *Journal of World Trade Law*, vol. 4 (July–August 1970).
9. *Proceedings of UNCTAD*, vol. 2, p. 43.
10. For terms of trade figures see *Handbook of International Trade and Development Statistics, 1969*, UNCTAD, Geneva.
11. OECD Secretariat estimate, quoted in Pearson, *Partners in Development*, p. 376.
12. Albert O. Hirschman, *How to Divest in Latin America and Why*, Essays in International Finance, no. 76, Princeton University, November 1969.
13. OECD Secretariat, quoted in Pearson, *Partners in Development*, p. 375.
14. About 20 percent for the American economy and 13–14 percent for the Indian, according to a lecture by John Kenneth Galbraith given in India in 1961 (*Economic Development in Perspective* [Cambridge, Mass.: Harvard University Press, 1962], p. 33). Since then, the dividing line "between the federal government's sphere of operations and the rest of the economy—and between public and private activities in the United States—has become increasingly blurred" (statement by Murray Weidenbaum, Assistant Secretary for Economic Policy in the United States Treasury, quoted by the *Times* [London], October 16, 1969).
15. Antony C. Sutton, *Western Technology and Soviet Economic Development, 1917 to 1930*, Publications Series no. 90 (Stanford, Cal.: Hoover Institution Press, Stanford University, 1968).

INDEX

Afghanistan, 221, 284, 285
Africa, 14, 15, 17, 33, 60, 68, 74, 94, 125, 171, 172, 221, 257, 285; arms imported by, 117–18; *coup d'état* in, as method of changing government, 90; education in, 101, 104, 105; elites in, 86, 94; profit remittances from (1965–1967), and absorption of foreign aid, 80
Agency for International Development, U.S., 37, 115
agricultural revolutions, 14, 18
agriculture, 6, 9, 13, 14, 83, 102, 103, 267; modernization of, 7–8, 238, 239; neglected in underdeveloped countries, 153
aid, foreign: *see* foreign aid
Algeria, 15, 219, 284, 287
Alliance for Progress, 73, 216
Americo-Liberians, 224
Angola, 49
Antilles, Netherlands, 49
Argentina, 61, 80, 116, 123, 124, 143, 172, 175, 204, 257
Aristotle, 149, 267
Asia, 14, 15, 33, 38, 72, 73, 94, 169, 221, 257; Commonwealth countries of, 38; *coup d'état* in, as method of changing government, 90; East, 15, 60, 70, 72, 73, 248, 257; education in, 101, 105; profit remittances from (1965–1967), and absorption of foreign aid, 80; South, 70, 72, 169, 257; Soviet, 173
Australasia, 33
Australia, 45 *n.*, 72, 123, 127, 176 *n.*
Austria, 45 *n.*, 273

Bali, 172
Belgium, 10, 39, 45 *n.*, 56, 69, 71, 120
Berlin blockade, 34
Biafra, 121
Bird, Richard M., 238
birth control, 239, 275
birth rates, 23
Bolivia, 61, 62, 96, 221
brain drain, 122–9, 241
Brazil, 61, 80, 102, 116, 126, 143, 171, 172, 175, 199, 204, 225, 273
Bretton Woods Conference, 31
British Commonwealth, 38, 68, 123, 257
Buddhist institutions, 99
Burma, 73, 171, 210, 226

Cameroon, 102, 123
Canada, 33, 45 *n.*, 56, 116, 120, 123, 127, 257
capital-output ratio, 155, 156, 158 *n.*; defined, 155 *n.*
Caribbean islands, 17, 171, 199, 219
Carnegie Endowment for International Peace, 114
Castro, Fidel, 73
Central America, 117, 219
Ceylon, 17, 73, 94, 102, 143, 172, 217, 253
charitable and voluntary organi-

zations, as alternatives to official governmental aid, 240 *n.*
Chile, 61, 80, 90, 94, 126, 144, 175, 204, 217, 253
China, 10, 14, 177, 205, 208; Communist: *see* Communist China
"China-watching," 209
climate, as factor in sociocultural patterns, 176
cocoa: fiscal duties on, 244; imported by Communist countries, 232; imported by France, 16
coffee production: international agreement on, 231, 232; in West Indies, 15; of world (1840–1880), 16
cold war, 34, 39, 72, 73
Colombia, 61, 123, 125, 126, 142, 143, 144, 146, 157
Colombo Plan, 38
colonialism, 18, 87, 93, 99, 169, 178, 182, 275
Common Market (European Economic Community), 25, 231, 242, 244, 249
Commonwealth, British, 38, 68, 123, 257
Communism, 4, 11, 35, 72, 134; *see also* Soviet Union
Communist China, 26, 27, 34, 68, 73, 74, 115, 168, 176, 178, 207, 208, 209, 221, 249, 255, 256, 261, 268; aid program of, 281, 282, 287–8; arms exported by, 114, 120; Cultural Revolution, 103, 178, 208, 287; Great Leap Forward, 178; Hundred Flowers experiment, 178; nuclear weapons produced by, 183; and Soviet Union, 254, 288
Congo (Kinshasa), 117, 221, 223, 268
copper production, 232
corporations, multinational, 195, 215, 219, 249, 257, 258, 259, 260, 265, 272, 273
Costa Rica, 90, 117
cotton production, mechanization of, 7
Cuba, 72, 74, 105, 112, 168, 253, 281, 282
Cultural Revolution, in China, 103, 178, 208, 287
Cyprus, 49, 219
Czechoslovakia, 34, 120, 253, 283, 285, 286, 287

DAC (Development Assistance Committee), 44, 45, 48, 49, 57, 58, 70, 244 *n.; see also* Official Development Assistance
death rates, 23, 188
demographic explosion, 265; *see also* population growth, world
Denmark, 45 *n.*, 49 *n.*, 56, 191
Depression, Great, 197, 204
Development Assistance (DAC publication), 44
Development Assistance Committee (DAC), 44, 45, 48, 49
Development Decade, first, 55
development economics, 3, 133–43 *passim; see also* DAC; foreign aid; technical assistance; third world; underdeveloped countries
Development Program, U.N., 284
diffusion effect, in economics, 6, 8, 20
"divestment companies," international, 258
Dominican Republic, 61, 67

East Asia, 15, 60, 70, 72, 73, 248, 257
ecological disequilibrium, 269, 271
Economist, The, 40
Ecuador, 221

Ecumenical Council, 76
education, in underdeveloped countries, 100–7, 170
EFTA (European Free Trade Association), 244
Egypt (United Arab Republic), 15, 67, 74, 112, 123, 124, 219; Aswan Dam, 285, 288; cotton exported to Communist countries, 289; Soviet aid to, 284
El Salvador, 117
energy: consumed in United States, 268; world production of, 268
engineering, in underdeveloped countries, 102, 103
England: *see* Great Britain
Ethiopia, 90
Euro-dollar market, 110
Europe: Eastern, 280, 281, 282, 283, 285, 287; Western, 33, 37, 168, 219, 222, 268, 269
European Economic Community (Common Market), 25, 231, 242, 244, 249
European Free Trade Association (EFTA), 244

films, patterns of demand stimulated by, 23
Finland, 49 *n.*
food: as foreign aid, 236; shortage of, in underdeveloped countries, 82, 267, 270; synthetic, 266
foreign aid, 29–30, 34–40 *passim*, 42–66 *passim*, 79–81, 88, 90, 91, 92, 96, 154–61 *passim*, 228, 231, 234, 235; apparatus for, size of, 130–1; Communism contained by, 72; costs of, 43, 46, 55, 56; and DAC states, net flow of financial resources from, 291–2; food as, 236; and international influence of donor country, 70–1, 73–4; and intervention, 96; and "Other Official Flows," 45, 46 *n.*; and "Private Flows," 46 *n.*, 291; by Soviet Union, 278, 280–90 *passim;* tied, 46, 47–8, 56, 156; trade as motivation for, 68, 69; *see also* DAC; development economics; technical assistance; third world; underdeveloped countries
Foreign Assistance Act (1968), Symington Amendment to, 116
foreign exchange, and underdeveloped countries, 79, 90, 155, 188, 196, 234
Foreign Relations Committee, Senate, 115
Formosa: *see* Taiwan
France, 5, 6, 7, 8, 10, 14, 15, 16, 20, 39, 45 *n.*, 49, 68, 71; arms exported by, 111, 119, 120; automobiles in, 268; and brain drain from underdeveloped countries, 123; investments of, in underdeveloped countries (1966), 257; technical assistance supplied by, 50, 51; United States investment in (1965), 259
freight rates, 20, 23
Funds, private-development, 238, 239, 240

Gabon, 221, 223
GATT (General Agreement on Tariffs and Trade), 82
General Motors Corporation, 257
Germany, 10, 39, 45 *n.*, 69, 72; investments of, in underdeveloped countries, 257; technical assistance supplied by, 50, 51
Ghana, 102, 221, 287
Great Britain, 5, 6, 7, 8, 9, 14, 15, 20, 68, 71; arms exported by, 111,

117, 119, 120; foreign doctors in, 122, 123; investments of, in underdeveloped countries (1966), 257; *see also* United Kingdom
Great Depression, 197, 204
Greece, 49
green revolution, 92, 144, 189, 237
Greenland, 49 *n.*
Guatemala, 144, 253
Guinea, 67, 74, 221

Hirschman, Albert O., 238
Holland: *see* Netherlands
Honduras, 117
Hong Kong, 24, 77, 172, 209
Humphrey, Hubert H., 116

Iceland, 49 *n.*
IDA (International Development Association), 32, 60, 236
illiteracy, 101, 105 and *n.*, 139
India, 14, 15, 31, 62, 67, 68, 73, 74, 77, 96, 126, 172, 208, 211, 217, 225, 226, 253, 254, 268, 272; anglicized minorities in, 94; antibiotics produced in, 286; arms imported by, 112, 115, 120; Bhilai and Bokaro steel complexes in, 285; brain drain from, 122, 123, 124; education in, 102, 103; exports by, to Communist countries, 289; five-year plan in, third (1962–1966), 285; food situation in, 82; and *Report of the Education Commission* (1966), 103, 105; saving habits in, 144; Soviet aid to, 284, 287; and United States, comparison with, 199, 260
Indians, South American, 211, 226
Indochina, 114, 121
Indonesia, 62, 72, 74, 96, 172, 199, 220, 223, 284
industrial revolutions, 4, 7, 9, 10, 11, 13, 15, 24, 135, 137, 205
inflation: in industrial economies, 245; in underdeveloped countries, 147
International Development Association (IDA), 32, 60, 236
International Monetary Fund, 31, 59
Iran, 62, 67, 114, 115, 123, 126, 171, 223, 284
Iraq, 253, 284
Ireland, 49 *n.*
iron ore, 19, 224
Islam, 94, 169, 173, 211
Israel, 11, 24, 62, 74, 112, 120, 126
Italy, 45 *n.*, 68, 71, 120, 257
Ivory Coast, 25, 221

Jamaica, 172
Japan, 10, 15 *n.*, 25, 26, 27, 34, 39, 45 *n.*, 69, 151, 168, 176, 184, 205 and *n.*, 210, 219, 220, 222, 249, 256, 261, 268; ascendancy of, over East Asia, 72, 220, 248; development of, 176, 177, 183, 189, 205–7; exports by, 205, 256; investments of, in underdeveloped countries (1966), 257; isolation of, 205, 208, 261; after Meiji Restoration, 27, 183, 205; raw materials imported by, 220; during Tokugawa Shogunate, 205
Java, 16, 171, 172, 173
Johnson, Harry G., 195, 197
Johnson, Lyndon B., 35
Jordan, 67, 120, 123

Kennedy, John F., Foreign Aid Message of (1961), 35–6
Kenya, 106, 221
Khrushchev, Nikita, 289
Korea: eighteenth-century, 14; North, 281, 282, 287; South, 25, 26, 62, 73, 96, 123, 124, 126, 220, 222

Korean War, 26, 34, 222
Kuwait, 114
Kuznets, Simon, 138

Laos, 67, 73
Latin America, 14, 15, 17, 27, 33, 60, 61 *n.*, 70, 73, 100, 172, 176 *n.*, 204, 226; in arms race, 115–17; brain drain from, 122, 123, 125; *coup d'état* in, as method of changing government, 90; education in, 101, 102; elites in, 86, 94, 172; middle classes in, 172; and outflow of private domestic capital (1946–1962), 111; profit remittances from (1965–1967), foreign aid canceled by, 80; sociocultural pattern of, 169; United States investments in (1966), 257
Lebanon, 219
Liberia, 67, 223, 224
Libya, 24, 117, 219

maize, high-yielding, 237, 238
Malaya, 17, 94
Malaysia, 25, 80, 220
Mali, 285
malnutrition, extent of, 265, 266
Malta, 49
Mao Tse-tung, 34, 68
Marshall Plan, 34, 35, 36
Mauritania, 221
McCarthyism, 34
medicine, 22; in underdeveloped countries, 102, 103
metal industry, expansion of, 8
Mexico, 11, 25, 61, 77, 80, 90, 105, 123, 143, 171, 172, 199, 204, 219, 222, 248, 257
Middle East, 68, 74, 114, 120, 121, 257
Mill, John Stuart, 15
mining industries, 19
Mongolia, 221, 281
Morocco, 173, 219
Mountbatten, Lord, 31
Mozambique, 49
multinational corporations, 195, 215, 219, 249, 257, 258, 259, 260, 265, 272, 273
Mutual Security Act (1953), 37
Myrdal, Gunnar, 100, 154

Nasser, Gamal Abdel, 89
nationalism, and ideology, 254
natural resources, growing scarcity of, 270, 271
Nehru, Jawaharlal, 89
Nepal, 221
net flow, defined, 45 *n.*
Netherlands, 39, 45 *n.*, 49, 71, 257
New Delhi, UNCTAD conference in (1968), 57
New Guinea, 72
New Zealand, 49 *n.*, 176 *n.*
newspapers, patterns of demand stimulated by, 23
Nigeria, 62, 102, 117, 123, 172, 221, 226
Nixon, Richard M., 36
North Korea, 281, 282, 287
North Temperate Zone: dispersion of modern power throughout, 255; industrial civilizations of, 176, 192, 262, 264
North Vietnam, 281, 282, 287
Norway, 45 *n.*
Nurske, Ragnar, 144
Nyerere, Julius K., 106

OECD (Organization for Economic Cooperation and Development), 44, 281
Official Development Assistance, 45, 49, 291; *see also* DAC
olive oil, international agreement on, 231
Organization for Economic Cooperation and Development (OECD), 44, 281
Outer Mongolia, 72

Pacific Islands, U.S. Trust Territory of, 49 *n.*
Pakistan, 62, 67, 68, 73, 96, 102, 112, 115, 120, 122, 123, 126, 217, 284, 287
Papua, 72
Paraguay, 221
Paul VI, Pope, 76
Peace Corps, 53
Pearson, Lester B., 197
Pearson Commission, report of, 45, 46, 48, 57, 64, 139, 150, 151, 154
Peru, 62, 116, 217
petroleum production, in underdeveloped countries, 257
Philippines, 36, 72, 73, 123, 124, 126, 220, 223–4
plantations, 17, 18; in Java, 16; in West Indies, 16
Plato, 267
"Point Four" program, Truman's, 35
Poland, 283, 287
Politics (Aristotle), 267
pollution, environmental, 269
population growth, world, 15, 265, 271
Populorum Progressio, 76
Portugal, 45 *n.*, 49, 117, 118
Protestantism, economic influence of, 11
Public Law 480 programs, 48
Puerto Rico, 24, 173, 223

radio, patterns of demand stimulated by, 23
re-colonization, economic, 263
Republic, The (Plato), 267
resources, natural, growing scarcity of, 270, 271
Rhodesia, 117, 118
rice: high-yielding, 237, 238; Japanese, export of, 243
Ritchie-Calder, Lord, 32
Robinson, Joan, 154
Rostow, W. W., 150, 151
rubber: consumption of, 16 and *n.*; exported by Liberia, 224; exported by Malaysia, 25
Russia, 10, 27, 177, 205; *see also* Soviet Union
Ryukyu Islands, 49 *n.*

Saudi Arabia, 24, 114, 123
Second World War, 29, 205, 230, 272
Senate Foreign Relations Committee, 115
Seneca, Lucius Annaeus, 174
Senegal, 102
Sinkiang (China), 173
SIPRI (Stockholm International Peace Research Institute), 113
SIPRI Yearbook of World Armaments and Disarmament 1969/70, 114 *n.*
Six-Day War, 114
Somalia, 71
South Africa, 49 *n.*, 117, 176 *n.*
South Asia, 70, 72, 169, 257
South Korea, 25, 26, 62, 73, 96, 123, 124, 126, 220, 222
South Temperate Zone, industrial civilizations of, 176 *n.*
South Vietnam, 67, 73
South Yemen, 287
Soviet Union, 68, 72, 105, 168, 176, 177–8, 207, 208, 221, 249, 254, 255, 256, 261; aid program of, 278, 280–90 *passim;* arms exported by, 111, 114, 115, 117, 119, 120; and China, 254, 288; Western technical assistance to, 261; *see also* Russia
Spain, 49, 273
Stalin, Joseph, 72
State Department, U.S., 37, 281, 284
Stockholm International Peace Research Institute (SIPRI), 113

structural intercommunication, in economics, 6, 40
Sudan, 117, 287
sugar production, 233; international agreement on, 231, 232; in West Indies, 15
Sukarno, 89
Sumatra, 173
Sweden, 10, 39, 45 *n*., 56, 120, 151, 235, 257
Switzerland, 10, 45 *n*., 120, 151, 257
Symington Amendment, to Foreign Assistance Act (1968), 116
Syria, 284

Taiwan (Formosa), 11, 25, 26, 123, 126, 220
Tanzania, 67, 106, 118, 217, 287, 288; and "Tan-Zam" railroad, 288
tariffs, 23, 78, 194, 229, 233, 241–4
technical assistance: by Communist countries, 285; by West, 50–1, 261
technology, 151, 170, 203, 211, 219, 220, 238; anti-insurgency, 275; imported into labor-abundant societies, 22, 260; miniaturization of, 232; sophistication of science-based, acceleration of, 10
Temperate Zone, 14, 17; North, *see* North Temperate Zone; South, industrial civilizations of, 176 *n*.
textile production, 20–1; mechanization of, 7, 8
Thailand, 25, 90, 112, 143, 171, 220, 223
third world, 113, 114, 167, 168, 218; *see also* underdeveloped countries
tin: exported by Malaysia, 25; international agreement on, 231
Tito, Marshal, 72
Togo, 123
trade-versus-aid debate, 234
transforming industries, 18, 19
transportation, acceleration of, 10
Truman, Harry S, 35
Tunisia, 62, 96, 219
Turkey, 49, 61, 96, 105, 125, 126, 143, 172, 284

UNCTAD (United Nations Conference on Trade and Development), 57, 61, 76
underdeveloped countries, 3, 4, 19–27 *passim*, 33, 42, 59, 83–4, 89, 148–56 *passim*, 160, 161, 162, 167, 174, 181, 194, 196, 198, 200, 248, 258, 272, 273; agriculture neglected in, 153; arms imported by, 111–22; autonomy of, as alternative to foreign aid, 251; basic needs of, 185–6, 187; brain drain from, 122–9, 241; breakdown in self-confidence of, 182, 203; and capital-output ratio, 155, 156; Communist aid to, 278, 280–90 *passim*; corruption in, 107–10; debt situation in, 59–65, 237, 260, 286–7, 289; development strategy for, 184–93 *passim*, 203–4, 210, 228–9, 230; education in, 100–7, 170; engineering in, 102, 103; exports by, 79, 90, 92, 194, 234, 255–6; flow of resources to, statistics of (1970), 291–2; food situation in, 82, 267, 270; and foreign exchange, 79, 90, 155, 188, 196, 234; GNP growth rates of, 138, 141, 142, 143; humiliation, sense of, 182, 201; imports by, 145, 146, 256; and income redistribution, 147, 216; inflation in, 147; investment stake in,

Western, 256–7, 259; labor-intensive production in, 145–6; and land reform, 185, 191, 216; medicine in, 102, 103; needs of, basic, 185–6, 187; nepotism in, 108; net flows to, statistics of (1970), 291–2; population growth in, 15, 199; private investments in, 80, 81, 82, 156, 157, 195, 291; radicalism in, 257; ruling elites in, 86, 87, 91–2, 93, 97, 98, 121, 128, 152, 219; savings in, 143, 144, 155, 156, 157; secret transfer of funds from, 110; slums in, 153, 259; structural changes in, 78; tariffs on imports from, 242; technical assistance to, 50–1, 261, 285; tourism in, 219; trade deficit of, with Communist countries, 286–7; unemployment in, 161, 259; weapons imported by, 111–22; Western investment stake in, 256–7, 259; *see also* DAC; development economics; foreign aid; technical assistance; third world

unemployment: and technology imported into labor-abundant societies, 22; in underdeveloped countries, 161, 259

UNESCO (United Nations Educational, Scientific and Cultural Organization), 123

United Arab Republic: *see* Egypt

United Kingdom, 45 *n.*, 55 *n.*, 123, 127; technical assistance supplied by, 51; *see also* Great Britain

United Nations, 20, 31, 32, 40, 44, 94, 113, 121, 132, 140, 141, 213, 230, 263, 281, 284; Charter of, 30, 34, 38; Economic and Social Council of, 30, 214; General Assembly of, 57; Special Fund of, 31; Technical Assistance Board of, 31

United Nations Conference on Trade and Development (UNCTAD), 57, 61, 76

United Nations Development Program, 284

United Nations Educational, Scientific and Cultural Organization (UNESCO), 123

United Nations Institute for Training and Research, 126

United States, 10, 20, 33–5, 36, 37, 48, 56, 68, 69, 70, 72, 73, 123, 168, 219, 249, 267–8; arms exported by, 111, 114, 115, 116, 119, 120; and brain drain from underdeveloped countries, 122, 123, 125–6, 127; energy consumed in, 268; and India, comparison with, 199, 260; investments of, in underdeveloped countries (1966), 257; and Liberia, special relationship with, 224; net flow from, 45 *n.;* and Puerto Rico, special relationship with, 223; rubbish produced in, 269; technical assistance supplied by, 50, 51

Uruguay, 94, 175

Venezuela, 68, 221, 223

Vietnam, 251; North, 281, 282, 287; South, 67, 73

Vietnam war, 26, 73, 259

violence, spread of, in Southern Hemisphere, 191

voluntary and charitable organizations, as alternatives to official governmental aid, 240 *n.*

West Indies, 15

wheat: German, export of, 243; high-yielding, 237, 238; in-

ternational agreement on, 231, 232
Woods, George, 68
World Bank, 31, 59, 60, 68, 101, 105; International Development Association (IDA), 32, 60, 236
World Health Organization, 123
World War, Second, 29, 205, 230, 272

Yemen, South, 287
Yugoslavia, 49, 72, 74

Zambia, 80, 106, 118, 221, 288; and "Tan-Zam" railroad, 288

About the Author

Born in Hungary, educated in England, Tibor Mende is today a French citizen. From 1965 to 1971 he was a senior official of the Secretariat of the United Nations Conference on Trade and Development. The author of eleven books, including *Conversations with Nehru* and *China and Her Shadow*, he is currently a professor in the political science faculty of the Sorbonne and at the Centre d'Études Industrielles in Geneva.